Why Johnny's Can't Read, Write, Or Do 'Rithm

Degree

An Account Of The Fraud Of Higher Education

by Professor Doom

Why Johnny's Can't Read, Write, Or Do 'Rithm

Contents

Introduction

It was a special day on campus. We were giving a fundraiser, and students could pay $5 or more for the privilege of smashing a pie into the face of a faculty member, or even an administrator.

I know mathematics isn't a popular subject, and thought to raise some money for charity by offering my face as a target. One student, renowned on campus for not being exactly clever, paid his money, and approached me with a pie. He got excited at being the center of attention, shouted, and swung the pie, along with his fist, full force into my face, cracking a tooth and nearly knocking me to the floor.

Administration saw no need for disciplinary action, and I concurred: this student had real psychological issues, and there was no malice in his blow. Besides, it was his 7th year of going full time at the college, and he was close to graduating.

The college offers no degrees that require more than two years of full time attendance to achieve.

A small introduction is in order. I've been teaching mathematics at colleges and universities for over twenty years. I've taught at large public institutions like University of South Florida and Southeastern Louisiana University, private institutions like Tulane University, and spent the last decade at a small community college. I worked hard to bring that college through accreditation; once accredited, administration saw no reason for integrity or education to be a part of the campus, and faculty, once treated with respect on campus, were suddenly irrelevant. The realization that accreditation was a detriment to education shocked me into researching what, exactly, is going on in higher education today.

One of the first courses I taught, in 1989, was a non-college credit "Algebra for College Students" course, a remedial course for unprepared students coming to the university. It covered the material common to 10th grade algebra classes in my area, less some topics (like circles, matrices, hyperbolas, inequalities, ellipses, sequences, series, binomial expansion, combinations, permutations, and a few other things—every few years, a topic is removed, never to return).

I teach basically all undergraduate math courses, but the most common course by far for the last decade has been "College Algebra," identical to the remedial course I taught so long ago, except now it's considered college level material. The remedial courses of yesteryear are now college courses, and my campus offers three additional levels of remedial courses, covering material from around the 3rd to 9th grade. Money pours into "higher education," but much of it goes to teaching pre-high school material.

I do teach other, actual, college courses, but the material, both in quantity and complexity, is nothing like what I used to cover many years ago. I still have some of my course material and tests from then, so I know it's not simply my memory playing tricks on me. College material today is simply not what it once was.

Other than old course material, I see other evidence that something has changed dramatically. In 1977, I begged my father for a board game, *Code Name: Sector*. I wanted it because it had a computer (little more than an LED display in those days, running off of a 9 volt battery), but he was reluctant. The game was for ages "12 and up," you see, and I was but 10 years old; eventually he relented, and I had the toy. Why the age restriction? Well, the computer gave out the coordinates of two points, which you had to plot on a grid, and then connect the dots with a crayon. This is what is known in mathematics as "graphing a line." That's not even addressing the rest of the game, which was about tracking down submarines, drawing a line segment representing the course of a warship was merely a small part of it.

The issue: in 1977, corporate America (never accused of overestimating consumer intelligence) had no doubt every interested 12 year old could read a page of instructions explaining how to plot two points and draw a line between them, confident enough that this task could be a small part of a game.

In the 21st century, a large portion of my job was trying, and often failing, to teach high school graduates how to plot two points and draw a line between them—a concept most have never seen before. To emphasize: college administration sees nothing strange in having an experienced professional spend a week or more training rooms full of normal adults how to do what any child can do with just a bit of effort. If I was 80% successful in teaching adults skills that children used to have, administration would be thrilled.

Something has changed.

Yes, it's a cliché to say that "students these days are terrible", but in no way do I blame students for what's happened. It's very clear that the last decade or so has been very special, with standards falling fast, measureable-from-one-semester-to-the-next fast, too fast to simply blame a generation. This is no figment of my imagination, or local to my school, or even my state: my associates at other institutions across the country see it as well, but someone needs to speak up.

The Occupy Wall Street movement had many college-degreed protestors, unemployed and with heavy student loans, protesting that they were not getting the good life despite their degree. They don't know what was done to them, and nobody answered their questions about why they have a college degree, but nothing to show for it but a large student loan. It's not a simple answer, but it's a very fair question, and they deserve to be told. I hope a few of them read this book so they can know.

It's easy enough to point fingers at faculty who don't put any effort into their teaching, or students more interested in partying and drugs than learning, or in high schools that don't teach students anything, but none of these excuses give the whole story, or even comprise more than a small percentage of an explanation for what has changed.

Throughout history, even mediocre minds have made discoveries and written fascinating books without hardworking teachers to train them. College students have been notorious for excessive partying for centuries, as long as there have been institutions of higher learning. The public school system, sometimes more accurately called the "government" school system, has been failing since it started a century ago. None of the standard excuses can explain the last ten to fifteen years, and there were no protests equivalent to Occupy Wall Street in prior economic downturns.

Something is far bigger to the story, a confluence of events and circumstances that have allowed the American college and university education system, once renowned as the greatest in the world, to begin sliding into an abyss. It's been falling sharply for at least ten years, unnoticed both because it started so high, and because those who should have noticed are the ones that take much of the responsibility for the fall. Step by step I'll take the reader through the immense fraud I've seen and, regrettably, been a part of, hoping, all but futilely, that by illuminating the rot that has infected the system, it can be removed. Failing such removal, perhaps the small healthy part of the system can be preserved, so that some aspect of the greatness of the American higher education system can survive.

Chapter 1: What You Were Told About College Is Wrong

"I can't believe I wasted two years of my life there. I should have just gone straight to a technical school."

—from one of the best students I had. Many of my students never realize that we don't actually teach any direct job skills here.

A great scam needs a great sucker, or a great many suckers, to succeed. The scam is the American higher education system. The suckers are the students. There have always been a minority of students in college who've wasted years of their lives and small fortunes, but the numbers of such victims have exploded in the last few years.

Before we can begin to explain what happened over the years, we need some statistics to highlight how bad the situation is, right now. According to the United States Department of Education, student loan debt exceeded one trillion dollars in 2011[1]. To put this kind of debt into perspective, realize that at this point it exceeds credit card debt in this country; more people are going into debt for college than for most all (other) consumer goods put together. The average student loan in 2011 is around $25,000, slightly less than the median starting salary for a college graduate. A student graduating with such a loan will take years to pay it off, assuming he can even get a job that pays well enough to do so. Getting such a job is a rather big and dangerous assumption since, unlike credit card debt, student loans cannot be erased by bankruptcy.

That bears repeating: you can't get rid of student loan debt by bankruptcy. A person going into debt for an education has that debt, forever, or until he pays it off...even if he doesn't get an education. Even if there was fraud involved in the institution, and there was never any chance of getting an education, the student gets that debt.

"Student loans = Debt bondage"

--OWS protest sign, showing at least some grasp of how mathematical relationships work.

Anyone who goes into debt for a college education, and does not quickly acquire a well-paying job thereby, will be in debt for the entirety of his life, paying multiples of his original loan due to penalties and interest. Considering that, according to the Bureau of Labor Statistics (BLS), this country has over 600,000 low paid waiters, waitresses, and cashiers with college degrees[2], being caught in this debt trap is a reality, *right now,* for a great number of college graduates—and those are the ones lucky enough to get a job. It won't be any better for the students indebting themselves and still in college today—they'll be competing with all the previous college debtor/graduates for the same jobs, with the same qualifications (plus a few years' experience working as a waiter and such).

Why would so many people get trapped like this? What is it about college education that enthralls so many to mortgage their entire lives when the risks are so great and rewards often so questionable? The answer lies in the myths of college, myths that were told to everyone since they were small children, and believed to their very core. These myths may well have been true in the past, but like so many other myths, certainly aren't true today.

A great scam needs many suckers, and the many collegiate myths in American culture created those suckers, 300,000,000 of them it seems, ready to be victimized. Without these suckers, the scam would not have been so awesomely successful. Here are some of the most important myths allowing for this scam to succeed:

Myth #1: "You need good grades to get into college."

"I hate math. I failed this course four times in school, why do I have to take it again?"

--typical complaint from my students.

Decades ago, college or university admission was not a certain thing, and high school graduates would eagerly await the mail, hoping to get an acceptance letter. Applying to college was nearly pointless unless the prospective student took "college preparatory" courses in high school—what educational institution would accept a student who had not already troubled to acquire the basic skills of higher learning? A student with good grades, and having the appropriate coursework in high school, still could not be certain of acceptance, and would almost certainly also need high scores on standardized tests like the SAT and ACT. Even all these put together might not be enough to assure acceptance, and students wishing to improve their chances of acceptance still further would engage in extracurricular activities like charity, volunteer, and honor society work.

Those days are long gone. Now, "open admission" policies are common at most public and many private institutions. Online, accredited *graduate* schools like Capella require nothing from their applicants besides a check that doesn't bounce. Grades and transcripts mean nothing in an era where grade inflation and widespread cheating scandals in high schools barely make the local news. Around half of students enter college unprepared on some level, requiring a semester, a year, or *more* of "developmental" courses before they can even take actual college courses[3]. The amount of remedial coursework required by many students means the majority of incoming students won't receive a four year degree within six years of admission. Standardized tests are no longer relevant to admission, instead serving to determine where in the remedial course sequence a student should go. Extracurricular activities are completely irrelevant.

"Fill in this application form. Check this box if you're a degree seeking student so that you can qualify for student loans."

--the primary means of getting into many institutions of higher learning.

Decades ago, having a child accepted into college was a point of pride for a family, since it served as validation of that child's hard work. Today, getting into a college is about as significant an achievement as purchasing a refrigerator, and about as much effort. If the check clears, you're in...and ultimately that's all you need to get into college or buy a refrigerator. A far more accurate myth is "Any college will take your money, no matter what." This hardly sounds better than those easy credit loan schemes by businesses of questionable integrity that are often advertised on TV, and for good reason, as we'll see later.

A child raised on this myth will, without good grades, enter early adulthood believing college is beyond his reach. This makes him particularly vulnerable when a recruiter tells him the truth: his grades count for nothing, a college will take him no matter how poorly he did in school. And so another student enters the college system, thinking he's getting a "lucky break" by getting to go to college...when the reality is his poor grades in school were an indicator that academia is a poor choice for him, and that he'll probably not learn anything that will help him pay off the loans that are paying for his classes.

It's little different than all the smiling customers P.T. Barnum fooled when he put up a beautiful sign, "This way to the Great Egress!" Ignorant of what an egress was, his customers cheerfully followed the sign to see the great thing. After exiting the circus, they were in no position to do anything about being tricked. If they really wanted to complain, they'd have to pay an entrance fee to get back in the tent. A few did so, to Barnum's delight. Students likewise are completely helpless, years later, when the loans start coming due and there is no way to escape the loans. A few students, unable to pay their loans, take out more loans to go back to college. "There's a sucker born every minute," to steal another line from Barnum, and this myth is the first to creating many of the suckers in the higher education system.

Myth #2: "You'll have to work hard to get through college."

HEY I HAVE CAME UP WITH A MAJOR PROBLEM AND I NEDD YOUR HELP PLEZ....MY MOTHER WAS DIGNOSED WITH CANCER AND IM DA ONLY CHILD AT HOME AND I HAVE BEE MISSIN ALL MY SCHOOL AND I WAS WONDER WOULD YU

BE KINDA ENUFF TEW HELP ME REPLACE ALL MY MISSIN GRADES AND ASSIGMETS PLEZ!!!

--actual e-mail from a second year student at my college, yes, it was in all capital letters, and not the first semester where such an excuse was offered by this student.

Having achieved the precious admittance to college, further prestige is granted to the student for staying in college, even if a college drop-out in times past didn't have nearly the stigma of, say, a high school drop-out. "Dating a college boy" was a prestigious goal for a high school girl of decades ago, or at least was often presented as so in films of the era.

The reality is quite different today. A full time course load at most institutions is 12 credit hours, which represents 12 hours a week of sitting in a classroom. Actually, it's more accurate to say 10 hours, since a class that meets for "an hour" really only meets for 50 minutes. More than a third of students spend less than 5 hours a week studying alone, and only a minority spend more than 10; the overall average time studying is less than half what it was decades ago[4].

Think about that: the vast bulk of full time college students spend less than 20 hours a week on college work; more than a third spend less than 15 hours a week. That's little more than what a serious hobbyist might spend on his weekends building model trains or the like. Half of students report they've *never* read more than 40 pages a week in a course—that's perhaps the equivalent of reading a few newspapers a week...again, less than what many people do in their spare time. Similarly, about half of students didn't write a paper of at least 20 pages in a given semester[5]. The introduction and first chapter of the book you're reading now represent more writing than many degree-holders have ever done in a single semester, a few graduates probably didn't do so much writing their whole career. How can students be to blame for not being able to read or write meaningfully when they're not asked to read or write meaningfully?

Dropping out of college now is quite an achievement, probably more so than getting into college years ago. Failing college courses in the past was certainly grounds for academic probation, and failing courses in multiple semesters could easily get a student removed from college. Certainly, students could get in over their head by signing up for a course beyond their ability, so many institutions had "withdraw" policies where a student could drop a course a week or two into the semester, after he'd had time to see if he could handle the material. While available, withdrawing like this was frowned upon in the past: there was often a financial penalty, and a student could only exercise this option a limited number of times throughout his entire college career (the limit was three at my alma mater). Under these conditions, staying in college was an achievement—the college student was clearly working towards his goal, progressing towards a degree, and had no opportunity to waste semesters taking and dropping courses.

Today, the withdraw rules are very different. A student can withdraw as many times as he wishes, and the last day to withdraw from a course is well past the halfway point in the semester. Under these conditions, it's all but impossible for a non-comatose student to fail a course, and it's no surprise that students commonly take six years or more to get their four year degree. What prestige can there be to staying in college when ultimately this just means the student drops courses repeatedly? Consider the student quoted above: taking and withdrawing from courses semester after semester, learning nothing but getting student loans all the same. If the myth were "A good way to waste four to six years of your life and be in debt forever is to go to college," would people be quite so willing to indebt themselves for a degree?

Excerpt from student paper: "...a new double barrow shotgun. Like Doom, Doom II offers Multiplayer support..."

--This particular passage, with its odd typo, allowed me to find the old web page a student had cut-and-pasted from, and submitted as her writing assignment. The thought of a shotgun that fires great mounds of dirt, burying an enemy, was amusing, but I hardly knew how to respond to this level of plagiarism. I asked administration for advice. Response:

Administration: "Please allow this student to re-submit the assignment. She needs this course to graduate."

The other way to get expelled from college, cheating, is a relic. Even extravagant cases of cheating on tests or plagiarism often mean little more than a slap on the wrist; worst case scenario is an F in the course, but the student can retake the course for a higher grade. He probably won't be caught cheating the second time around, and even if so, it's still highly unlikely he'll be expelled for it.

While the first myth pulls students into the system, the second myth, that college is supposed to be hard work, traps students into staying in a system far past when it was clear they should leave. It's such a pleasant surprise when the student finds out how many classes are complete blow-offs requiring no effort at all, and the looks of pride and respect from family and friends at being "in college" surely help the student to remain as well. Yes, there are a few courses that take some effort, but those can be easily avoided, or dropped if the student, through some accident, finds himself enrolled in one.

To avoid taking anything too difficult, most institutions' course catalogues have pages and pages of "elective," content-light, courses to fill out that schedule, to keep students coming on a full time basis. And so the student stays on for years, long past the point where he knows he's not going anywhere, with everyone proud of his "hard work" taking courses in Women's and Gender Studies, Human Sexual

Behavior, The Learning Environment, Creative Expression in Early Childhood Development, Language and Literacy in Early Childhood, Child Psychology, Adolescent Psychology, Social Psychology, Abnormal Psychology, Contemporary Social Problems, Marriage and Family, Criminology, Human Relations, Fundamentals of Speech, Techniques of Speech, Personal Communication, and others (those are all courses on my tiny campus, just a sampling, and larger schools have much more to offer in introductory courses).

I know, as a mathematician I'm a bit biased in what I think is useful, but it isn't (entirely) the subject matter of these courses, it's how little these courses build on each other or lead to anything else. They're all introductory dead ends, or nearly so.

How does the student take these courses, go to an eventual employer and say "My degree took 6 years to get, and most of the material was subject matter that anyone could master in three months with no prior skills needed, and I don't know it now because none of it was needed for anything else. Now will you hire me because I'm educated and have a huge loan to pay off?" These courses with minimal entry requirements lead, quite often, to nowhere, and offering them really facilitates students not having to work much to stay in college, facilitates retention. I'm all for electives, students should be allowed to experiment with knowledge...but the system is trivially exploited to the student's detriment (and the college's advantage).

The myth of "You need to work hard to get through college" traps the student, who thinks it's an achievement to stay in college, even though often all it does is just allow ever larger student loans to pile up while the student takes pointless courses, considering himself lucky (or smart) at not having to work as hard as he thought would be necessary to stay in college. He's not being clever by staying in college...he's being a sucker, racking up more money for the institution.

Myth #3: "College degree earners earn a million more dollars over a lifetime."

"You pay your fee and get your B."

--description of less than reputable schools in my area

This myth was posted on the walls at my college and, I suspect, is posted at many institutions. Money is a powerful motivator, for learning or anything else, so the intentions are good by posting it...but this is a deceptive myth. There's nothing wrong with viewing a college degree as a financial investment, any more than viewing a college education as a source of personal growth. Unfortunately, institutions are not above using the myth of making so much more money with a degree to justify the ever increasing cost of tuition[6], and, in turn, the likewise increasing loans taken on by students.

This myth is far more damaging than the others, and people honestly believe that because they'll be ultimately making more money, it's worthwhile to take out loans. Secretary of State Hillary Clinton even quotes this myth in a speech on college affordability (implicitly justifying the cost of college)[7], so it must be true, right? There's a grain of truth to this insidious myth, but only a grain. If you subtract "super-earners" from the college graduates (the upper 1% of the top 1% of college degree holders), the rare souls that earn a great many millions or even billions, the actual average would drop substantially, but the true deception is the "over a lifetime" part of it. Allow me to write something that terrifies my students, and many administrators: let's do some math!

The average annual income for a janitor is $25,000 (and there aren't any "super earner" janitors). Consider the six years it takes an "above average" student to get a degree. If, instead of going to college, an 18 year old coming out of high school worked for six years as a janitor ($150,000), took that money and invested it for forty years, at 4%, compounded annually, he'd have over $720,000. (As an aside, most incoming students, even with a calculator and the formula directly in front of them, cannot perform this calculation.) If this janitor could get 5% annually, he'd have over a million dollars and still not be 65 years old, better off than a college graduate, according to the myth, and with another decade or so of life still to live!

And yet going to college is presented as economically a good idea for everyone.

Think about that: many a college graduate would be better off financially if he had just scrubbed toilets instead, and *that's not even factoring in the student loan*, or accounting for those that don't graduate. I've left off life expenses as a janitor, but life expenses for a student are probably no more than for a janitor. Granted, in the 2012 economy making a secure 5% a year is not a given—but with over half of college graduates unable to find a relevant job in the current economy, scrubbing toilets is still a better deal than being un- or under-employed with a vast student loan to pay off. If children were told a more honest myth, that "People that go to college generally don't do as well financially as janitors," would so many be willing to sacrifice years of their life and enter eternal debt slavery to go to college?

Particular jobs (engineering, for example) do require a college degree, and those jobs tend to be higher paying. If you're specifically going to college for the specific degree for exactly one of these jobs, and you can get that degree, and that job, then college and a loan does make financial sense. But to extend the favorable risk/reward calculation for these particular jobs to all degrees, even those in such generally unprofitable fields as Ufology, is foolish.

To repeat the myth of how much money there is to be made just because of having a degree, any degree, is to repeat a lie. For institutions to rationalize raising all tuition for all coursework on the basis of higher salaries for a few jobs based on a tiny minority of that coursework is unethical at the very least, and just pulls in suckers.

The Final Myth: **"You need a college degree to succeed in life."**

"I had stuff to do."

--*Excuse given by a bright student for why he missed a test. I learned later he had a court hearing. He did graduate eventually, and is now a successful purveyor of recreational chemicals. I don't imagine his coursework is all that relevant to his occupation.*

"You need a college degree to succeed in life" is the core myth, the one most responsible for so many people ultimately destroying themselves by going to college. Children are told in certain terms that they *need* a college degree, and this imposed *need* is why so many sacrifice so much for a degree. They *need* it, you see. Without a degree they are doomed to failure, or so they've been led to believe.

I don't imagine my generation is particularly special in this regard, and I've certainly encountered many students who firmly believe that to fail at college is to fail at life. I remember one day when I was a child, and my father, not a jovial man, was visibly happy. I asked him why, and he said it was because he was now certain that he would have the money to send me to college: his son would have a chance of success. I was perhaps 12 years old, and he was happy to have achieved that goal for me. *That's* what going to college meant to people of a generation or more ago. The entire purpose of pre-college education is to learn enough to get into and succeed at college, to *succeed at life*, or so we've all been told repeatedly. A look around at the real world shows how this cannot be true.

Bill Gates and Steve Jobs are household names. Bill Ellison of Oracle is worth over $30 billion. Karl Rove's political career will be in history books for generations. These extraordinarily successful people never completed college. Dave Thomas (founder of Wendy's restaurants) never even went to college. From a business or political point of view, it's very clear lack of a college degree or even entire lack of college education is not an impenetrable barrier to success. Alternatively, there are tens of thousands of MBAs, people with at least two degrees, who have not achieved any comparable success in their business or political ventures.

Those success stories are of people that worked for themselves, self-made men at the very least. On the other hand, a student intending to work his whole life for someone else might still be well served by learning particular skills, very expensively, at a college, so that someone will hire him. While being someone else's employee does grant a level of security, the risks there are much higher than you've been told—just ask employees of Enron (or most any Detroit auto-worker) how safe it is devote your lives and livelihood to a boss at the top who cares nothing for you. If the myth were "Get a college degree to go work for someone else and hope you don't get your pension ripped off at the end," I imagine a college degree wouldn't be held in quite the same esteem, even though it's every bit as accurate as the current myth.

Perhaps my examples are all geniuses, congenital masters at what they do. Do you need to be a genius to work for yourself? Not at all, not even close. My karate instructor, at 71 years old, can casually beat me in a fight even though I'm much larger and faster than he is. He has worked for others, but he's also been his own boss often. He's had a barber shop, gym, rental properties, and, of course, dojo...done it all. He can barely write outside what is necessary to fill out government forms, and if I ask him "What is 3 − 3?" he's not very confident of the answer, thinking about it carefully before taking a guess. By any measure, this is a successful man. And yet, he too, succumbed to the siren song of a college degree, spending nearly 20 years of his life struggling to get one despite the fact that he has no real talent for academics and it never did him any good. I feel grief when I consider all the time and money extracted from this man in pursuit of a worthless degree in Criminology. At least he started before the "easy loan" craze that has harmed so many of the more recent students.

My mother also has no college degree, and yet managed to run a very successful antique mall, sell real estate, and raise a family with my father (whose college degree helped him only marginally, as he quit working for others, retiring before he was 40 to run his own business). My mother never took a single college course. She also never did require an accountant at her antique business, which had millions in sales and many thousands of customers (my college, incidentally, even when it had less than a thousand students, still required multiple accounting professionals, many with advanced degrees, just to get by).

The average person doesn't *need* college to succeed. Yes, it can help, but the vast majority of degree fields will not financially help in the slightest, and a person absolutely doesn't *need* to start adult life four years older and much deeper in (inescapable) debt than he would be without college. Only a sucker could be talked into disadvantaging himself so, a sucker raised from childhood being told he *needs* it.

"It's not that I'm the oldest student that bugs me. It's that all the professors are younger than me, too."

--comment from a non-traditional student, nonetheless receiving financial aid. If all goes perfectly well, she'll get her teaching certificate just as she hits 65. For the vast majority of students, all does NOT go perfectly well.

Institutions now aggressively pursue "non-traditional" students. This is not an officially defined term, but usually applies to students over the age of 24. Certainly, 24 is young enough to re-tool for a new career, but I find it troubling how often I see students 50 years and older in my remedial courses, "FA" ("Financial Aid") marked by their name, showing that they're being loaned money to learn material they haven't seen since they were in the 8th grade, thirty or more years ago.

I see no reason to restrict older people from learning whatever they want but...if they're truly seeking a degree, why hasn't someone done the math for them? It'll take at least five years for them to complete the degree (assuming the very unlikely event that they pass every course on the first try), and they'll only have a few more years after that to get any use out of the degree in the workforce. Going into debt just makes no financial sense, particularly when these older students, the few that have actually thought about picking an actual field of study, say they're going for degrees in fields (for example, psychology) that have few job prospects, much less prospects where paying back the money is even slightly possible. Many of them quit their jobs or reduce their income for the privilege of going into debt—so now the lost wages should also factor into the cost of education at this age. It's painful to watch these nontraditional students bury themselves in years of debt and college, because they were told as children that "good jobs" only went to those with degrees, so they believe they *need* the degree to be a success in life, and are willing to sacrifice everything to satisfy that need.

Even more frightening for these older students is the little known detail that the Federal government can recover its loan money through social security payments. There were a mere 54 cases of social security being withheld due to student loans in 2000, but that's shot up quite a bit in the last decade. In the first eight months of 2012, there were 115,000 retirees that saw their benefits reduced due to student loans[8]. People aren't just mortgaging their homes to pay for a college education, they're risking their retirement as well. While most of these people are at least paying for their own student loans, some of them are having social security payments reduced because of loans they took out for their grandchildren's education.

It's difficult to comprehend the raw power of the myth of "You need a college degree to succeed" to overcome what should be obvious. Grandparents are destroying themselves to give a college education so their grandchildren can "succeed in life," even as the grandparents in many cases have already demonstrated you don't need a college degree to succeed in life. Even social security isn't safe from the destruction of student loan debt. As the younger generation holds more student debt than ever in the history of the world, this probably will only get worse as the years go by.

Anyone past the age of 50 and employable in any capacity, should think long and hard about going back to school and taking on debt for it, as it is seldom a wise career move. They should also be made aware of the risks they take when they support student loans for their children and grandchildren. Loan money changes college from a life fulfillment issue to a financial issue. Institutions won't, of course, warn older people against the trap they're entering, instead encouraging them to "just click the box saying you're a degree seeking student."

Should people get a college education for personal growth? Sure, if that's what they want. But putting loan money on the table makes education a different matter entirely.

The pervasiveness of these myths in American culture created a whole population believing that college is ultimately desirable for everyone. These myths might have been true at some point, but college administration introduced policy after policy, snuffing each myth out while creating ever more suckers for the system.

Most other consumer products have regulations on them, to prevent customers being victimized. Food is inspected to make sure it's healthy (or at least safe-ish) to eat. "Lemon laws" and other regulations keep car buyers from being scammed. Health care is heavily regulated to make sure people don't get hurt too easily.

"Tell us your life experiences, and we can give you a Ph.D. for it."

--typical advertisement from a not-very-legitimate, unaccredited, institution.

What's the protection suckers have against being scammed into a lifetime of debt when they buy this intangible commodity, "education"? Accreditation. Accreditation is also the only way colleges can get federal student loans to their "degree seeking" students. Accreditation represents the seal of approval for an educational institution, a guarantee of legitimacy. Degrees from unaccredited institutions are definitely worthless in the marketplace, but accredited institutions give valid degrees, and their credits for coursework often easily transfer to other institutions.

At least, that's what the suckers are told. Accreditation might establish that the institution has a huge bureaucracy, but, as we'll see in the next chapter, does nothing to prevent suckers from being scammed into buying a bogus education. It means nothing.

Chapter 2: The Accreditation Myth

"[That professor's] courses were a waste of time, every one of them. No reading, no writing, we passed out candy for credit, and talk about racial shit in class when she didn't cancel class, which was at least once a week. I took five of her classes, they were great for my GPA."

– a good student, speaking of a very favored professor at an accredited institution.

A great scam needs suckers, particularly vulnerable suckers with money. The culture provided the suckers, and the Federal government provides the money, although only for suckers going to an accredited school. Vulnerability is supplied by the myth of accreditation, the belief that accredited schools protect people from buying a bogus education.

College education is big business, with lots of money changing hands from the taxpayer to the government to the students to the workers in the industry. Of course, where there's money, there are criminals and fraudsters there to take a piece, and education is no exception. "Diploma mills" and similar operations have always been around, and the primary way for a student to determine if his school is legitimate is accreditation.

Of course, with this being the bar, scammers will naturally (and trivially) self-accredit their schools by setting up their own accrediting organization, but outside of these, regional accrediting bodies, in their own way "accredited" by the Federal government, are well known. When a student, or prospective employee, shows up with transfer courses or credentials from an unknown school, the very first thing a suspicious employer or registrar will do is check the accreditation of the school. If the organization granting accreditation is legitimate, then it's immediately assumed the credentials are legitimate, that that person has a real education from a real school.

Rubbish.

Accreditation is mostly hokum. At best, accreditation shows that the institution could--theoretically and at some point in the past--offer a legitimate education, but the vast bulk of accrediting regulations have little to do with actual education. What little could be construed as verifying the school educates the students is easily worked around as institutions self-report their efforts at education, and, once the school is accredited, the school generally has no more interest in caring about education beyond the effort it takes to convince the accrediting body that the school cares about education.

The preceding paragraph may sound shocking, but it's the simple truth. Schools in my area are accredited by SACS, the Southern Association of Colleges and Schools, so most of what I have to say here applies specifically to SACS. While only SACS is addressed in detail here, there are many accrediting agencies, each responsible for a defined region or area of specialization. They all are legitimized by the Department of Education, and so they all generally conform to the same set of rules coming from that department, although each accrediting agency does have some differences in how they address accreditation. One of the goals of accreditation is to facilitate students that migrate from one institution to an institution in a different region, and this further serves to homogenize what accreditation means. In short, accreditation agencies, like public schools, fast food restaurants, and big box retail stores, all generally follow more or less the same practices even if there are some differences, so the SACS guidelines for accreditation are largely analogous to accreditation guidelines given by other agencies.

My own eyes, and years of experience, had long since told me that accreditation meant little as far assuring an established institution was really providing an education to the students. I had thought these established institutions were defrauding the accrediting agency, but something happened to change this opinion: I began working at an unaccredited public institution. I started in my current position before the college was accredited, and worked on many of the projects necessary for my college to achieve accreditation through SACS. My going through the accrediting process from the ground up showed me that those older institutions were not defrauding the accreditation agency, or at least not very much. Accreditation, the whole process of it, has little to do with education.

For a school to gain accreditation from SACS, it must comply with SACS' *Principles of Accreditation: Foundations of Quality Enhancement*[1], an extensive document. Going through the accreditation process is extraordinarily time consuming, taking years and the hard work of many administrators (who often hire helpers) to document and answer every issue raised. To demonstrate the assertion that accreditation has very little to do with authentic education, most every point in this long document is addressed in this one chapter. For the uninitiated into the doldrums of bureaucracy, you can take it on faith that most of accreditation has nothing to do with education, and just move on to the next chapter, Remediation. If your faith is lacking, read 2.5, 2.7.3, 2.12, 3.3.1, 3.5.1, and 4.1 in detail below, as these sections represent areas where, possibly, some education takes place at the institution and is verified, laughably, by SACS.

The document begins with an extensive preamble of terms and descriptions before finally discussing precisely all the conditions that must be satisfied before an institution can be accredited, and how such conditions will be assessed. To be accredited, a college must satisfy the following (bold face represents excerpts from the document, with comments following):

1. **Principle of Integrity**

    "I will not lie, cheat, or steal, or tolerate those who get caught."

    ---Slightly altered military oath. One year I taught a class full of ROTC students, and one of them cheated on an exam; I couldn't prove it, so I let it go. I received a series of calls after that from

other students, wanting to make sure that one student cheating wouldn't affect the other student's grades. I was initially non-committal, but finally decided that it would (since I curved grades in that course). Only after telling students that a cheater could indirectly affect other student grades did I receive a call from the commanding officer of the ROTC students, asking that I drop the cheating student.

Integrity, like education, is difficult to define precisely, it's usually easier to identify what is not integrity or not education. While qualitative, integrity is necessary to education; learning will always boil down to an opinion of what is knowledge or skill. Thus, the educators must act with integrity, basing their decisions and opinions in an intellectually honest way. The value of a diploma is nil if the institution granting it has no integrity.

Because integrity must be part of education, SACS only accredits institutions that act with integrity, whatever that might mean (and accreditation rules by other agencies have similar language). This section of the SACS document begins with a two page discussion of integrity, verbosely saying "don't hide stuff and also, you should act like you have integrity." Certainly a decent if somewhat circular way to address integrity, but the section makes it clear SACS will simply trust the institution not to hide stuff and will assume that the institution will act with integrity. In a vague way I suppose, if this were followed, this would set some sort of example to the students for their education, but it's rather odd that one assumes an accredited school acts with integrity...and the accrediting body likewise just assumes the school acts with integrity.

"Trust, but always cut the cards" is good advice for a reason; the accrediting agency never actually cuts the cards, as shown below and in other places in this book, and this in part explains why it's easy to find students with college degrees from accredited institutions but nothing that qualifies as an education.

It probably should go without saying that there's not a lot of integrity at the schools I've taught at, but I'll give a few examples of the institutional chicanery I've witnessed with my own eyes (student cheating will come later):

--A permanent position was available in my math department. A committee was formed, candidates chosen, documents reviewed, and a candidate was voted upon to receive the position. The Dean overruled the committee (almost causing a fistfight to break out by committee members) and someone not qualified, or even on the list of candidates, but a "personal friend" of the Dean, was given the position instead.

--A Dean had made a series of grotesque errors in implementing a policy regarding a promotion candidate. As per policy, the Dean served on the promotion committee, which rejected the promotion based on all her errors. When the candidate appealed since the errors were not his, the Dean, in explicit violation of the policy, somehow got appointed to the Appeal committee, and threatened and otherwise influenced the committee to likewise reject the promotion due to the errors, rather than acknowledge and correct the errors (to emphasize: the Dean served as judge regarding the validity of the promotion

documents, and as jury on both the Promotion and Appeal committees, in direct violation of written policy, integrity, and common sense concepts regarding "conflict of interest").

--A faculty member was found to be unqualified for his position, not having so much as a Master's degree, but it was not realized that he had no idea what he was doing until he was assigned to teach Calculus. He went through the entire semester without getting to "the derivative" (in other words, he covered about 2 weeks of material in 16 weeks). The teacher's whole class was excused from the Calculus departmental final because there was no way they could pass it, although they were still given credit for the course. The faculty member was a valued teacher because he passed all his students, so rather than be rid of him, administration saw to it that he received several individual "independent study" graduate courses over the summer, instantly making him qualified to teach collegiate mathematics.

The rumor mill is as productive at educational institutions as it is elsewhere, so I've avoided, above, the non-integrity things I've only heard about and stuck with just a few of the things I have personal knowledge of, spreading out my references amongst institutions. These are but a few examples of "integrity" at accredited schools, and I know full well these sorts of activities are covered up as much as possible by the administration. I've left out the many "students" that have been talked into taking on a life-destroying amount of debt while spending many productive years in pursuit of a pointless degree; more than a few of these students are not intellectually capable of understanding what they are doing to themselves and what institutions are doing to them when these students agree to accept student loans. I doubt seriously this sort of behavior satisfies SACS' definition of integrity, or anyone else's, outside of administration. I also doubt that these incidents, even if/when SACS is made aware of them, would cost an institution its accreditation. The SACS document concludes with a handwave, a statement that **"The institution acts with integrity in all matters,"** and then moves on to the next topic. As is always the case in this document, there are no teeth: an already accredited institution can violate the rules with relative impunity, with no penalties given. When caught, the university has plenty of time to show it's not violating accreditation any more, but need not compensate victims or otherwise be concerned about consequences of violating accreditation.

2. Core Requirements

Admin: "You've failed this student five times, and he needs to pass College Algebra to get his degree."

(the core requirements for graduation force most students to take at least 3 hours of math)

Me: "He can't pass the course, and, frankly, having seen his writing skills, I don't see how he can pass most any other college course."

Admin: "He needs to pass College Algebra."

Me: "I don't want to say this student is capable of doing things he clearly cannot do. "

Admin: "Well, can we just make up an independent study course, and use that to give him credit for his math requirement?"

Me: "That would satisfy the core requirements."

--Conversation with administration; I'm rather disappointed in myself that this didn't even occur to me as another example of questionable integrity.

SACS Core Requirements aren't quite the same thing as the requirements a student needs to get a degree. Instead, these are the basic things an institution needs to get accreditation, almost none of which has much to do with an education.

2.1 The institution has degree granting authority…

While this is desirable to have from the student's point of view, it's not related to getting an education. It simply means the institution has governmental authority to print out a piece of paper saying the student has some sort of education. Such authority is worth something, but the reputation of the degree-granter is worth so much more. Most people would find an "unofficial" degree in Computer Design and Programming signed by Bill Gates as vastly superior to a similarly named degree granted by a community college, even if only the latter has the "authority" to grant a degree.

2.2 The institution has a governing board of at least five members…the presiding officer and a majority of the board are free of…financial interest in the institution.

The ellipses are abbreviations to make the statements more manageable, but enough remains to get the gist of the clause; I'll do this often, for the sake of brevity. It's interesting that before a single classroom is opened, there need to be five administrators (almost certainly making vast amounts of money in the system) ruling over it. At least only a few of them can have a direct financial interest in the institution. Despite this wording allowing for some possibly questionable behavior, I've never seen anything more than just a little shady, and I'm not sure having a financial interest is such a bad thing.

One wonders how for-profit institutions deal with this requirement. If they hire the board and pay them to govern the institution, how is the pay completely not a financial interest?

2.3 The institution has a chief executive officer...not the presiding officer of the board.

This is almost one more person necessary before the college can open an accredited classroom, since the CEO could also be just a board member. Of all the administration, the CEO is the only one that merits mention in this entire document. As far as accreditation is concerned, no other administrators are necessary. Keep that in mind.

2.4 The institution has a clearly defined...mission statement....addresses teaching and learning.

At least an accredited institution has a mission statement, although the SACS requirement doesn't indicate the statement need be followed.

Here is my college's statement, suitable as a template for most 2-year institutions: *"[This] Community College is an open-admission, two-year, post-secondary public institution serving the [region]. The College provides transferrable courses and curricula up to and including Certificates and Associates degrees. [This] Community College also partners with the communities it serves by providing programs for personal, professional, and academic growth.*

An additional part of the statement addresses how it will achieve its mission ("Retention" is the fifth word, mentioned before education), and talks a bit about how there will be learning. It's nice that all institutions are obligated to have a statement where teaching and learning is talked about, but this is just some words on a piece of paper (or computer screen, for online students), and that's all accreditation requires here.

You won't find a mission statement saying how the institution intends to provide high paying jobs for as many administrators as possible; in light of what we'll see later, this is something of a surprise, since it's a mission many institutions clearly aspire to achieve.

2.5 The institution engages in...evaluation processes that...demonstrate the institution is effectively accomplishing its mission.

"I hate reviewing [Professor]'s work for SACS. Most of her students just cut-and-paste their papers, and I don't want to fail almost everyone. Does she even care her students cheat that much?"

Finally we come to something that might relate to education—this is "institutional effectiveness", showing that perhaps the institution is actually educating students. Interestingly, my college is the only institution where I've witnessed any attempt to show giving an education. Every other institution self-reports it to the point that general faculty don't seem to be part of the process.

Although it's not said here, institutions can't simply use grades for the courses as evidence. It's too easy to submit bogus grades, I suppose, so SACS requires some other evaluation process….with the same instructors that could give bogus grades completing the process.

What my college does to show institutional effectiveness is every faculty in every class gives a simple assignment that complies with our general education requirements. I repeat: this is a very simple assignment, where the student is walked through each question to show specifically that we're doing what we say we're doing. To make sure the students do the assignment, they're collected and graded—students quite understandably won't do assignments if there's no grade involved. It's a very mild form of grade inflation, acceptable in the name of pleasing SACS.

Then the SACS assignments are turned in to our compliance person. Then, next semester we all get together, and the assignments are passed back to their respective faculty. The faculty member then rubber stamps his own assignments for his own students, and passes it back.

SACS doesn't want to use course grades due to easy manipulation of results, but I just don't see how this method is any less vulnerable to manipulation.

In times past, we were grading each others' students' work to give a veneer of legitimacy to it all, but that's mostly not done now. It really is madness to have me grade an art student's work, or for the theatre professor to grade a physics assignment, so this is forgivable chicanery.

Now, for SACS, we basically grade these assignments pass/fail (beyond whatever grading is used in the course), and then report what percent of our students we say are capable of answering an easy question in a controlled situation. The whole faculty gets together and is literally grading 5,000 assignments in an hour or two, so there's just no way to have grading be complicated. Despite the obvious practical concerns, we have near constant intrusion from Educationists asking us to use a complicated multi-dimensional grading rubric packed with gobbledygook; this sort of discussion is saved for later.

This is how we demonstrate that we're educating our students. There are three big issues here. First off, we're encouraged to give our SACS assignments early in the semester; this is so that we can collect this data before the drop-off of students that comes when the checks get cashed. My pointing out to administration that it's not exactly fair to "demonstrate" we're educating students that, in many cases, are just here for the checks falls on deaf ears.

We often do these SACS assignments for every class (even pre-sub-remedial courses). The typical mission statement, above, says nothing about bringing students to the high school level, the statement says post-secondary education. With nearly the majority of students in developmental courses, we should be excluding these as not part of our mission. Our results with these students shouldn't even apply for SACS.

Finally, it seems blatantly obvious that we should focus on demonstrating we're educating our students by only looking at the students that are graduating (i.e., looking at the students that we *claim* we're educating) as opposed to everyone with a pulse, but such is only obvious to faculty and not the decision makers. Semester after semester, we show that we're accomplishing our mission on students nearly as quickly as they come on campus, with nary a question asked about how silly that sounds.

Nonetheless, this is how "institutional effectiveness" is satisfied, by showing that we actually achieve our mission on basically every student within a few weeks of that student walking in the door. For added laughs, note that we self-report this by self-assessing how our own students do on assignments of our own choosing.

Being accredited is taken to mean the institution is legitimate, but this legitimacy is verified not by SACS, but by the institution...talk about foxes guarding henhouses. But at least with this clause there is something in accreditation that has something to do with education (or at least the institutional mission), so there is that.

(Graduate at commencement, in halting speech): "I am so gla' that I went to this here Commun'ty College. I love my time here. And sad that I mus' go. Thank you Commun'ty College!"

(After polite applause, another graduate, same commencement, to cheers of adulation): "Never give up! Never give up! Never give up! Never give up! If I can do it, so can you! Never give up! Never give up! Never give up! Never give up!"

--two students were invited to talk at graduation, to share their experiences at my Community College.

Imagine if instead of all the self-reporting, SACS actually took a look at the graduates, and verified with their own eyes that the graduates really were capable of doing work comparable to what we're saying they can do. Accrediting might mean something if accrediting agencies really verified that degree-holding students had some sort of verifiable education.

"Trust, but cut the cards."

2.6 The institution is in operation and has students enrolled in degree programs.

I certainly agree this is something a student would want. This does set up something of a death-trap for students that require remediation (or "developmental") work. These students, if they want to go to an accredited institution, must go to a degree granting institution, which can't focus its resources on remedial students. Students that failed to learn to read at the 5th grade level, but nonetheless have a high school diploma, and legitimately want to learn, probably should go to a special school more able to handle their needs, instead of being poured into postsecondary education schools that must have and support degree programs to be accredited.

Too bad, since people with such a low level of education might need special help the most.

Of course, "We want to build a special school to teach adults the things they should have learned in primary and secondary school, charging them a second time for the privilege" probably isn't as easy a sell to a community than "We want to build an institution of higher learning", even though the former is often a more accurate representation of what's going on in college.

2.7 This is a large section, broken into smaller components:

2.7.1 The institution offers…degree programs.

Me: "I see you have 165 hours now. You know we're a 2 year college, and all our degrees take less than 70 hours?"

Student (with at least some shame): "Yep."

For a time, faculty could easily see the number of hours each student had already passed. This student was my record for that semester, although others had over 100 hours, many getting financial aid.

It's interesting that there's no such thing as an accredited school that doesn't offer a degree. It really seems like certain subjects (industrial chemistry, for example) might be a singular focus for a school, without forcing the school to also have to cover various other topics. In any event, having a degree program is no guarantee that an accredited college will actually push the students towards getting a degree, and I've seen many students with hours far beyond what should be necessary to get a 2 year degree...and, like my example above, a few that have enough for a 4-year degree.

2.7.2   **The Institution offers degree programs that embody a coherent course of study...**

Me: "Ok, once you finish your first Statistics test, you can hand it to me and go."

Student: "You mean this isn't Physical Sciences with [another professor]?"

--Exchange between me and a student, a month into the semester. The student had attended at least ten classes, and had the syllabus as well as book for my course.

It rather makes sense that the degree program covers the right subject, but it really seems like a student could figure this out quickly, even if my example above shows that is probably a bad assumption.

This isn't a difficult requirement to be met, most institutions have no trouble just copy the degree programs of previously accredited institutions.

2.7.3   **In each undergraduate program, the institution requires the successful completion of a general education component...**

"I really wish we could get rid of the math requirement. It would help our passing rates so much."

--administrator bemoaning one of the few checks on administrative avarice, in an address to students.

This is an important section, the general education, or core, requirement, the primary reason colleges and universities look the way they do, with their "ivory towers" scattered across campus, each devoted to a particular field of knowledge.

This is the section that forces students to take a few hours of math, a few hours of English, and so on. This is the section that motivated the Vice-Chancellor at my college to announce to his students how much he wanted to get rid of math. This is the section that caused the Dean at another university to publicly criticize the math department for being such an "impediment to graduation." At some point in ages past, educated people got together and agreed that there was a body of knowledge that all educated people shared. This body of knowledge can shift over time—Latin was important to the educated of a century ago, while today knowledge of statistics or even how to type on a keyboard might be argued as more necessary knowledge to an educated person in the modern world.

This is the section that gives me and my colleagues so much job security, I know thoroughly that most students wouldn't take my math classes if they could avoid it. I'm hard pressed to feel hypocritical about forcing students to give me a job, but I have a handy rationalization: I went to college much like my students, and I had to take many courses in fields I cared little about.

Like all other students, I was forced to take a year of another language. Even though I took two years of Spanish in high school, my alma mater had me take a year of French. I've never actually used French, but it did help me to gain a better understanding of English and European languages—knowledge of two European languages gives me a shot at translating the gist of passages in Italian or even Latin. When I try to convince my students that math is just another language, that when the student sits down and learns how to read and write in the mathematical language, he needs to use the same skills he used when he's learning a new language, I get blank looks: students no longer are required to learn an additional language in high school, or in college (some of my English professor associates assure me that learning English isn't a requirement, either).

I was forced to take a political science course, despite my caring very little for politics at that age. All I remember is the very first day, when the professor announced "Nixon is the most brilliant president this country has ever had." Still, I did learn that even the most reviled person can have admirers. Writing a paper on a subject I cared little about and memorizing a timeline of important events at least showed me I could do such things, even if I don't consciously remember the political paper or events. The knowledge that I can be competent even far out of my experience and interest may even have helped me in graduate Education and Administration courses, addressed later in this book.

Despite my miserable handwriting (a problem in an era before computers and printers everywhere), I was forced to take English courses as well. Failing to convince an English professor that "facet" can apply to various sides of an argument, and doesn't strictly refer to gemstones, is partly how I ended up majoring in mathematics, and if I learned little English, I did at least learn to be more careful dealing with people that may not be the most reasonable.

"Why isn't Mr. [author] here? I have 85 students on this roster. One is missing. Where is he?"

--physics professor in 1985, noticing that I had dropped his class. Friends passed on his disappointment to me.

I also took a year of Physics. I dropped Physics the first time I took it, on the first day, not even showing up to class. A single student dropping was noteworthy in 1985! Compare that to 2012, when 20% of students not coming to the first class doesn't raise an eyebrow, and a 50% drop rate overall is standard. I loathed the lab work, although I did appreciate seeing a proof of Einstein's Theory of Relativity, the $E = MC^2$ part of it, anyway. Freshmen and Sophomores are exposed to *fractions* as college material in the 21st century, but a generation ago they were shown the most important concepts of the modern world. Of course they were, that's what education used to mean.

These are just a few of the courses I was forced to take, "impeding" my graduation with a mathematics degree. I, and most all academics, were subjected to these general education requirements. In retrospect, there are many gaps in those requirements, gaps I filled in adulthood, but the requirements did give me the foundation to learn whatever else I wanted to learn.

"...in the upscale neighborhood was an ice cream store. One of the confections on sale was ice cream in the shape of a very large female breast, covered in a chocolate coating.

This shows how wealthy white people, even in the 20th century, still long for their huge black mammies of the slave-owning days."

--paraphrased excerpt from a textbook used in another course on my campus. My family came to this country well after the Civil War, but I promise you I have no particular longing for black mammies. I do like chocolate covered ice cream, however. I feel the need to point out: this passage was not in the book as an example of ridiculous thinking for educated people to point at and laugh.

Back to my own field, I still feel a little hypocrisy about forcing students to learn rudimentary math just because of this arbitrary accreditation rule. Learning another language might arguably be more useful, and I don't know how loudly I would have protested the removal of that requirement, not that my protestations would have been noticed. The math requirement is singled out often as the most onerous requirement, but so many of those general education requirement courses are so bogus and content-free that the problem isn't that math courses are so hard...it's that so many other courses are a joke, to judge by assignments, textbooks, and other materials I've observed from them, along with discussions with students over the years.

"It's just common sense stuff."

--Faculty member, describing her course material. I thought it an odd thing to say at the time.

SACS, of course, looks at what the college course catalogue and syllabi say about the course to see if it meets the standards of a legitimate college course. Even if the course looks like it might be legitimate by reading the course catalogue, this means nothing. There are topics in the course catalogue for, say, "College Algebra" that I've never covered, and administration doesn't care, instead I receive pressure to cover even less material than what we self-report to SACS that we cover.

Even the course syllabus passed out by the instructor means nothing. At my school in Spring 2012, another math professor only made it to Chapter 2 for the whole semester (I get to chapter 5), not even coming close to what the catalogue or his own syllabus says the course is. He gets special consideration from admin (and that's money) indirectly because he passes so many students, and from personal knowledge I know he isn't the only math instructor who has done the like.

"It's all common sense."

--Different faculty member, describing material in his course on a different subject. I don't even consider my basic remedial courses just common sense, instead being knowledge that humanity worked to understand, a long time ago.

Back to the point, SACS does force colleges to inflict a wide range of subject matter, at least in theory, on their students. Are there students actually learning the material, or faculty actually teaching it, leading to an education? No, that question isn't addressed by accreditation, so accreditation has nothing to do with that at all, Administration rather discourages such activity for the most part, instead self-reporting that institutions are doing their job.

"Everyday knowledge, most things anyone could guess at. Look 'em in the eye when you talk, stuff like that."

--Another faculty member, describing material in his course, unrelated to the previous two common knowledge courses.

SACS does send people on campus, providing long advance notice for their arrival. The SACS people look, I'm told, at some turned in assignments and things, but if accreditation were taken seriously, why not just enroll some SACS people in a decent sampling of the courses offered, and **see with their own eyes** that the coursework and grading is valid? There's no excuse for not doing so at an open admissions institution, particularly with so many courses offered online. Thousands of hours of form-filling out by administrators and faculty for SACS, and a nearly like amount of time is spent by SACS employees filling out their own forms...but SACS can't spare the time to do a direct check at what is really going on at the institution.

Administrator: "Congratulations to [student], for her degree, with a concentration in math."

--my college has given many 2 year degrees with concentrations in math. This is curious, as the most advanced course we've ever taught on campus is Elementary Calculus 1. While this is the most advanced course our "math students" see in their two years, this used to be the course non-math students took their first semester on campus.

The general education requirement gets trimmed every few years. Recently in my state, the math requirement has been scaled back to 3 hours, just "College Algebra". Twenty years ago, this level of algebra was typical for a high school graduate (or at least a 10th grader). Now this ability to think abstractly is going to be the theoretical maximum of what can be expected from a college graduate. As I struggle to address concepts in calculus and statistics with students that cannot add fractions, I imagine fractions will be reserved for people with graduate degrees in another decade or two.

The reason for the scaling back is straightforward: doing so will increase passing rates. Administrators influence the general education requirements, after all.

"They don't need this."

--typical administrator complaint, justifying the removal of another chapter, or a whole course.

Algebra isn't necessary for leading a successful life. Neither is being able to speak a foreign language, nor understanding the basics of modern science, nor is being able to write a coherent essay, nor is being able to read and comprehend a work of literature from a prior century.

As we cut back the general education requirement further and further, it becomes that much easier to find college graduates who have no, or minimal, skills in reading, writing, mathematics, or any other measurable knowledge.

Conferral of a degree is an assertion that a person has an education, knows the things "all educated people know", with perhaps some concentration in some area. "All educated people know" may well be a matter of opinion, but "nothing," the educational goal of many institutions, seems to be an awfully small amount considering the kind of money being spent on education.

2.7.4   **The Institution provides instruction for all coursework required for at least one degree program...or...uses some other alternative approach to meeting this requirement...**

"I need this course to graduate, and it's full again. Why is it offered only once a year?"

--common student complaint.

This fits in nicely with forcing only degree-granting institutions to get accredited, they must also actually offer the courses with instruction. What's interesting here is that is there is no requirements that provision need be in a timely manner, and quite often my students that move on to four year degrees complain that the courses they need to graduate are seldom offered in a way they can take them.

2.8 **The number of full time faculty is adequate to support the mission of the institution ensure the quality and integrity of its programs. Upon application for candidacy, the institution demonstrates that it meets the comprehensive standard for faculty qualifications.**

"As you know, this university has experienced major growth in the last few years. To support this growth, we're going to allow our Developmental Department instructors to teach some of our introductory-level college courses."

--One accredited institution's method of making sure there were enough sections available; developmental instructors need not even have a Master's degree.

The first sentence of this clause is rather poorly defined, which is why most institutions get away with hiring vast numbers of part-time employees to cover their courses. What's "adequate"? Nobody but administration knows, but supporting the quality and integrity of programs is fairly low on the list of goals for many institutions. While the institution must demonstrate they use qualified faculty when applying for accreditation (**"upon application for candidacy"**), this clause makes it clear that afterwards, no such effort need be made.

2.9 The institution…supports…library collections.

It certainly is good that every accredited institution must have a library and other such resources. I emphasize this is typical of what accreditation assures: it asserts that the institution could theoretically give an education if it so desired.

2.10   The institution provides student support programs…

Again, this just theoretically means the institution can help with learning; these programs are poorly defined, although many institutions do have vastly bloated support programs, constantly begging students to come and use them. Even with very minimal (at best) participation, these programs seem to go on forever.

2.11   This section is broken into smaller sections:

2.11.1 The institution has a sound financial base…

This is simply an assurance that the institution won't just blow away, certainly of value to students. Of course, a few accredited institutions in New Orleans did just that when Katrina came through.

2.11.2 The Institution has adequate physical resources….

"Can I have even one class this semester not in a trailer?"

The influx of students and growth of administration and support means that classroom space (and parking space) can be very limited at institutions, but this clause at least forces administration to provide trailers for the students, even if providing such might cut into other things the administration could do. Online institutions have an easier time with this, and doubtless the lower overhead is why online offerings are strongly encouraged at many institutions.

While I've seen many a classroom converted into administrative or support offices, not once has a classroom trailer ever been considered good enough for an administrator to use as his office. Hmm.

2.12   The institution has developed a Quality Enhancement Plan (QEP)...

"What does this have to do with math? And why do we keep having to do this every class?"

--common complaints by student upon receiving a QEP assignment. Some students at my institution have completed over a dozen QEP assignments now.

The QEP is quite an annoyance at my institution. Each semester, each faculty member, in every class, has to issue a QEP assignment (in this case, it's to "Improve Information Literacy"). It doesn't matter if the course has nothing to do with information literacy, we have to give the assignment, and, of course, it has to count for a grade (otherwise the students won't do it). Every class. Every student. Every semester. This means every student (or at least those taking more than one course in a semester) has to perform multiple QEP assignments, every semester, for years.

All faculty grade these en masse on a single day. As you might expect, these assignments are very simple. Much like the SACS assignments mentioned above, to facilitate grading thousands of such assignments in a very brief time, each member quite often grades his own assignments and structures them for easy grading. Many just give the same assignment every semester (I switch a number or two around on mine), so many students perform the same assignment three or more times. Naturally, our assessments of our students' ability to complete QEP assignments are generally improving, and this pleases administration.

We have the same students literally answering the same questions semester after semester...and the rising scores are taken as evidence that we're accomplishing our QEP, and giving an education to our students.

After the Core Requirements come the Comprehensive Standards. As we'll see, very little of this does much to ensure the institution is really educating anyone:

3. Comprehensive Standards

3.1 The mission statement is current and comprehensive...

Certainly all well and good, but this is of little value to students. What's interesting is many of these statements are very similar from institution to institution. Well, it might be interesting to outsiders, but from the inside, it's little surprise, as many institutions, at inception, just "cut and paste" the sorts of gook that form mission statements from other, accredited, institutions, and modify it slightly, so that it's one less hurdle to clear to get accreditation.

3.2 Governance and Administration

This entire section covers relationships between the governing bodies, chief administrative officer, and administration. There's quite a bit here, but all of it is far removed from anything relating to students and education. The title alone should be sufficient indication there will be nothing here regarding education. There is a clause mandating "periodic" evaluation of administrators; this evaluation would be done by administrators, of course, and the criteria are not published. Compare this to faculty, who are "regularly" evaluated (with no explanation of the different word), by criteria that are published (3.7.2).

While "regularly" and "periodic" can be viewed as synonyms, why is the true manner of evaluation of administrators a big secret? Because of this, one can only guess administrative goals by administrative actions: grow the institution, get more students by any means possible, retain more students by any means possible, get more pay...probably not in that order.

3.3 Institutional Effectiveness

3.3.1 The institution identifies expected outcomes, assesses the extent to which it achieves those outcomes and provides evidence of improvement based on analysis...

Here we come to a section where an accredited institution actually has to show in some way that it is improving in five different subsections, including "student learning outcomes". The first one, 3.3.1.1, "Educational Programs, including Student Learning Outcomes", is the most important subsection, as it partially addresses the education of the students (three of the other four subsections have nothing to do with students and education, with the remaining one partially addressing student support. One subsection, 3.3.1.4, addresses administrative support, leading one to wonder if supporting the students truly is less important than supporting the administrators).

In 3.3.1.1, not only is the institution required to identify "outcomes" (i.e., identify what is desired in the way of education), the institution also needs to show evidence of improvement. These outcomes are often reduced to easily quantifiable terms, for example, student retention.

It must be this way. Most of actual education is impossible to precisely define, much less precisely quantify the levels of education. It may be possible to say one student poem is better than another, for example, but to say with certainty that it's objectively 2 points better, or 5 points better, or whatever? This is all but impossible in a single course, much less over several semesters of courses.

For the sake of argument, let's assume this is possible and that steady improvement (necessary for accreditation according to this clause) is possible, and note the incredible lie that follows: there are accrediting bodies that ask for this as part of accreditation for decades, and yet we are to believe those accredited institutions are generally showing improvement in educating their students. If there is so much improvement in the manner in which education is provided, why is there endless evidence of grade inflation and greatly reduced coursework on college campuses? Improvement means doing more, not less.

How can such improvement exist when *literally everyone* familiar with the topic acknowledges students coming into college are weaker and less prepared than a generation or two ago? Institutions are improving their outcomes with less all the time, apparently.

So, the definition of "improvement" is kept simple…but the end result is accredited institutions always show improvement.

Where are the big breakthroughs that all this improvement should have? In addition to being less prepared, students study far less now than in years past. Probably as a result of the reduced student workload, measureable improvement in learning is minimal for a large percentage of students in their first two years[2]. And yet we're to believe that education is "improving" at accredited institutions in a documented way, and that this improvement has been shown year in and year out for a very long time.

Even though improvement is completely impossible to legitimately show, I believe every accredited institution provides evidence of improvement on a near constant basis. I've sat in on many a meeting and been told by administrators that we need to show improvement. Even back when my school offered no government student loan money (because we weren't accredited), and passing rates in my classes were higher than reported than at any accredited institution (because our students were primarily the ones that wanted to learn and paid with their own money), still administration was asking for improvement. I could have a 100% passing rate and still improvement was asked for. Yes, without student loans I might only have five students in my class (granting 4 As and a B, for example)...and I was asked to improve. Now, with all the loan money, I have 25 students in my class (giving 4 As, a B, a few C's, and everyone else dropping)...and still I am told to improve.

Now this clause is basically impossible to satisfy, so it's no great harm that, obviously, the "improvement" that accredited institutions show must be bogus. It may be forgivable that institutions give bogus results, but accrediting bodies forcing institutions to be deceptive in this category detracts greatly from the integrity of the rest of the process.

3.3.2 The institution has developed a Quality Enhancement Plan that (1) demonstrates institutional capability for the initiation, implementation, and completion of the QEP; (2) includes broad-based involvement of institutional constituencies in the development and proposed implementation of the QEP; and (3) identifies goals and a plan to assess their achievement.

I addressed my college's particular QEP in 2.12, above. Note carefully what's being asked here: the institution has to develop a QEP, prove that it can start, implement, and finish the QEP, include much of the institution in the QEP, and have a purpose to the QEP.

Comparatively speaking, the QEP and all it entails is five times as important as showing students are receiving some sort of education at the institution. Of course, in theory an institution could make "providing an education" a goal of the QEP, but this would be impossible to show quantitatively, and thus it would impossible to satisfy the requirements of this clause.

3.4 All educational programs.

3.4.1 The institution demonstrates that each program...is approved by the faculty and the administration.

ever It's interesting that my college is the only institution I've been at where my approval has

been asked regarding a program. Granted, I'm probably not qualified to approve an entire program, but considering the massive influence administration has over faculty, I do have my doubts about how important this is.

3.4.2 The institution's continuing education, outreach, and service programs are consistent with the institution's mission.

Note that the mission can be easily changed, so even if there is a problem here, it's easily fixed.

3.4.3 The institution publishes admission policies that are consistent with its mission.

This is why most every institution has a line about how they admit everyone, regardless of race, gender, or whatnot. Since they all use basically the same mission, it rather follows they'll have the same policies...and what college actually restricts admission all that much? Again, if there is a problem, it's easy to change the mission statement.

3.4.4 The institution publishes policies that include criteria for evaluation, awarding, and accepting credit for transfer...ensures that course work and learning outcomes are at the collegiate level and comparable to the institution's own degree programs. The institution assumes responsibility for the academic quality of any coursework recorded on the institution's transcript.

"I'm a transfer student from [another institution]. I just wanted to touch base with you before the semester started. I'm really good in math, my girlfriend calls me a human calculator."

--student entering my remedial math class, with credit from an earlier remedial course coming from elsewhere. You don't get many "human calculators" taking remedial courses, and throughout the semester he demonstrated all 4,000 known human facial expressions for "complete confusion," failing the course. I often wonder at the skills of his girlfriend, to evaluate him so highly.

Most every institution has hard posted rules regarding transfer credit; I've seen institutions refuse to accept their own coursework for degree programs, and I've seen transfer rules violated, with credit granted where it clearly shouldn't be, despite written policy; it all depends on who you know in administration. The key here is "comparable to the institution's own degree programs", so in theory a college need not accept any transfer credit....all that is required for accreditation is that the policies be published, not that they be fair in any way.

You can usually count on accredited schools accepting at least some credit from other accredited schools, even if that credit won't count for a degree. Nevertheless, a student wishing to transfer credit should resolve that issue first, before even applying to the school, and get that resolution in writing. The driving institutional need for more students usually will make it easier for transfer credit rules to bend if that's what it takes to get a student.

I often get students utterly unqualified to take the courses they're in, but were allowed to register based on transfer of credit from elsewhere. I can't recall a single time the institution where the credit came from had to "assume responsibility" for the bogus coursework by returning the student's money or the like.

3.4.5 The institution publishes policies that adhere to principles of good educational practice...

Certainly this is a reasonable thing to do, although "publish" and "follow" are very different things, and SACS doesn't require following of policies...keep in mind always, that accreditation is supposed to be an assurance that the institution really is a place to get an education, and how very little of accreditation is about the one thing a student should care about. With so much of their money going to accredited institutions, taxpayers probably should care about it as well.

3.4.6 The Institution employs sound and acceptable practices for determining the amount and level of credit awarded for courses, regardless of format or mode of delivery.

The phrasing here is to support, presumably, online and correspondence courses, which are very different than traditional classroom courses, enough to merit discussion on online courses in a different chapter.

There are still serious institutions that offer correspondence courses, with students literally completing the course material through physically mailing their work; these "dinosaur" courses are unchanged from when they first were created, decades ago. I can only guess that there was a time when accreditation meant something, and these courses represent the standards of that time. I do some tutoring on the side, and students taking correspondence courses are often overwhelmed enough to hire me for an hour or more a week while they struggle through the concepts. I've yet to see a correspondence course that wasn't *much harder* than a traditional course offered today.

For now, however, note that this clause assures, sort of, that the student will get the same credit for a course regardless of delivery method.

"Online schools? Like University of Phoenix, those guys? Right in the trash..."

--HR director describing treatment of resumes with online degrees.

This is all well and good I suppose, but I bet students would quickly avoid a method (say, online) if that method awarded zero credit. Curiously, online schools, even accredited ones, give no notification that their coursework is held in minimal esteem in the real world. Sometimes this low esteem is for good reason, though it's fair to consider in light of the evidence, "brick and mortar" schools may be getting too much credit. Whenever there's a faculty position open at my college, we get numerous applicants who have one (or more) online graduate degrees from often really odd-sounding fields; administration generally don't call such people in for interviews.

3.4.7 The institution ensures the quality of educational programs and courses offered through consortial relationships...

This is actually a fairly relevant clause, since otherwise a legitimate school could simply contract out to a non-legitimate school most or all of their students and coursework. Still, a school that does this will probably lose its honest student base long before it loses accreditation, and once again the institution self-regulates its own legitimacy.

3.4.8 The institution awards academic credit for coursework taken on a noncredit basis only where there is documentation that the noncredit course work is equivalent...

I guess this applies to some small percentage of students, but realize that "documentation" is just words on paper, it's easy enough to provide, and all it takes past that point is a compliant administrator, faculty aren't a factor in this decision.

3.4.9 The institution provides appropriate academic services.

"You can get a good education here, if that's what you want and you work to get it. You can also get a not-so-good education here, if that's what you want or aren't careful."

--another faculty member, describing the situation at an accredited institution I taught at.

Insofar that "appropriate" is in the eye of the beholder, this is a fine line. Accredited or not, a prospective student should check and see what the services are, verifying that they're appropriate to the particular student.

One academic service that is often lacking is academic counseling. After twenty years, I can't count the number of student complaints I've heard regarding getting bad counseling advice what courses to take to further the student's academic career. I don't recall a single student ever saying he got good advice, though I admit a student would have little reason to tell me such a thing.

Still, with most students taking 6 or more years to get a degree, it's clear administration isn't doing much of a job when it comes to advising students what classes to take to get a degree in a timely manner.

3.4.10 The institution places primary responsibility for the content, quality, and effectiveness of the curriculum with its faculty.

"This course is bogus."

"There's no content here."

"How are we supposed to spend 16 weeks on a course with only 4 weeks of material?"

--Faculty responses to a highly gutted mathematics course introduced by administration. Nonetheless, the course was forcibly approved, as a small minority of faculty were willing to teach it, for bonus considerations.

This is a questionable clause, and I've certainly seen it violated in practice. For the most part, faculty have nothing to do with the curriculum, outside of elective courses of their own construction. Degree programs must have about all the same courses, and those courses must all have about the same material in them, at least on paper. What actually happens in those courses is nowhere addressed by accreditation, and even if faculty object to the curriculum, they can be easily overruled.

3.4.11 For each major in a degree program, the institution assigns responsibility for program coordination, as well as for curriculum development and review, to persons academically qualified...

Degree programs and majors are almost all cut-and-pasted from institutions that already have such degree programs and majors, not that there's anything wrong with that (a bachelor's in psychology should mean nearly the same thing from State University or Harvard, after all). Academically qualified is a nice restriction, although you don't need to be qualified in the actual field of the program. There are Ph.D. degrees in "curriculum" or "education," and these fields somehow make the recipient qualified for this responsibility regardless of knowledge of any subject material.

3.4.12 The institution's use of technology enhances student learning and is appropriate...students have access to and training in the use of technology.

While at first glance this seems like a nice thing to have in an accredited institution, note how nothing here is really defined. "Appropriate" and "technology" are almost meaningless, and access could just be a single computer in the campus library. It would seem a degree program that specifically uses technology would have training, but what does that constitute for a random student? My college offers a course that helps the students identify the disk drive, the tower case, and the mouse (to judge by questions from a test in the course), and the course is used to satisfy this clause. This is "training", I suppose.

Computer training used to be a general requirement of our students, but it was removed. A factor in removing it was the extreme difficulty in finding qualified, degreed people willing to teach these "Mickey Mouse" (as the teachers of those courses describe them) courses for the money the administration is willing to pay. A Master's Degree in Computer Science opens up doors to well paying, legitimate, jobs, leaving few recipients of such degrees available for teaching. The skills are simply too economically useful for people with such skills to have much interest in teaching, so institutions get rid of the courses, rather than make teaching the skills more attractive. A simple look at job openings reveals a plethora of openings for people with real computer skills.

Meanwhile, the college course catalogues are jammed with completely worthless courses, filled with skills and knowledge taught by people that can't get a job in the real world with such skills and knowledge.

Isn't it fascinating how useful skills are taken *out* of the college curriculum, and useless courses inserted in, by administration? How is it even a puzzle that so many college graduates are unemployable?

3.5 Undergraduate Educational Programs

3.5.1 The institution identifies college-level general education competencies and the extent to which the students have attained them.

This is somewhat redundant to what was addressed above, so forgive a somewhat redundant commentary here. One might think the grades assigned from the course would address these competencies. This is not the case, instead, there is a general competency for a course, say "the student can solve a word problem", that is given. A faculty member at my college would then create a problem, assign it to his own students, and assess if the student can do it.

Almost exclusively these competencies are addressed with students that have not graduated, and in many cases not even been on campus but a few weeks. Nevertheless, these competencies are met with a high proportion of students. As I discussed above, this is all self-reported, at no point does SACS actually create a competency, or verify that students can demonstrate such competencies in anything like a controlled situation.

And, of course, SACS never seems to wonder why we need years to train a student when we consistently document competencies being shown after but a few weeks of classes.

3.5.2 At least 25 percent of the credit hours required for the degree are earned through instruction offered by the institution awarding the degree.

This just keeps a student from earning all his credits at one institution, and transferring it over to another and getting the degree quickly; the vast bulk of institutions put such restrictions on transfer credit that this would be a difficult clause to violate, and this is about the only advantage that non-accredited schools have to offer: a quick degree.

3.5.3 The institution publishes requirements for its undergraduate programs, including its general education components. These requirements conform...

Much like before, it's almost impossible not to have conformity in programs, and it's already pretty natural to put such requirements in student handbooks and elsewhere.

3.5.4 At least 25 percent of the course hours in each major…are taught by faculty members holding an appropriate terminal degree.

This is nice clause, but self-reported, easily manipulated, and for all that easy enough to satisfy with adjuncts. It is interesting that clauses like this mean you really need a Ph.D. in math to teach 10th grade algebra; it's hard to be upset at such outrageous efforts at my own job security.

3.6 Graduate and Post-Baccalaureate Degree programs.

This particular section is of little interest to the new college student and parallels 3.5, so not covered in detail in this book. The only interesting clause is the first, where it is specified that the graduate courses are more advanced in content than the undergraduate programs. This alleged "more advanced" content is self-reported, of course, and I'll look at online graduate courses in a later chapter.

3.7 Faculty

3.7.1 The institution employs competent faculty members…

"Any function that is differentiable is continuous, and any continuous function is differentiable."

"The probability that the population mean is in the 95% confidence interval is .95."

"Every function has an inverse."

--quotes from three different qualified (via "Math Education" degree) and experienced faculty regarding material in three different mathematics courses they were actually teaching, at an accredited institution where I was employed (for the uninitiated, these are all embarrassing things to say for a professor in this field, comparable to a history or geography expert saying in all seriousness "George Washington conquered Tokyo and then marched the Continental Army to nearby Moscow in less than a week.")

The competence of faculty is, of course, self-reported by the institution. I've observed more than my fair share of faculty members of questionable knowledge of the topics they teach. Every few years, another bogus "Ph.D." who has been teaching in academia for years is discovered. Yes, those fake professors are caught, so that could be taken as evidence the system works…but they're not caught by the accrediting agency, they're caught by the institution (because this is self-reported), and the years it takes for such frauds to be identified don't give me much confidence, even if, as I suspect, they are fairly rare people. Of great interest to me is how often these frauds are popular with students and administration, almost as though popularity facilitates surviving and prospering when competence is questionable. Key to this: there is no mechanism for identifying if a professor is teaching a bogus course.

Pensacola State College fired a tenured professor Tuesday amid allegations that he presented college administrators with an unaccredited master's degree from an online diploma mill...[3]

The University of Pennsylvania's vice dean, Doug Lynch, tricked school officials into believing he held a master's degree as well as a doctorate from Colombia University.

UPenn discovered Lynch's deceit, however, they kept him on in a leadership role regardless of his false claims.[4]

---isn't it fascinating that faculty with bogus degrees are fired (and he had tenure, to give an idea how long it took to discover), but not administrators, who can still be kept on "in a leadership role." Since administrators hire and fire both faculty and administrators, it's not much of a surprise at all. Administration has complete control over education now, and it shows.

This SACS clause, of course, only regards flat out bogus degrees, not competence. It's quite possible for someone with a bogus degree to nevertheless be a competent teacher, although I'm not sure SACS would take kindly to such a possibility. Bogus faculty members (or even the administrator, above) can work for years before the fraud is discovered. In any event, it's more common for me to see people with "legitimate" credentials to have no knowledge of the material they supposedly teach.

3.7.2 The institution regularly evaluates...each faculty member....

"[The professor]'s courses are a snap. Tests are all multiple choice, no writing. You learn nothing in class, just read the book. Easy."

--description of the classes taught by a professor that gets generally perfect evaluations every year, moving smoothly up the promotion ladder.

This is just the annual job evaluation, no different than anyplace else. You might be wondering if somewhere in the SACS document there's a clause where each administrator is regularly evaluated by faculty. No, there is not, certainly not in a meaningful sense.

These evaluations are interesting things, and almost entirely depend on how well the faculty member is doing what the administrator wants. "Not having to hear students complain" is very high on the list of administrative desires. Realize this is nearly interchangeable with "not having failing students" (i.e., "high retention")--my personal estimate for the probability that a given complaining student is also failing is around 0.95, and a faculty member with few complaints and high retention can find himself getting high marks in other categories of the evaluation, say for publishing, community service, or whatever, regardless of actual efforts in those categories.

On the other hand, generating student complaints for any reason can result in lower ratings everywhere else in the evaluation; it's not a random thing, and faculty quickly learn what not to do.

Me: "I see I'm docked a little under teaching policies. What's the problem?"

Administrator: "Your grading policy uses a weighted average. You need to use points."

My grading policy has 5% of a grade from attendance, 5% from homework, 60% from the three best tests of four in the course, and 30% from the cumulative final—thus the final grade is a weighted average, with tests (demonstrations of skill and knowledge) getting the most weight.

I have to make attendance/homework worth something (or else students won't show up or do the work). If either is worth too much, I have to deal with a host of excuses, and any excuse I reject causes the student to complain to administration.

"I want a make-up for that last test. My brother beat my sister-in-law to death, so we all had to go to Mississippi to give moral support for the trial..."

--I'm not kidding, an actual excuse for missing a month of classes.

As I drop the student's lowest test grade, no questions asked (to avoid hearing excuses), I have to make the final exam cumulative or else students that took the first three tests will consistently just blow off the last month of the semester (covered by the last test).

Thus, I use a weighted average. Actually demonstrating skills via tests is the most important part of a course to me, as it demonstrates student knowledge and skills. I'd prefer to treat my students as responsible adults, but I know they can make bad decisions. I help them by making homework and attendance worth something, even if it's a little insulting to "make" an adult behave a certain way (in actuality, all students get full credit for homework and attendance, but I don't tell them that).

Back to the point, I'm "graded" by my administrator using a published policy where I get 5% from volunteer work, 10% from committee work, 15% from the in class observation, and so on. My annual evaluation is a weighted average, given by an administrator who penalizes me for using a weighted average. Perhaps administration feeds on hypocrisy.

Anyway, SACS mandates every faculty member is regularly evaluated, and I agree that this is reasonable. I do wish the word "**regularly**" was replaced by "competently", however.

3.7.3 The institution provides ongoing professional development of faculty...

"When Alexander the Great conquered Alexandria, it was called Memphis at the time, he found the Great Library there, and took the knowledge back to Greece to form the foundation of Western thought. How many of you were unaware of this?"

--Diversity speaker provided to us by our institution, with a Ph.D. in African History and decades of experience. Regrettably, only a few of the faculty were familiar enough with history to realize the issues with these claims. Fewer still had the guts to dare risk annoying administration by challenging the claims.

The institutions I've been at provide development, in the form of speakers that come by once or twice a year. I don't know how it is elsewhere, but at my college, these speakers, often deeply ignorant of any subject, are there to tell us how to teach. I've been told many times to put less math (and more writing) in my math classes, to use more group projects==even if, as *Academically Adrift*, and common sense, says this negatively correlates with learning by the student[5]--and to give more credit for non-course things, like attendance. These speakers tell me these things, to "develop" my teaching skills.

Even with 20 years of experience I'm not a perfect teacher, and I still come across concepts that I know I'm not addressing clearly enough. I know "make attendance 20% of the course grade" is not improving my teaching, even if administration and these teaching experts believe otherwise. Luckily, I've always been able to find faculty, people with actual knowledgeable of my subject, to give real help in explaining topics when I was at a loss for ideas. This sort of development, or any other sort, isn't mandated by SACS. Not once in a score of years has an official speaker helped me to address any concept I teach in my courses.

Multiculturalist: "On this page is a list of various types of people. Check off the ones you would teach."

(The list has homosexual, black, murderer, pedophile, Catholic, etc).

Faculty: "Is this a joke?"

Multiculturalist (surprised): "No."

--The multiculturalist happened to have his apartment near mine. He really likes The Cranberries, playing "Linger" at insane volume for hours on end.

The accreditation document doesn't specify how the development will take place, which means the "development" will only be what administration wants it to be. At every institution I attended, such development was composed of invariably dubious talks on diversity, multiculturalism, political correctness, methods to increase retention, and patently absurd alternatives to teaching the subject material. As my quotes above show, sometimes this "development" can be completely outrageous in content.

Administration rarely, if ever, attends these discussions.

It probably would be better if faculty development were at the choosing of the self-serving faculty, instead of the self-serving administration, although either way it doesn't necessarily do much for the student and can be very counter-productive when it comes to education.

3.7.4 The institution ensures adequate procedures for safeguarding and protecting academic freedom.

"[The professor] told us Jefferson had sex with his slaves. I didn't need to hear that."

--official complaint, impacting the professor's annual evaluation (and not in a positive way).

I suppose for the most part there is academic freedom at my college and elsewhere. You're free to do whatever you want as long as the students don't complain and you have a high passing rate in your classes. Past that, I honestly haven't seen any real restrictions on freedom.

3.7.5 The institution publishes policies on the responsibility and authority of faculty...

Not much in the way of rights, but certainly faculty have responsibilities. Faculty authority is very questionable, however. How can faculty have any authority over anything when it's the administrators that have ultimate authority over the faculty in all things?

3.8 Library and Other Learning Resources

This section, in three parts, simply details that the institution theoretically has the tools so that if a student wants to get an education at the institution, he can do so on his own time using the resources at the institution. Between public libraries and the internet, this isn't hardly granting much more than what anyone with a car or internet connection can achieve.

3.9 Student Affairs and Services

3.9.1 The institution publishes a clear and appropriate statement of student rights and responsibilities...

Note how students specifically get rights; not so much for faculty (see 3.7.5, above.)

3.9.2 The institution protects the security...of student records...

"Those printouts we hand you at the beginning of the semester? Please don't throw them away, they have student records on them."

--administrative warning, explaining why faculty offices have piles of papers in them. Some faculty offices are pristine, but administration has yet to figure out how that happens.

What's interesting here is there is no prescribed penalty for failure to protect student records. There have been quite a few security leaks at institutions, and many grade-changing scandals, with nary a hint of a school losing accreditation over it.

3.9.3 The institution provides a sufficient number of qualified staff...

PR director at my institution: "Did that reporter ever get in touch with you? He asked me to help, but I didn't know your contact information."

Me: "Luckily I was in the phone book and he thought to look there. The interview was in the paper yesterday."

PR director: "It was? Can I get a copy?"

Me: "Sure."

(She had a copy of that very paper sitting on her desk, which I picked up and handed to her. A few days later, a local television reporter interviews me. I bump into the PR Director on campus:)

Me, to PR director: "Thanks for directing the TV reporter to me."

PR director: "You were on TV? Did you get a recording?"

Me: "What is your job, again?"

--I didn't say that last line, but did provide her with a recording of the interview. I created an elective "Game Writing" course, which attracted some local media attention before a shooting on another campus drowned it out.

"Sufficient" is in the eye of the beholder, but I suspect this clause is often used to justify the massive administrative and support bloat discussed earlier. "Qualified" is also self-determined by administration, leading to all sorts of bizarre people attempting to do jobs they don't know much about.

Student In My Writing Class: "You know that reporter that was here with the TV camera?"

Me: "Yeah, what about her?"

Student: "I paid her to write my papers for me in high school."

--the student, incidentally, was in the Education program, hoping to become a physical education teacher.

3.10 Financial Resources

This section covers the various financial aspects of the institution, in four sections. There's nothing here that addresses education, or even in the way of stopping student loans to customers that clearly aren't at the institution to learn anything.

3.11 Physical Resources

This section, in three parts, merely assures that the institution has the physical resources to do whatever it feels like doing. A safe environment is mandated, which, if one were to really scrape hard, could count as contributing to education a little. It's interesting that there's nothing here addressing parking, which is a severe problem at almost every institution

Parking is a funny thing at institutions. A campus with 10 classrooms open at a given time, and 30 students per class, will need a place for 300 students to park their cars at the beginning of the semester at that time—300 cars, basically. By the end of the semester, those 10 classrooms will only require perhaps 100 spaces. Administration quite understandably doesn't see the need to have 300 parking spaces when they're only useful for the first few months of the semester. As long as administrative and faculty parking spaces are reserved, I guess it's not a high priority for the institution. It's probably the same for restaurants and grocery stores, as these places also don't care to provide enough parking to handle peak use. Oh wait, they do care.

3.12 Responsibility for compliance with the Commission's substantive change procedures and policy.

When an institution is accredited, it is only done so for the programs it has at the time it is accredited. Thus, a liberal arts school, once accredited, can't immediately change over to a medical school and claim to be likewise accredited. This section details what to do when an institution wishes to add a new program, or otherwise wishes to make major changes in what it does. There's nothing here of relevance to a student wondering if accreditation means education.

An institution that wishes to make major changes (say, by adding a new degree program) doesn't lose accreditation for its other programs, it merely has to go through the relevant hoops detailed in this document to get its accreditation extended to the new program. It is theoretically possible to lose all accreditation by making substantive changes, but realistically this is as likely as a doctor accidentally amputating his own hand during an appendectomy.

3.13 Responsibility for compliance with other Commission policies

This very interesting section basically states that refusal to accredit can only come from not adhering to the clauses in the entire document or otherwise not following policies. Accreditation can't be rejected based on simply not liking the institution; of course, so many of the above clauses are so ambiguously defined, it would be pretty trivial to put the squeeze on an undesirable institution if SACS so wished.

As the accreditation process generates $15,000, and annual fees, quite possibly much more, I don't imagine SACS dislikes any institution whose check clears. Overall, the fees are actually fairly modest considering just how much money accreditation eventually grants to the institution via loan programs. The operating budget of accrediting bodies is usually just a few million, miniscule relative to the hundreds of thousands of students in the institutions in a region.

3.14 Representation of status with the Commission

This just states that the institution accurately represents where it is in the accreditation process, if it is accredited, and various other things relevant to accreditation.

One line is particularly fascinating here: "**No statement may be made about the possible future accreditation status**…" An institution cannot make a statement about a possible future accreditation status, for good or ill. Note that carefully: an institution that knows it is about to lose its accreditation due to gross violations is under no obligation to notify students, and in fact is not allowed to do so. An institution telling you that it is accredited not only is saying nothing about education, it's not even saying much about it being accredited in the near future.

4. Federal Requirements

As mentioned before, all accrediting agencies need to be recognized by the Secretary of Education, and thus have to follow Federal guidelines as well, which are passed right on to the institutions they accredit.

4.1 The institution evaluates success with respect to student achievement consistent with its mission. Criteria may include: enrollment data; retention, graduation, course completion, and job placement rates; state licensing examinations; student portfolios; or other means of demonstrating achievement of goals.

While many clauses are heavily abbreviated and edited, this clause is included in full to emphasize: education is *not* a recommended part of any success measure. *Lack of education as a goal is baked into the system.* Enrollment data could count towards success--just get the warm bodies. Graduation can be success--just print out the slips of paper. Course completion can be success--it's just graduation on a smaller scale.

I get the feeling few institutions use job placement rates and state licensing examinations (outside of technical schools), since those are outside the control of the institution. Student portfolios could well be a means of showing education, although no institution at which I've taught or attended uses them in general. Other means could be used to show success, but I doubt an administration would use the imagination to consider other means with so many easily quantifiable methods provided.

4.2 The institution's curriculum is directly related and appropriate to the mission and goals of the institution...

"I know for a fact I'm never going to use this."

--common student complaint, often accurate. In a physical education course, students do hundreds of jumping jacks, an exercise with no direct application in the real world. Similarly, students do many exercises in my math classes that have no specific applications.

While it's nice that accreditation assures this, this clause is somewhat redundant to the above, and most students can usually figure out if it's not the case. So much of what is taught is questionable when it comes to directly practical applications, both in my field and others.

My college has a Business (sometimes called "Elementary") Calculus course, for example, and one might think such a course would relate to having a business. I've owned and run a variety of businesses (including a restaurant), I know in perfect detail that nothing in Business Calculus really helps with a business. I can mumble some half-hearted apology about how the course does teach attention to detail and rigor...but this isn't enough to justify calling the course "Business Calculus".

As always, institutions self-report the appropriateness of what they're doing, so this sort of shenanigans is quite common.

4.3 The institution makes available to students and the public current academic calendars, grading policies, and refund policies.

Good to have, although this probably isn't an issue with institutions.

4.4 Program length is appropriate for each of the institution's educational programs.

"I have to take this senior level course to graduate, and it's only offered in the Fall; it takes up every weekday afternoon from 1 to 4. I have to take this

other senior level course to graduate, and it's also only offered in the Fall, from 2 to 3 Monday, Wednesday, and Friday. What the hell?"

--student complaint regarding a program at a nearby state university

While every program I've ever seen could theoretically be completed in 2 or 4 years (depending on the credit hours required), what penalties does the institution face if withdrawal policies are such that few students actually complete in that time? None. What happens if critical courses are offered so sparsely that it would be miraculous if a student managed to line up everything year to year to complete it in that time? Nothing. What happens if students manipulate loans and course taking so that it takes them quadruple or more the "appropriate" time to complete a program? Nothing.

These events are all very common, however, and it doesn't take much imagination to guess which part of the institution sets the policies that allow for it.

4.5 The institution has adequate procedures for addressing written student complaints and is responsible for demonstrating that it follows those procedures when resolving student complaints.

"[The professor] did not say 'Good evening' quickly enough to me when I said 'Good evening' to him."

--written student complaint that required a response from the professor, who was encouraged to reply more quickly in the future.

Certainly, this is nice to have, but do realize that the main time administration really cares about complaints is when they've an axe to grind against a particular faculty member (and "not passing enough students" has forged many an axe). Note that complaints against administration have literally nowhere to go and no required policies for dealing with them.

4.6 Recruitment materials and presentations accurately represent the institution's practices and policies.

As there is no oversight, it's difficult to violate this clause; institutions self-report this, after all, although outside of athletics recruiting (and those types of students generally know where they're going and why), there's not much that can go wrong here.

4.7 The institution is in compliance with its program responsibilities under...the most recent *Higher Education Act* as amended.

The Higher Education Act, signed into law in 1965, provides educational resources to educational institutions, and sets guidelines for whom should get federal student loans. The terms of these loans are statutory: there is no risk assessment to them. This Act is re-authorized and modified by Congress approximately every five years.

In 1998, the Gear Up authorization *guaranteed* financial aid for students who had a high school diploma. And here we have direct evidence for the death of the myths regarding what it means to go to college and be a college student. Anyone with a diploma and no place else to go, can come to college and pick up a check.

4.8 An institution that offers distance or correspondence education documents each of the following...

Broken into three parts, this clause provides special requirements for this type of education.

First, there is some effort made to verify that the student submitting the material is the same as registered for the course (secure login and pass code is primarily how online distance courses do this, and note how trivial it is for a student to simply pass that code off to a ringer if need be). In practice, this is meaningless, as we'll see later.

There also needs to be a written policy for protecting the privacy of such students (no prescribed penalty for violating such policy).

Finally, there needs to be written notification of any additional costs for taking these types of courses. Most correspondence courses, relics of an older age, are offered at a discount—these courses are not actually taught by a professor, after all, so charging for teaching would be unfair. This differs from the shiny new online courses, that often likewise have no actual teaching...but are just as expensive as traditional courses.

Note that no effort is made here to verify anything educational is going on in these courses.

4.9 The institution has policies...for determining the credit hours awarded for courses...

All institutions follow basically one of a few types of protocols for awarding credit hours for courses (the most common is 1 credit hour for each 50 minutes of class time for most lecture courses, with exceptions for labs and other special courses). This is hardly much of a requirement.

Summary:

An appendix defines some more terms, but the above is, in brief, all that is required for an institution to acquire accreditation under SACS. Very little of the above has anything at all to do with education, or showing an education is being provided. What little might arguably apply is all self-reported by the institution, SACS never sends representatives into classrooms and sees with their own eyes what's really going on. SACS never sends people to take the courses and sit in the classrooms to see exactly what the coursework entails. SACS never takes online courses and establishes there is learning and teaching going on there, or that there is no cheating going on in such courses. SACS never takes a look at all the course materials from actual courses and sees with their own eyes what students truly are expected to learn in a course (I've heard rumors that they sometimes look at samples). SACS never considers the graduation/grades of students and thus is never in a situation to consider if a school is merely a diploma mill with only the veneer of legitimacy that, at most, does all that is required for accreditation.

Individuals in the following areas receive the highest priority for inclusion in the Registry:

Governance and Administration
Administrative Services (financial resources)

---SACS is always seeking evaluators for their Registry of evaluators, with some types of evaluators in more demand than others. Faculty can become evaluators, but only with the express approval of the administration of their respective institution.

It's also worth noting that while faculty have various responsibilities and restrictions placed upon them in accreditation, of all the administrators only the chief administrator merits specific mention above. Administrators can apparently do whatever they wish, provided their activities go towards goals of, say higher graduation or retention rates (from 4.1).

The Principles of Accreditation is something of a living document, and is subject to change, albeit incremental. Just a few years ago, administrators needed, as part of accreditation, to have the experience, competence, and capacity to lead the institution, while the current document no longer requires capacity—an odd requirement to drop. Institutions now need "a sufficient number" of qualified staff, instead of in the past where it only needed to be sure the staff were qualified—almost as though accreditation were trying to add to the number of staff at the institution. Institutions also used to have to provide financial profile information on an annual basis, but not now[6]. There are other, minor, changes, and perhaps it is only imagination that would lead one to believe that, even in the last few years, accreditation requirements seem to be dropping.

Accrediting agencies usually only have a small permanent staff (a few dozen at most), and recruit personnel from administrators at accredited institutions, so perhaps it isn't such a surprise that administrators have few restrictions via accreditation, or that accredited institutions get nearly a "free ride" when it comes to violating these principles, or that there is at least the appearance of steadily dropping requirements for accreditation.

To be fair, accreditation was never about education, even a century ago. It was a self-regulated process, where faculty at institutions (back then, faculty *were* the administrators) got together and examined each others' practices, to learn from each other and reach agreement on best practices. This was an era when "get rich" wasn't part of education, so there few temptations to not be honest in endeavor. Now, with a trillion dollars of loan money on the table, and with many administrative positions regularly paying $100,000 a year (and *much* more as you go up the ladder), the time is long past to have accreditation be such a trusting process.

There might not be a lock on the Poor Box in church, when donations are only a few dollars. But if the box has a trillion dollars in it? That's completely different.

A population seduced by myth into dreaming college is the yellow brick road to a successful, honest life. Mandated guaranteed funds allow the population to follow their dreams at the college of their choice, or nearly so. The legitimacy of these college dreams is certified by accreditation programs. Throughout the entire country, accreditation is considered the gold standard for determining if an institution is legitimate. And it addresses nothing beyond asserting that the administration is determined and capable to do whatever is necessary to get those checks flowing.

Accreditation is as much a slip of paper as a degree from a diploma mill.

Can you get a legitimate education from a non-accredited institution? If they charge for it, probably not. There are many non-accredited "institutions" that will cheerfully sell you a degree, for perhaps 2% of the price of getting a degree from an accredited online institution; considering an unaccredited degree is often worth about as much in the marketplace as an accredited online degree, this might be a bargain and thus less of a fraud, but a degree is still not an education.

Something never said in a college admissions office is how a person can get an education for free if he wants. The public library has nearly every book a person could need for a bachelor's degree, and the internet has basically all human knowledge available. Even people that don't like to read books can still learn something from Khan Academy's 3000 free videos on coursework from basic English to Organic Chemistry (and tens of millions of views says these videos are generally good). University of the People is nearly free and offers coursework and programs comparable to other schools. It's not difficult to just get a course catalogue from any college, ask for the syllabus, buy the textbook for an exorbitant fee (if the library can't get it) and learn. Harvard and MIT, among other respectable institutions, provide the content of many of their courses online for free. A self-motivated person has endless opportunities to learn even very advanced topics for free. Such a learner won't have the benefit of "a degree from an accredited institution", but in all seriousness that's neither the point of education nor is accreditation much of a seal of approval.

Self-learning is a hard way to get an education, and what of the remedial student? A student that hasn't been able to learn much in the first 18 years of life might not have the skills to give himself an education. College student population growth has gone hand in hand with the growth in the number of students that require at least one remedial course when they come to college, so if educational institutions really are interested in education, they should be doing something for remedial students.

Accreditation doesn't protect the average sucker from getting into deep student debt for nothing. A remedial student, a "below average sucker" if you will, forced to spend at least one additional semester in remedial courses, will of necessity get even deeper into debt. Because of this additional expense and risk, institutions acting with integrity should be taking care to see that treat these particularly vulnerable students properly. Let's now take a look at remediation, and see if it's really doing the job of helping these people get an education, or preventing them from unduly hurting themselves.

Chapter 3: The Myth of Remediation

A student came to me for my developmental math class, and passed, with hard work. He took me again for College Algebra, and Trigonometry, passing both. He graduated, off to a local university. Two years later, he came to me for help in his latest math course, Differential Equations.

--A rare success story for me. At one institution, not one student in four years went from developmental math to successfully passing Calculus I, much less Differential Equations, which is taken after Calculus III.

A great scam needs suckers, and the more suckers, the better. It didn't take long before administrators realized that the big, big money was in broadening the market, dragging remedial students into the pool of victims.

The easily acquired and plentiful student loan scheme means anyone can go to college, but what if the student has little in the way of academic skill or interest? A popular TV commercial hawking college education has the would-be student sing about not doing great in high school—enough to keep a student out of college, years ago, and evidence the myth is still alive. It's not just late night TV commercials that target these potential students (or should I say victims?) for enrollment, although there has always been some option for remedial classes at college or university. Only a few such classes were offered, since "in the good old days," only a few students lacking in basic skills could nonetheless gain admittance to an institution.

No matter the era, no matter the subject, no matter the class, there are always going to be some students weaker than others. Both faculty and administration were against students being in classes beyond their capability, albeit for different reasons. Even a few weak students force the teacher to slow down, and reduce course content, and that harms the prepared and hardworking students, who need that content to succeed in later courses...and the weaker students still fail. This lowers passing rates, which administration cannot tolerate.

Answer: "The Rapist."

Question: "How does a remedial psychology student pronounce the word 'therapist'?"

--Campus joke.

An aberration emerged from the unholy alliance between faculty and administration: institutional remediation. The weaker students, the ones more likely to fail, would be identified and shuffled off to special classes, so that faculty wouldn't have to deal with them in the "regular" courses. Administration could still claim a large student base, and better course passing rates as well. This is a win-win situation, in theory, and absolutely there needs to be an option for students that legitimately have reasons for not knowing basic material, material they'll need to know if they want to learn the concepts of higher education. As long as the numbers of students requiring remediation are small, the system was fairly effective at giving borderline students a chance to prove they really could excel in a college environment, despite a rough start.

In today's college environment, entrance restrictions are minimal, so most anyone can get accepted into an institution of higher learning. Student loans are not strictly acquired by people who "want to learn," even if they don't know all that much to begin with. Instead, student loans are granted to anyone who can "check a box saying you are a degree seeking student." Administrations at many institutions have become very successful at talking people into checking that box, and remediation has come to dominate "higher education" now, with a great number of incoming students requiring one or more remedial courses before beginning a real college education. There would be many more remedial students, a clear majority even, but administration has "defined down" college material over the years to keep this from happening.

Even institutions with admission standards still admit remedial students. To take a college math course the student might need to score 250 on a placement test, while the admission "standard" requires the student to score 200 to get admitted to the college. While one has to chuckle at a college "standard" that admits students not ready for college, such is quite common. Having a great number of students going into remedial courses looks bad for institutions of higher education, but administration tirelessly works to fix this problem, but not in a way that a person of integrity might think:

"We're going to reduce the score necessary on the placement test to get into College Algebra so that even the weakest students will be told they can skip developmental courses if they want to. They'll still be competitive."

--Administrator, explaining a clever plan to reduce the number of students taking remedial courses. Until I heard this, I had no idea that getting an education was a competition. This change in policy led to several disastrous years in the entry level mathematics courses.

When a student tries to enroll for an entry level course, often he'll take some sort of placement test to see where he fits as far as reading, writing, and mathematical skills. There are many sorts of tests, each with their own special scoring system, ultimately translated into either "good enough for a college level course" or "should take a remedial course." Amongst the many choices, most institutions favor some form of standardized test, paying a dollar or two per student for the privilege of having an independent company quickly grade and administer the test online. These tests are far from perfect, but have been around for decades, with constant improvement by many private corporations legitimately interested in providing a better, more accurate product. They are quick, cheap, and about 95% accurate for determining which mathematics course a student should take next. Quick and cheap are important factors—the days of real "entrance examinations" for incoming college students are long over, students want to be admitted quickly, and administration complies. The advantage to online grading is there's no need to wait for faculty to come in to grade the test; even if no faculty are around, the test can be administered and graded in a matter of minutes, an hour at most and often less. The 95% accuracy might sound very good, but it means that in every classroom of at least 20 students, you'll expect one student was misdiagnosed by the test.

I admit that's high, but institutions have no choice in the matter: they really need way to figure out where a student belongs. It's not feasible to administer to every student a 3 hour comprehensive test and hand grade it (this would be around 99% accurate, and costly, assuming an incoming student would take such a test). A fast, cheap test that costs almost nothing to administer is a fine solution, and this as good a way as any to determine the extent of mathematical education a person received in 12 years of public school. To get around the "low" accuracy of the test, any student who complains bitterly enough can take any course he wants, going into remedial if the test says he should be in College Algebra, or vice versa. This event is rare, but happens, usually to the detriment of the student—at some point you have to let a person make his own mistakes.

As hinted at above, administration hates losing control of students to placement tests, and is always looking into ways to take back control. The most likely way in the future will be through PARCC, a placement test that will allow students to place out of placement tests. It probably will be more accurate, as some parts will be hand-graded, making it harder for a student to look knowledgeable with just a few lucky guesses. A planned trial on 20 million tests will take place soon. It doesn't take a calculator to see the amount of money being poured into re-inventing the placement tests is huge. Administration clearly wants this control, and a reasonable person might wonder how well they could be trusted with this power.

A student that does poorly on a placement test, no matter how poorly, is never turned away. "No problem," says college admissions, "you'll just need to take a developmental course or two and then you'll be fine!" Years ago, these types of courses were called "remedial," and this is a more accurate word, since it indicates a correction of something deficient, in this case deficiency of skills and knowledge that should have been gained in public school. "Remedial" became something of a slur, so they started calling them "developmental," which administration insists means the same thing, just not a slur. Whatever the name for these courses, administration certainly never tells students that fewer than 1 in 10 remedial students will get a 2 year degree within 3 years[1]. That's above a 90% failure rate...these are not good odds for making a low-interest loan. That's just getting the degree, even with a degree it's not at all certain the graduate will get a job that pays sufficiently to address the loan.

And those are the successful students! 40% of students that start in remedial *never* make it out of remedial courses. Of course, the college gets the loan money, while the student gets the debt, so the college has no reason to tell the student such depressing information…he might change his mind about going to college, and there goes that sweet check.

"Someone's making a lot of money off this. Not us."

--Mathematics department head, at another daylong meeting addressing ways to improve remediation.

Another dirty little secret of remediation is the sheer size of it. College remediation is a 3 billion dollar industry, and over half of incoming community college students will require remedial coursework (around 20% of university students will require remediation, but this is a little misleading since most weaker students get directed towards community college)[2]. Keep this in mind when a community is being sold on opening up a community college for "higher education": the majority of the students there will be learning high school level material—material the community already paid for their children to learn in high school. Universities even have tried to justify rising tuition costs due to all the additional remediation they do[3]. If remediation were truly that expensive, the university could just, well, not admit the remedial students in the first place, although administration would never turn down a warm body.

Actually, to call the material high school level is rather generous. It makes sense to look at remedial courses in some detail, to make it easier to see what's going on in this critical stream of institutional revenue. I'll focus on the math courses since I know them well, although the situation is only a little different in the English courses:

1. **College Algebra**

    "It's called College Algebra because nobody would pay for a course called The Algebra You Should Have Learned in High School."

--Faculty member (not me, though I wish it were).

Algebra is the basic language of mathematics, it's all but impossible in the modern world to accomplish much in math without some familiarity with the syntax of algebra. I was a bit slow in math, and a year behind the "top" students. Thus, I took algebra in the 11th grade, instead of the 10th grade like the better students, but the point is college material today used to be early high school material.

"[That professor]'s math class is hard. You'll have to come to class for it."
--overheard student comment, defining what makes a course hard, relative to other courses, no doubt.

College Algebra is a necessary course, the language, notation, and attention to detail learned there is critical to almost every other field. It is the prerequisite to over a 100 courses, and yet administration is perpetually trying to get rid of it, unable to understand that doing so shuts students out of many of the most profitable fields of study.

The "College Algebra" course offered at my college (and elsewhere) is little different than the remedial algebra course that I taught at University of South Florida in the 80s...it's also little different than the algebra course I took in high school. The primary differences are that College Algebra has less information than my high school course, lacking discussion of several topics, like matrices, circles, hyperbolas, inequalities, and a few other things. This is actually representative of many low level college courses: they have less than what used to be taught in high school courses of the same name. I also teach a college trigonometry course for example, and it similarly covers far less material than the trigonometry I took in high school. In any event, I include a discussion of College Algebra in the chapter on remedial courses because, at one point, it was a remedial course.

Passing rates in College Algebra courses usually run a bit more than 50%, although not much more (at one university I taught, the rate went from 50% to above 85% from one semester to the next, due to extensive pressure and threats from administration to pass more students). This is certainly lower than many other classes, especially the classes where, like my student quoted above, attendance (or, likely, any learning of the material) isn't needed for passing.

Pitchman: "What we know for sure is, the students who score high enough for College Algebra usually took courses past College Algebra in high school. The students who don't quite make it into College Algebra took it in high school, and so on down the line."

Faculty: "Wait a minute. You mean there's hard evidence for what we know to be true: that to achieve a goal in learning, you must push past that goal to succeed? Why haven't these results been published?"

Pitchman: "That was off the record."

--Exchange between faculty and pitchman, discussing results learned from a very popular standardized test very often used to place students.

Because the passing rate of College Algebra is so unsatisfactory in administration eyes, many campuses offer an "Explorations in Algebra" type course, a fake course with "Algebra" in the title so it at least sounds like it might be a real course. These courses are rationalized by "removing material the students don't need," and it's no small amount of material. There are variations, but the course seldom has significantly more in it than a remedial course, but it's for college credit all the same. Well, sort of college credit: the course is seldom transferrable and doesn't prepare the student for anything (remember, College Algebra is a prerequisite for over 100 courses). That said, the fake Algebra course generally has a much higher passing rate, which makes administration very happy...and is worthless when the student tries to apply it towards most any degree anyone would be willing to pay for.

The quote above hints at a truth, at least in mathematics and probably in other fields: the most advanced skill a person has mastered *cannot be* the most recent skill that was learned. In order to be comfortable with high school algebra, a student must push past the concepts in high school algebra. After years of diligently working to make a college degree represent no more than a high school diploma of years ago, college administrators, by promoting "Explorations" type courses, are now working to make a college degree as meaningful as graduating from the 8th grade.

"Dammit. I studied for two hours and STILL failed that test."

--student angrily telling me my test was too hard. The two hours represented all the time he'd put into the course over the last month. How did he get the idea that two hours of study would be sufficient to understand a month of material? Hint: other courses he was taking.

Although the passing rate is relatively low, College Algebra really isn't that tough a course. Every semester, I've had multiple students that failed the course before take it again, come back and pass the course, often with a B or better. They're only too willing to tell me the difference is they actually studied the second time around. For most students, passing this course is simply a matter of study and effort, which can be quite the confusing barrier when compared to other courses.

On the other hand, there are absolutely people (perhaps 10% of the population) that have a real problem with math. They've come to my office literally unable to tell me the slope-intercept equation for a line ("$y = mx + b$"), and then shown me a page where they've copied "$y = mx + b$" *hundreds* of times the day before. It doesn't matter how hard they study, they just won't get it.

The most common issue they claim to have is they "can't remember anything" when it comes time to take the test. They are not lying about this lack of memory, but in speaking with them, asking for demonstrations of knowledge outside of test time, they can't remember anything outside of test time, either. It's a real problem, and I do think it's cruel of administration to force such people to take this course, but in administration's defense, for accreditation, they have no choice to force students to take it. Quite often, these students eventually pass by taking an "Independent Study" course, "fishing" for an easy instructor, or some less reputable means. I'm glad these students eventually find a way, but I do wonder what kind of education a person can have when he remembers none of it, and how administration can claim to be acting with integrity when they go out of their way to sell an education to such a person.

"How much is 2/5?"

--Student question, a high school graduate who passed a remedial course the previous semester. I tried to explain via a pie graph and other examples, but I'm not convinced I helped her even a little. A history professor jokingly offered the best answer: "3/5."

Many students come into College Algebra unprepared, either by catching a break from a remedial teacher, getting lucky on the placement exam, or by simply not wishing to take a remedial course in the first place. I try to accommodate these students as much as possible (for example, for every single problem that has a fraction, I have no choice but to stop and review how to work with fractions), but the end result despite my efforts is most unprepared students fail the course. With no ability to work with fractions or distinguish between multiplication and addition in algebraic notation, there's little chance they can pass. I'm hardly the first faculty to complain how hard it is to teach a class with such unprepared students, and complaints like mine led to the creation of remedial courses, to address the material that all students, theoretically, learned in public schools. This leads to our first official remedial (nowadays) course:

2. **College Preparatory Algebra II**

"The Civil War was inevitable, but it didn't have to be that way."

---quote from a student history paper. A month before the paper was

written, the history professor ranted extensively to the rest of the faculty how annoying it was that he had to stop his lecture, and spend time defining the word 'inevitable' to his class. This is common to remedial students: they can look you dead in the eye, nod in agreement that they understand, and still not comprehend a word you're saying. Remedial students generally can take other college classes, even if they have yet to take, much less pass, the remedial courses.

This is the most common developmental math course for a student to take. It covers basically the material that public schools address in 7th-9th grade, from graphing lines to the basics of the quadratic formula. A great number of students are in this course because they failed this material (or failed to take it) in the 7th, 8th, 9th, 10th, 11th, and 12th grade. Again, I pass around 50% of the students, which should be considered amazing considering the student's history of failure, but the pressure from administration to pass, pass, pass, pass the students is very strong, and the majority of meetings regarding math instruction are about how to increase retention (i.e., passing) in this class.

What's particularly funny about this is how much time faculty spends in state meetings, presenting information and material that the high school teachers need to give their students, so their students will be prepared for college. Somehow, we think the pressure college faculty face to pass as many students as possible isn't nearly as bad as the pressure high school teachers face.

A large minority of students in College Preparatory Algebra II are non-traditional. They took and passed the material years ago, but have simply forgotten it, or at least are extremely rusty. While spending four months reviewing in college is a painfully slow and expensive way to go about regaining these skills, I can appreciate not everyone has the initiative to go down to the library, check out a book, read and re-read and practice for a few hours until the skills come back. I'm sure administration would never suggest such a course of action to a student, not with a sweet student loan check on the line.

Me: "A quarter of my remedial class was high school students…."

(other faculty chuckle)

Faculty: "Doesn't administration know you can't remediate when they haven't had a chance to learn it the first time around?"

I also have non-traditional students that are young, not even old enough to have graduated high school. My college successfully recruits high school students into taking this course, oblivious to the fact that the material here *has* to be offered at the high school already, for less money. As the high school schedule is different from the college schedule, I have to change my course presentation just for these students. Year after year I do what I can to offer an abbreviated course (almost 2 weeks less material because of the schedule conflict), simultaneously with the other students, who so far don't seem to notice when a handful of very young students disappears towards the end of the semester. Putting high school students in remedial courses isn't restricted to my campus, my associates at other schools report administration is doing the same elsewhere.

"I co ming offise to day AAAAaaaa?"

--E-mail from a Vietnamese student. She got an A in my trigonometry class, dominating the other students despite not knowing much English at all. Yes, she did work in a nail salon when she wasn't in class, and no, she didn't graduate the equivalent of high school in her native country. She asked one question the whole semester, coming to my office to do so: "How come students that know nothing are in this class?"

Another small percentage of students are in College Preparatory Algebra II because their English is very weak; I often get a few Spanish-speaking students, and on rare occasions someone with a different native language. These students, like the non-traditional students, tend to do better than the other students because their reasons for doing poorly on the placement test, for example, have little to do with a fundamental lack of interest in learning. These students care, but through not being born to the English language just don't happen to be prepared for advanced material presented in that language. Even if this course is less than ideal, it does serve students that care.

Disciplinary problems, almost completely absent in college courses (I've had perhaps two significant incidents in twenty years), are strikingly common at the remedial level. Loud talking to the point of interrupting class (and ignoring the instructor's requests for quiet) are everyday events, and students becoming hostile and engaging in shouting matches with the instructor during class are not unheard of.

Student: "Is Mr. McTurkey in?"

Faculty Member, looking at list of names on the door: "Who?"

Student: "Mr. McTurkey."

--Students often have trouble with my last name, which is why I introduce myself as Mr. [first name]. This particular student had taken me for the previous remedial course, but was having trouble and came to my office for help. I wasn't in, but the faculty member who shared my group office was happy to let me know the student was looking for me, albeit a little confused on my name. I firmly believe reading is more important than mathematics, although educated people should have proficiency in both.

Remedial students will even initiate calls or answer their phone during class. In College Algebra, upwards of 20% of the class at any given moment will be texting/playing on their cell phones, but the percentage of students engaging in this activity in this level of remedial class is usually around 50%, at least in my classes (it's rather amusing how many students think they are fooling me by keeping their hands in their crotches for 50 straight minutes, or digging in a purse every five minutes of class). Various rules make it difficult for faculty to do much about this, and faculty, for many reasons, are loathe to try anything that might lead to a student complaint.

3. **College Preparatory Algebra I**

Me, addressing class: "Ok, so last class we learned about complementary angles, worked some problems with complementary angles, and I assigned homework problems on it. Any questions on the homework?"

Student: "Yeah, problem #1."

Me, reading the problem: "Angles A and B are complementary...before going to the rest of the problem, what does complementary mean for angles?"

(I go to the whiteboard to write down the definition, and wait. Several moments of silence, then a student responds)

Student A: "They're equal?"

(Three other students, echoing): "Equal?" "Equal?" "Equal?"

Me: "No. The mathematical word for 'equal' is 'equal'. This is a different word, and it means something different. Take out your books, and look in the index or the section the homework is in, and find the definition of complementary."

(I sit down and wait. Sixty seconds of page flipping passes, and a student responds)

Student B: "They're the same?"

(Three other students, echoing): "Same?" "Same?" "Same?"

--I believe the most frightening thing about this incident is that nobody even laughed, no student in the course understood how this answer could not be right, or had the initiative/capability to look up a word in a book even when directed to do so.

College Preparatory Algebra I basically covers material from the 6th to most of the 9th grade. If that seems to overlap with College Preparatory Algebra II above, that's because it does; years of my explaining this to administration accomplished nothing, because the course as-is had a higher retention rate. Recent initiatives in higher education may make this course obsolete (but will come back again in a few years, as addressed below). The only thing missing from this course relative to the more advanced developmental course is a discussion of the quadratic formula.

Despite this being nearly the same course as College Preparatory Algebra II, the students that place into this course are clearly weaker than in the "advanced" remedial course—those placement tests are pretty good, all things considered. The students in this course, whether I pass or fail them, spend years on campus, going nowhere but deeper in debt. I did have one student, her grasp of English shaky at best (Spanish being her first language, and non-traditional as well), take this course, and she earned an A. I offered her the chance to just read the few pages that differentiates this course from College Preparatory Algebra II, and she did so, passing the final exam for the latter course without actually taking it, and moving directly to College Algebra (saving her four months of time), which she also passed in her first attempt.

For a small minority of students, these courses can be the start of a successful college career, but for the rest, being told to take one of these courses is a warning. Usually if a student comes to enroll, and needs a year of remedial courses before he can take what used to be a remedial course, maybe administration should ask "Are you serious about learning?" rather than telling him "Check this box stating you're looking for a degree, so you can start getting student loan money." It's a long hard road to higher learning from the 6th grade, and I just don't see the economic sense in loaning everyone money to spend so much time learning material that is available for free in the public library, and that most people already had years of opportunity to learn in public school. While I don't see the sense in it, administration sure does, for some reason. Oh yeah, the checks.

4. Basic Mathematics

"It's dummy-dummy math."

--this course as described by a student.

This course covers perhaps 3rd to 5th grade material, from how to add and subtract whole numbers, to plotting points on the number line. While many of these students may well have serious learning disabilities, I've often observed a learned helplessness to these students, as though they've been trained to stop all activity as soon as a question is asked. No exercise is too simple, no question anything but insurmountable, and every homework problem I assign must be done in class because, well, no understanding of the material can be taken for granted.

Even as I acknowledge that, perhaps, the college is justified in offering this course, I again don't understand why there are no moral reservations about loaning people money to take it, or interest in directing them to cheaper methods of gaining these rudimentary skills. What's interesting is disciplinary problems actually drop off here relative to the other remedial courses; while there is some unruliness, it's not as severe as in the other remedial courses, nor is cell phone use during class nearly as prevalent.

I've never seen or heard of a student going from this course to anything like a successful college career. With over 90% of "normal" remedial students failing to have a college career, this isn't surprising.

My college is currently in the process of reworking the entire remedial math system, again, based on yet another theory of presentation that, if followed, will supposedly increase retention, so these remedial courses may not even exist at the publishing of this book; they were part of my college for 10 years, however, and many institutions have similar courses.

There's nothing wrong with trying to improve education and learning, but at some point, someone should think that "Gee, this student didn't learn this in 3rd, 4th, 5th, 6th, 7th, 8th, 9th, 10th, 11th, and 12th grade. Maybe he doesn't want to learn this and we shouldn't loan him money to learn it." Failing that, admissions should think "Maybe loaning this person money that goes right to us would be taking advantage of someone with a mental disability and it would be not be acting with integrity to do that." So far, these possibilities have never been raised at any meeting concerning remediation, and administration continues to sell these courses to anyone willing to go into debt to take them.

Let's go over that last issue again: an adult coming to college campus with skills comparable to a 2nd grader should still be treated with integrity, and not exploited. Putting such an adult into a contract of lifelong indebtedness is borderline criminal...and yet many college campuses have this level of remedial course for sale to incoming students, and don't even blush when asking the student to check that box. As a matter of principle, a college helping students to get financial aid for this course should have their accreditation reconsidered; taking advantage of people like this cannot possibly be acting with integrity. To satisfy the people that really need the help of this course, a college could just simply offer it, for free, as part of their obligation to the local community; I know I'd be more motivated to donate my time to such students if I knew they were there out of a legitimate interest in learning, instead of just for the check.

For one semester, we offered an even more basic math (a sub-pre-sub-remedial course, if you will). This course was promoted by one instructor as "taking out the math they don't need, like squares and rectangles," and allowed to offer it after singing the "better retention" siren song to administration.

Why so many remedial students?

"Hey. We're selling a plot of land, and thought we could ask our math professor friend for help. The land is a rectangle, 120' on one side, and 300' on the other. I know you need that much. What's the square footage and how do you get it?"

--question from the wife of a longtime friend, valedictorian at her school, and a

bright person. She and her husband just didn't take math in high school.

Now, it's easy to blame the high schools for the unprepared students entering college, but that's not fair. High schools offer College Algebra-level material, and often more advanced math, and also simpler courses, as well as other options. They tell students "this is what you need for college, this what you need to get by, and this is what you need to pump gas" giving their students the option to take the challenging material, something simpler, or no math at all. Students choose (or are advised by counselors or parents) not to take the challenging coursework, improving their GPA and chances of graduating high school. I don't blame students for taking the easy way out when asked to do so; I would have myself if my parents had let me. A student who puts effort into it can avoid having a math class for his last few years of high school, if he wishes; I commonly get students that tell me they haven't taken math since the 8th or 9th grade, and looking at their tests, I am in no position to disagree.

"Find the exact area under the curve of the graph of y = 3x^2 + 2 between x = 2 and x = 4, using the limit of sums method."

-- High school calculus problem. Using sums in this way is way beyond what I would attempt in an elementary college calculus course, where I often spend considerable time going over the quadratic formula.

I've certainly heard tales of bad teachers, teachers not doing their jobs, teachers that don't care about students, and, of course, teachers that succumb to the immense pressure to pass unprepared students. While I believe such teachers exist, I've met quite a few public school teachers, and through tutoring many high school students, I can only conclude that the vast majority of teachers are dedicated, hardworking, knowledgeable, and do a legitimate job in offering real mathematics courses to their students. In short, the vast majority of students that want to learn have a fair opportunity to do so.

Perhaps public schools shouldn't give students the opportunity not to learn, but I suspect they've long since figured out that forcing students into classes they have no interest in taking doesn't really help the students. If only that knowledge could be passed up to postsecondary institutions.

If a student chooses not to be prepared for college, it's no great surprise that such a student, when tricked into going to college, is not prepared for it. A student shouldn't be made to suffer forever for a poor choice made in high school, but…recall how years ago getting into college was not a certain thing. It was reserved for those who worked hard and studied, demonstrating they were willing to do what it takes to achieve higher learning. The great slobbering greed of colleges with open admission policies, and the "increase the student base at all costs" major goal of administration, has led to a massive influx of unprepared, often wildly unprepared, students onto college campuses.

These students, being unprepared for college, naturally do very poorly in college courses, and administration (with "graduation rate" being a goal of what makes a college good) clamps the pressure down on faculty to increase passing rates, as well as opening up an array of less regulated remedial courses, with no restraints on what goes into such courses. Unfortunately, the remedial faculty (often with less qualifications and job security than other college faculty) are bullied into having high pass rates, and the only surefire method of doing so is to lower the difficulty as much as possible.

(Two students at my door): "Hi. We're in your statistics class, and we have a question about lines of regression."

(Me, welcoming them in): "Certainly, those are some rough formulas, the key is to be very careful and not try to skip steps."

(I take out some paper and start setting up a typical problem)

Student: "No. We're not even going to try that. Our question is for when you already have the line, like for y = 2x + 1, because we can get that on our calculator. How did you get the points, and how do you graph the line? We've both had 6 hours of developmental and got A's in College Algebra, and neither of us had to do anything like that."

--Students at an accredited institution where developmental math wasn't handled at all by the math department, and College Algebra wasn't either, to some extent.

With no restraints, "reduce difficulty as much as possible" is results in very low difficulty indeed, which is why at one campus, it was quite common to have students with 4.0 GPAS, 9 hours of passed math courses...and still completely overmatched by what should have been basic concepts.

Since the flood of unprepared students doesn't stop at remediation, faculty in the higher level courses have no choice but to likewise reduce course requirements, or lose their position. So, in my case, it isn't just statistics students that can't handle graphing a line, nearly half of the students I have in calculus, for years now, are unable to add fractions, despite the high GPA and multiple prerequisites.

As long as administrators view everyone with a pulse as a source of a government check, with no concerns about how such a person can end up trapped in a lifetime of debt, remedial students will be a common feature on "higher education" campuses.

Has Remediation Helped?

"Many of our developmental classes have a 100% passing rate. Let's show the Developmental Department we can do just as well!"

--administrative encouragement to improve passing rates in college courses. Education is not an issue.

Remediation has greatly helped administration, as these easier courses are much easier to fill with students, especially students that don't realize the risk of taking on loans, leading to explosive growth in "higher education," if that phrase is taken to mean high school and lower level material. Perhaps it's more accurate to say explosive growth in the student base, which certainly helps administrators that get to show off how successful the institution is. Similarly, as non-college courses, it's easier to hire less qualified (and lower paid) instructors, with less accreditation oversight. Widespread remediation gives all the bonuses from being an administrator with many underlings, without the responsibilities, certainly a very attractive situation.

Does remediation help faculty? Not as much as was promised, even though initially faculty and administrators were on the same side in providing remedial courses. The point of remediation was supposed to be that a student graduating from it would come to a college course prepared. Unfortunately, most remediation is done without oversight, with the only goal of "pass as many students as possible." So faculty gains little from having remediated students, with the added burden of being told by a feckless administration, "If the remedial classes have a 100% passing rate, why can't you?"

Even without the pressure, faculty have little choice but to cover less material, at a slower pace, out of a sense of fairness to the unprepared students that are honestly struggling with the work; this ripple effect goes all the way up the chain of courses on campus. I get some small benefit from all the remediation, but it's primarily from keeping the disciplinary problems out of the real college courses. I still get wildly unprepared students in advanced classes, but the ones that care about the material almost always are able to pick up (or remember) the things they should have known coming into the course, within the first few weeks of the semester. To help these students, I can justify slowing down a bit, even as I know doing so harms the other students that intend to take additional courses.

Does remediation help students? The answer is an almost perfect "no." It's helped a few students, although I suspect these students would have been helped just as well before the "everyone goes to college" craze. Recall that less than 10% of remedial students get a degree in *only* a year more than "normal" students. Remedial students, even ones that complete a program, very disproportionately have no measureable improvement in their cognitive thinking skills from when they first entered college[4]. One could easily conjecture that these completed programs have merely been watered down to the point that cognitive skills are not necessary for completion, or never required such skills in the first place.

Every study on the subject has verified the obvious: remedial students are less likely to complete a program, and are more likely to spend more time than other students on any program completed or even attempted. They naturally also get further into debt, but as that translates into "make more money for the college," administration sees nothing wrong here.

Ever Changing Remediation: A Specific Example

"We've been doing it wrong, focusing on getting remedial students to pass remedial courses. This new process puts remedial students directly into college classes, and passes them from there!"

--Administrator, explaining the latest amazing new idea on August 6, 2012

Administrators are well aware that remedial students tend to fail college classes, and rather than take the choice of integrity (stop loaning money to so many remedial students), are always very eager to try something, anything, to get these students to pass. Improved passing, improved retention, is the only definition of a good education an administrator can understand, all those unemployed but degree-holding people occupying Wall Street notwithstanding. Almost every year I endure yet another cockamamie plan to improve retention, and so allow me to cover the most recent one in detail:

On August 6, 2012, I attended six hours of meetings to address the latest method: co-requisite courses for remedial math and English. I can't even guess at the money spent merely to have English and math faculty, along with administrators, travel from all over the state to Baton Rouge for this catered meeting. First, administrators present an array of statistics regarding how amazing the new idea is: at every level, "education" is ignored, and instead all improvement is measured in passing rates. The entire definition of a successful program is whether it passes students or not. Every statistic presented to us is all about the retention. After a flood of such data, impressive to administrators and irrelevant to educators, we're told of the new plan.

The new plan this time around? Instead of having students take remedial classes before taking college classes (for example, taking College Preparatory Algebra II before being allowed to take College Algebra), the new plan is to have students take both courses, remedial and college level, at the same time, and force them to get extra support. The remedial class is more like a lab, with teaching assistants giving more personal help. And the statistics show it works! Yay, passing rates are much higher!

It's so, so, trivial to manipulate and mislead the effectiveness of these programs via statistics, however, and most everyone outside of administration knows it—all the grey-haired faculty simply chuckle behind the administrators' backs, having seen this stuff dozens of times over their careers. It takes nothing to pass more students, for example one could just make "C" the lowest possible grade in the course.

The new English remedial program was particularly amusing—first, the salesman tells us how 15% of remedial students never take a college level writing course even after passing remedial writing. Then, he tells us his new program has 0% of these students not taking a college writing course. How does he achieve it? The new program forces all remedial students directly into college level writing courses. At least he knew that his success wasn't exactly surprising, given the requirements. Still, if success is defined as taking a college level course, a program that forces the taking of a college level course is guaranteed to be successful. It is, comparatively speaking, one of the more honest plans for improved retention I've seen.

The math co-requisite program likewise wasn't above manipulation to show how successful it was, although at least it put some effort into being misleading. Like almost all these programs, students were self-selected; only those that accepted the warnings that it would require hard work and dedication could enter the co-requisite program. Sure enough, this program showed greatly improved retention rates, 80% as opposed to the more typical 50%.

Restrict my classes to only hard working, dedicated students, and I'll probably do quite a bit better than average, too, no matter what special program I try. In twenty years of being subjected to these pitches, I've yet to see a program where they divided self-selecting students like these into two groups, with the program only being used on one group. This would go some way to showing it's the program, and not the self-selected students, that are making a difference. Why is this basic, rudimentary, *obvious*, idea seldom, if ever, implemented? I imagine it's because legitimate studies that use such controls don't show any major improvements among hardworking students relative to anything else (since the material at this level is learn-able by most anyone that puts effort into it), and thus aren't sold to administrators.

Next, we were shown how the co-requisite math students had much higher grades and passing rates, using a variety of poorly demonstrated interactive techniques and group projects. Group projects are a red flag that something is bogus about the coursework, there's just no real learning in group projects, merely, at best, a theoretical division of skills by students doing what they already know how to do. Nobody pays attention to the new activities that supposedly help so much, because everyone knows the ones running the program can give whatever grades they want and pass everyone on a whim. Higher grades and passing rates are meaningless in a controlled system with the person selling it giving out the grades.

Even administrators and the folks selling the new plan know passing rates are easily manipulated upward, so they back up the improved passing rates with an important-sounding statistic. Every incoming student had to take a standardized placement test, and the scores were recorded. The new students had an average score on the test of 211. At the end of the course, they re-administered the tests to the students that passed, and the students got an average score of 232. A 21 point improvement on a standardized test! The program works! Yay!

The pitchmen gloss over that 250 is the cutoff score for students to go into College Algebra for the placement test, so all they've done is pass students out of College Algebra who still don't qualify to take College Algebra despite having just passed it. Instead, the improved scores are celebrated. Without any question from administration, statistics like these are always taken as evidence, but a bit of critical thinking reveals these numbers from a standardized test still don't show anything worth believing.

Much like with the self-selected students, there's no control group, no set of students outside the program to compare test scores to. For all I know, a typical student that passes College Algebra has a 30 point improvement on that placement test, or that simply taking the test repeatedly will cause a 30 point improvement. In the latter case, numbers like administration provided could be taken as evidence that the co-requisite program is a massive disaster, with students worse off than if they'd never entered the program. For some reason, administration never thinks to ask such a basic question or administer this rudimentary control. It would cost a hundred bucks or so to double-administer those tests to a class or two of students, but I guess there's hardly any money left over after the many thousands of dollars spent implementing the program and pitching it to various states.

Even without a single control, there's another issue here. Only the students that pass the course are re-taking the placement test, and yet it's taken as evidence of improvement when the average score goes up. The students that failed (or dropped) don't retake the test, so we don't have their scores. Gee whiz, you take out all the F students, and the average grade increases. Practically everyone on the stage selling this to us has a Ph.D., a research degree, in Education, and none of them see this issue.

One of the pitchmen dares to complain that they're still looking for better ways to get statistics, but none of the faculty bother to try to help with any of the above suggestions about controls or factoring out the failing students.

An empowered faculty would point and laugh at administrators using such poorly compiled statistics in a vacuum to justify a major re-working of course programs. Instead, the faculty sit quietly and take it, for the most part. One brave soul asks "How do you expect us to teach the college material with the unprepared students sitting right there, doing nothing?"...the people giving the pitch mumble out a response that the answer to the question will come later, but it never does. Similarly, a question is asked about the failing students in the program, and we're told that the only students that failed in this program were the ones that didn't want help, disregarding how that conflicts with the self-selection process.

This program could affect every remedial student, as well as the non-remedial students who get put in co-requisite "college" courses along with the remedial students. In short, faculty are being strongly encouraged to follow a program that could affect a clear majority of college students and the best argument given to us for buying into this plan, beyond the meaningless "better retention," is a single feeble statistic from an uncontrolled experiment. Administration knows they can do whatever they want anyway, and just goes through the motions of convincing faculty that it works.

A statistician, would be embarrassed to present this sort of isolated statistic as useful, and yet, one of the pitchers of the new plan proudly tells us she's an actual mathematics professor, instead of saying that her doctorate is actually in Education. She gave no hint at all of her degree in the presentation or in any of the handout materials, as though she were embarrassed about it. I had to scramble around online to find that detail out. I found something else online, too.

Faculty: *"Did you see her students' comments on Ratemyprofessors.com?"*

Me: *"Crap, I was going to tell you about it. I didn't think anyone else goes there."*

Faculty: *"I thought I'd do some investigation."*

--Faculty are not stupid, we know better than to take anything from administrators at face value. We also know when administration wants us to "say something about" their new ideas, they only do so

because it's easier to cram things down our throat if we open our mouths first.

My online search also found what students had to say about her, and indirectly the program, at Ratemyprofessors.com. Despite the professor's presentation claiming great teaching skills, she has miserable ratings there. Now, I grant, only the most irate (and probably failing) students would go to an online site and post their complaints, but after being forced to watch videos of testimonials from students about how life-changing—*I'm not exaggerating their claims!*—the new program is, I think it's fair to present testimonials biased in the other direction.

She's rated in several categories at Ratemyprofessor.com, but "easiness" is by far her best category. Granted, "easiness" isn't on a collegiate student evaluation of teaching form, but this website caters towards student desires. An administration that was actually curious about challenging students-- critical to education!--would have such a question on the evaluations, and it's very telling that there is no such question on the evaluations. Qualitatively, here are some abbreviated quotes, some are obviously from students in the program with this teacher[5]:

"Hardly a teacher at all. All she does is talk, talk, talk. The second day of class she taught us how to turn on our calculator. The tests don't make sense."

"HORRIBLE!!! she is so rude and doesnt seem like she cares about anyone including her TAs. She acts as if she is better than everyone and her lectures are completely WORTHLESS. STAY AWAY!"

"A lot of people don't go to the lectures because they are extremely boring and attendence doesn't count but sometest questions ome straight from lecture. The labs are never fully coordinated. Tests are all about theory more than solving problems. Use the answer choices to solve test questions."

"Her tests are always about concepts with no actual calculations of answers."

"Her tests are all on principles and alghorithms. There were hardly any problems

you had to actually solve"

"stay away from this teacher taking this class with her will be the biggest waste you will ever come across"

"Wholly education/grant-funded class. Does a horrible job explaining in class. Try to get a different professor unless you enjoy being taught like you're in middle school."

Not a single student gave a positive review, not one, but I'll happily concede considerable bias at that site. Looking too closely at negative student evaluations usually isn't a good idea, but when the same specific complaints keep coming up over the course of years, that usually means there's some truth to it. Complaints like this had to have turned up in student evaluations administered at her school...and yet, administration never wonders at students consistently saying the course is strange in some way, instead only looking at passing rates. In reviewing her complaints and ratings, a more reasonable conclusion about her higher passing rates would be that she's just gives easy multiple choice tests where you can get the answer just by reading the questions, the program has nothing to do with it. All administration saw was higher retention, issues like "waste of time" in the course are insignificant next to the only goal of merit to an administrator.

After the pitch, the head pitchman tells us that when this program is tried at other institutions, retention rates vary from 25% to 77%; in other words, outside of controlled situations, the co-requisite plan doesn't seem to be working at all. He asks that if we get a high retention, we should contact him and tell us what we did so they can put that in their recommendations for the program. Some faculty drove *hundreds of miles* to be told how to implement this plan (sic) to improve retention, and the people pitching it already know it doesn't work and are looking for help.

Time and again, bad statistics, methods anyone with basic knowledge of the subject would know to be invalid, are used to justify a new change. Is it any wonder at all that education of remedial students hasn't improved under any of these plans?

Summary:

Year after year, colleges cycle through one plan to improve retention after another, as administration buys into one hokum plan after another. Never, ever, is it considered that maybe you can't teach people that don't want to learn, and that simply not accepting such people in the first place would help far more than admitting anything with a pulse and then optimizing the best way to extract the maximum amount of money from the victims of this "higher education" scheme.

The Cycle of Remediation describes remediation in higher education:

1. College courses with failing students in them have "low" retention.
2. To improve retention, failing students are pre-identified and shuffled off to remediation.
3. To improve retention in remedial courses, various plans are tried, but for reasons administration cannot fathom, remedial students still fail more than non-remedial students.
4. To improve retention, remedial students are put back in college courses.
5. Return to 1.

A remedial course, years ago, was an important tool, helping a student who just had a few weaknesses preventing him from going into higher education. Administration has taken that tool and turned it into a weapon capable of channeling herds of suckers into "higher education," where they are fleeced in the short term, paying way too much for courses that will benefit them far too little, and slaughtered later when the loan bills come due.

The population was given a dream of college education, and a way to follow that dream: student debt. They were misled about the legitimacy of college education and cheerfully took on that debt. Even those that never had any academic aspirations were told that they too could follow that dream, all they needed to do was spend a few months in special courses, and years of not caring about learning would be rectified even if they still didn't care about learning, making the non-learners every bit as qualified to pursue higher education as any hardworking student that had already devoted years to study and learning.

This fable might have been true if there had been serious advances in how to educate human beings. Unfortunately, the non-learners don't have the critical thinking skills to understand why this can't work, and administrators simply don't care as long as the checks keep coming in. I've always felt that you really can't teach a person something he doesn't want to know, but the field of Education, through the semantic tricks like redefining "education" into "retention," and "student" into "learner," and changing "grades" into "assessments," has exerted a demented control over higher education, influencing it in often macabre ways. This influence is particularly strong in remedial courses, but is felt through all college courses.

Let's take a look at the field of Education next, and see if knowing about Education, instead of knowing a subject besides Education, is the best way to become a great teacher of a subject besides Education.

Chapter 4: The Myth of Education as a Field of Knowledge

"My Ph.D. thesis, which was the only thesis that was shown to be true, showed that students who study tend to learn more."

Quote from an Education expert who came to tell us how to teach better. It isn't simply that this was considered a Ph.D. level thesis that worries me, it's all the wrong theses that still nevertheless led to successfully awarding a Ph.D. in Education.

With all the new suckers pouring into the system, one might think that all the new data from incoming students would lead to breakthroughs, real improvements in how course content is delivered, leading to better and easier learning by the students. A field that might do something like this is called Education, a field that seems to come from nothing in the last few decades.

The study of how humans learned used to be part of psychology, and is a legitimate mode of inquiry in a legitimate, if often qualitative, field. Education, on the other hand, is more about how to transmit knowledge, or at least it is taught that way. It might be more fair to say Education is more about getting high retention/passing rates, since that's the entirety of how the field is presented to other faculty.

Not once in years of being lectured by Educationists have I been told "teach how to graph a line this way, students understand it better," or "use this method to draw a parabola, it more intuitively relates to the functional definition" or even something as pathetically simple as "here's a mnemonic for the rational root theorem." Not once has an Educationist ever told me anything that would help students learn and understand the material in my courses, nor have I seen an Educationist offer up anything directly useful to another course. Instead, it's always "give more extra credit assignments that don't relate to the course, it will get more students passing," or similar advice that couldn't possibly require years of study to give.

Luckily, being at an institution of higher learning, I can go to someone else in my department (i.e., someone that actually knows the subject), and get help in finding additional ways to explain concepts. But Educations seems to have nothing to offer my students.

Student: "Why do I have to learn this crap? I'm only going to be teaching 8 year olds once I get my Education degree."

Me: "Because the parents of those 8 year olds want the teacher to know more than an 8 year old."

--I get a student that complains to this effect every semester, and my response never gets old.

At the undergraduate level, Education majors live in a world of their own, with most all subjects converted to a special format just for this special major. There's a Math for Education Majors course, with a few mathematical concepts. As mathematics is a basic skill useful in many fields, perhaps it merits a general course just for education majors. Similarly, many topics in psychology might well be justified as having special courses just for Education majors, and they are offered as such.

Why are there Chemistry for Education Majors and Physics for Education Majors courses? Shouldn't people planning to teach subjects like chemistry and physics have an actual knowledge of the subject, given to them by people that know the subject? Even music, apparently, is too technical a subject to be handled by specialists in the field, so campuses offer Music for Education Majors courses as well. In times past, a teacher of a subject was required to actually know the subject, but now a degree in Education is the starting requirement, and knowledge of a real topic no longer is considered necessary.

"1. If a 12 foot ladder is broken into 3 equal parts, how long is each part?

2. If you go the store and buy a 6-pack for $4.59 and a loaf of bread for $2.20, what is your total bill? Ignore sales tax."

---final exam questions for a "Math for Education Majors" course I proctored, calculators allowed. College Algebra was a prerequisite for the

course. The other questions were likewise simplistic, with no requirement to solve them in any particular way. Only the "extra credit" question was arguably at the high school level: "Write as an algebraic expression: A number plus three times the sum of the same number and three is twelve." No, they didn't have to solve it.

As one might guess by a discipline that requires so much "special help" for its students to get by, the coursework has been studied and found to be "intellectually thin"[1], and having directly observed so much of it, I tend to agree with that assessment.

"Needed: Math tutor."

"Needed: Chemistry tutor."

"Needed: Physics tutor."

"Needed: Writing tutor."

--various sites and places allow for postings of students needing tutors. I often frequent them, as I occasionally tutor for math. Not once, not one time, has there been a student looking for an Education tutor. As near as I can tell, the field covers no material so difficult that any student would need a tutor to understand and become proficient with it.

Graduate level Education degrees fare little better. Students entering graduate programs in education commonly score among the lowest on the GRE (Graduate Record Examination, a test comparable to the SAT, but for college graduates; public administration is the only field of study with incoming students scoring lower than education majors). It's worth noting that the majority of education programs don't even require applicants to take the GRE—scores would probably be lower if so. Education majors even score less on the qualitative (English comprehension) part of the GRE than non-native English speakers, and often score abysmally in the other sections[2].

Now, ordinarily it wouldn't be any concern of mine what goes on in other fields, but Education has a ridiculously powerful influence over what goes on in educational institutions, and that's where I work, so it matters to me. Administrators are easily enraptured by even the most marginal of Educationist topics, as long as the Educationist promises to deliver what administrators want. It seems every year another new method of teaching at my school is introduced by an Educationist for dubious reasons.

"You should put more writing in your math courses, it will improve retention."

--typical advice and justification from an Educationist training me how to teach.

Luckily, not everyone is under the influence of this field of study, and allow me to present an example where ignoring Educationists yields many beneficiaries:

Our written languages are phonetic; the letters on the page represent sounds. Thus, the deaf are at a strong disadvantage when it comes to learning how to read, and only with advanced training by an Educationist can they achieve even high-school level reading skills (with third grade reading level being acceptable even at high school graduation), and it's basically impossible to for them to learn more than one written language. Any Educationist will happily tell you this, and this is what is still taught in special Education for the Deaf courses.

Viataal (formerly called The Institute of the Deaf), in Sint-Michielsgestel, The Netherlands, begs to differ. Their deaf children learn to read three languages (Dutch, English, and German), reading at grade level in their native tongue by graduation, and graduating students typically read English at a 9th grade level. Surely such achievements are only possible using the best possible Educationists using the most advanced theories? No, not at all. While the school does have its own theories about how to teach the deaf, they simply do not hire people with education degrees, not even in special teaching for the hearing impaired...there are none at the school. When the school needs a physics teacher, they hire a physicist and train the new teacher on how to teach the deaf[3]. To that high achieving school, it just makes more sense to have the subject taught by someone that actually knows the subject, and spend a little time training that person how to teach, rather than spend years training someone in educational gobbledygook, and then have that poor soul try to teach a topic he knows nothing about.

"2 + 12 = 16"

"16 = 16"

"Are these the right answers?"

"Yes. One side equals the other side."

--Excerpt from Winning at Math, Fourth Edition, page 171, an otherwise good book by an excellent Educationist (seriously, he has relevant things to say). It's saddening that this book could make it to the 4th edition and still not have this error corrected.

While perhaps the school for the deaf is some isolated example that only applies in The Netherlands, consider how disastrous various new types of reading programs have been for teaching. Homeschoolers use "Hooked on Phonics" and raise children that read, while public schools try "Whole Word" and "Ebonics" methods to churn out children unprepared for the real world, much less college. Similarly, "New Math" has been of little use to helping public school age students. And yet, with this sort of track record, college administrators rapturously accept any idea coming from this field, especially one that improves the all-important retention of college students (and those sweet checks!).

What do Educationists do?

(The entire college faculty is gathered to hear the latest words of wisdom from another Educationist. This one specializes in multiple choice questions, and asked us to bring our course textbooks to help us make up a multiple choice question using her ideas—as though college faculty, like Educationists, don't know our basic material well enough without the textbook at hand.)

Educationist: "So, here we have a test I gave to my students. To each question, I've associated a number computed using my SPSS software. If the number is positive, that means students that did well on the test generally got that question right. If the number is negative, that means that the students who did well on the test generally got that question wrong.

Me: "These numbers your software is getting. These are just correlation coefficients, right?"

Educationist: "Yes, they're called that."

Me: "What conditions, say, certain class averages or scenarios, would allow for some sort of maximum to be achieved?"

Educationist: "I don't know."

Me: "Negative correlations seem fairly interesting, as they represent problems that good students tend to miss, more so possibly than poor students. What conditions or types of questions can lead to negative correlations in this case?"

Educationist: "I don't know."

Me: "Is there any known relationship between class scores and these correlations?"

Educationist: "I don't know."

Me: "Do you know of any research that might have led to some answers to these types of questions?"

Educationist: "I don't know of any."

--I bet another faculty member money that the Educationist knew very little about the topic she was explaining to us. He paid up. What a curious field where you can be an expert on a topic, but never to have considered in that topic, "What causes good things to happen? Or bad things? Or anything in particular?" The more mathematically inclined reader might want to consider what kind of class scores on say, a 20 question test would lead to correlations of 1, -1, or 0, to get an idea of just how little the educationist knows.

Educationists have their own language and terms. You know instantly when you're talking to one when you hear them refer to "learners"---a decidedly optimistic term for what us normal folk call "students." If their only influence was a mere change in vocabulary (no more noxious than exchanging "remedial" for "developmental," nor more effectual than exchanging "queer" for "fag"), they probably wouldn't be held in such low self regard by many faculty—even as I acknowledge I have met the occasional Educationist who does know what he's talking about. Unfortunately, Educationists very much influence college activity and coursework, seldom improving anything.

Suggested Group Project: Read A Book

Once again, the faculty is gathered to hear the words of wisdom of our latest Educationist, to tell us the wonder of Learning Communities:

Educationist: "I'm here to present to the latest methods on building Learning Communities. The foremost method by far is group projects, every course should be built around them. You should divide your class into groups of four or five learners within the first few class meetings, to get that community built as quickly as possible. Learners that form groups like this can have lasting friendships throughout their college careers. They stick together a long time, and that allows for better retention."

Faculty: "We lose at least a third of our students by mid-term, my groups won't last that long. I don't see how this works."

Educationist: "Might be best to reform groups if you have lots of drop-outs. By having groups, the learners can work together, taking advantage of each other's strengths and weaknesses."

Me: "But that won't help individuals gain skills. Each person does only what he's good at, and never grows. What is the purpose of everything being done in group projects?"

Educationist: "Research shows Learning Communities increases retention."

Me: "But how does it help with learning?"

Educationist: "If they're not retained, they're not learning, right?"

--Educationist using the ultimate trump card. The book Academically Adrift shows that simply being retained doesn't cause learning, although it most surely generates revenue for the institution[4].

In addition to taking math out of math courses, another tidbit of advice that comes up often is to have more group projects. The theory that each person in the group will contribute according to his or her strengths and leave the others to compensate for his weaknesses is beautiful, but it is also crap. Anyone who has been in a group project knows full well how it works: the one or two students that care about the course do all the work, and the other students coast along, learning nothing. Thus it's no surprise that there is a negative relationship between group study and learning[5].

Administration, of course, still pushes hard for group projects in classes. Negative impact on learning is not a concern because studies consistently show that being in group projects increases retention (i.e., warm bodies)...and that's all administration cares about. It's obvious group projects increase retention—it teaches the uncaring student that he can just coast by on the backs of his associates.

This coasting can go on for years, but is rather disastrous once the student encounters a course that either requires actual learning by the individual, or assumes the individual learned something earlier. If it goes on for a whole degree, the "lucky" student escapes into the real world, albeit with no skills or knowledge anyone is willing to pay for. You can see people like this on Wall Street, holding signs.

Bloom's Taxonomy, The Communist Manifesto, Phrenology, Unicorns, and Lysenkoism

(Again, the faculty is gathered to hear an Educationist how to satisfy our SACS requirements, using the beloved Bloom's Taxonomy of Learning)

Educationist: "To show we satisfies our core guidelines, we'll need to set up five columns for each objective identified, organized by Bloom's Taxonomy. Here's an example table I made. We just need to set up this kind of rubric for each objective and we're done."

Informational Rubric

Statement of issues	Does not state issues	States the issues	Lists the issues	Explains the issues	Expounds upon the issues
Organization	No structure	Some attempt to structure has been made	Poor attempt at structure	Structure developed well	Structure is clearly developed
Punctuation	Four or more	There are	There are	There is	There are

and Capitalization	errors in punctuation or capitalization	three errors	two errors	one error	no errors

(rest of rubric omitted)

Faculty A: "Can you tell me the difference between "States the issues" and "Lists the Issues"? Same for "Explains the issues" and "Expounds upon the issues"?

Educationist: "This is just an example, but "States the issues" just states what the issues are, while "Lists the issues" means the learner states the issues in a list.

Faculty A: "..."

Educationist: "Any other questions before we split off into groups to set up the rubrics?"

Me: "You realize that we'll have thousands of papers to grade, across a dozen general education goals, many divided into three or more sub-goals, and we're supposed to be grading work not in our discipline. Do you honestly propose a method with multidivisional arrays divided by subtleties that experts in the field cannot reasonably define?"

Educationist: "If you had my training, it would be easier."

Faculty B: "Where on this rubric of yours is passing? Can't we just do pass or fail?"

Educationist: "Pass or fail is not a rubric, we need to set this up according to Bloom's Taxonomy."

Me: "Pass or fail is a great idea, it's not like we're doing student grades here. Let's just define what satisfies our goal—in fact, we could just use the goal, like "student can solve a word problem", for our rubric. If the student can do it, then we'll say we've achieved the goal. Otherwise, not."

Educationist: " A rubric is a matrix. Pass or fail is not a matrix. You need to break it *down into smaller elements."*

Me: "We'll have two elements, one for pass, one for fail, and define what passing is. It works, and is simple."

Educationist: "That is not a matrix."

Me: "Sure it is, it's a 1 x 2 matrix."

Educationist: "You need more than that for a matrix."

Me: "No, you don't."

(Educationist leaves to complain to administration that we're not being cooperative...)

Year after year, an Educationist has come to explain to us the wonders of Bloom's Taxonomy, this amazing method that completely describes all learning. For the uninitiated, Bloom's Taxonomy is a classification system, and the important part of Bloom's is the system for the cognitive domain. The cognitive domain for knowledge, according to Bloom's Taxonomy, is a hierarchy. On the bottom is straight knowledge, remembering details and facts. Next is comprehension, understanding the facts. Higher still is application, using those facts you know and understand. Next is analysis, breaking facts down into smaller parts, to find relationships. Higher up is supposedly synthesis, putting facts together to create something new. Finally the highest form of cognition (although the last three are sometimes put on the same level) is evaluation, using your knowledge of facts, the understanding and applications of relationships of those facts, to create an opinion of the validity of new information.

Now, this is certainly an interesting model and not without merit, but it's quite often presented as absolute fact, to the point that you'll find Bloom's Taxonomized objectives splattered all over assignments, especially in online courses, since such courses generally have such rubrics mandated. While never have counter-arguments to Bloom's Taxonomy been presented (or welcomed) at an Educationist's demonstration, a tiny dose of critical thinking reveals there is much here that is questionable.

Allow me to take an example from the online world, for all to see that I'm not cherry-picking how ridiculous these things can get. This example (broken into three sections because rubrics can get extremely unwieldy past that) has been devised for faculty familiar with Bloom's Taxonomy (and if the Educationist above is reading this, note that it's not even presented as a matrix)[6]:

CATEGORY ONE: KNOWLEDGE AND COMPREHENSION (understanding the basics)

4—The work consistently demonstrates clear, accurate, detailed and comprehensive understanding of the relevant facts / data / theories/ terms as well as the ability to organize the information for application, presentation, documentation, and/or further examination.

3--The work demonstrates an adequate understanding of the relevant facts / data / theories/ terms as well as the ability to organize the information for application, presentation, documentation, and/or further examination

2-- The work demonstrates an uneven and shaky understanding of the relevant facts / data / theories/ terms as well as a limited ability to organize the information for application, presentation, documentation, and/or further examination.

1-- The work demonstrates an inadequate understanding of the relevant facts / data / theories/ terms as well as a limited ability to organize the information for application, presentation, documentation, and/or further examination.

CATEGORY TWO: APPLICATION AND ANALYSIS (attaining the concept)

4—The work demonstrates confident ability to work with the key concepts / information / process / theory -- applying or extending them to a wide variety of new problems or contexts, making predictions, recognizing hidden meanings, drawing inferences, analyzing patterns and component parts, communicating insightful contrasts and comparisons.

3--The work demonstrates adequate ability to work with the key concepts / information / process / theory -- applying or extending them to a variety of new problems or contexts, making predictions, recognizing hidden meanings, drawing inferences, analyzing patterns and component parts, communicating insightful contrasts and comparisons.

2-- The work demonstrates uneven and shaky ability to work with the key concepts / information / process / theory -- applying or extending them with mixed success to new problems or contexts, making predictions, recognizing hidden meanings, drawing inferences, analyzing patterns and component parts, communicating insightful contrasts and comparisons.

1-- The work demonstrates extremely limited ability to work with the key concepts / information / process / theory -- applying or extending them with very limited success to new problems or contexts, making predictions, recognizing hidden meanings, drawing inferences, analyzing patterns and component parts, communicating insightful contrasts and comparisons.

CATEGORY THREE: SYNTHESIZING AND EVALUATING (going beyond the given)

4—The work demonstrates surprising/insightful ability to take ideas / theories / processes / principles further into new territory, broader generalizations, hidden meanings and implications as well – as well as to assess discriminatively the value, credibility and power of these ideas (etc.) in order to decide on well-considered choices and opinions.

3-- The work demonstrates adequate ability to take ideas / theories / processes / principles further into new territory, broader generalizations, hidden meanings and implications as well – as well as to assess discriminatively the value, credibility and power of these ideas (etc.) in order to decide on well-considered choices and opinions.

2-- The work demonstrates uneven and superficial ability to take ideas / theories / processes / principles further into new territory, broader generalizations, hidden meanings and implications as well – as well as a limited ability to assess discriminatively the value, credibility and power of these ideas (etc.) in order to decide on well-considered choices and opinions.

1-- The work demonstrates little ability to take ideas / theories / processes / principles further into new territory, broader generalizations, hidden meanings and implications as well – as well as a limited and superficial ability to assess discriminatively the value, credibility and power of these ideas (etc.) in order to decide on well-considered choices and opinions.

You're supposed to actually use this to grade a student's work. The first issue apparent to anyone who looks at these rubrics with an open mind is how much these monstrosities rely critically upon semantic games. Does "uneven and shaky" really represent a whole new level of learning above "limited"? Exactly how? Some folks would consider "uneven and shaky" knowledge to be worse than "limited." There's almost no way to construct these rubrics wrong, so cranking them out is pretty trivial, requiring little more than an extended vocabulary or a handy thesaurus. Take it from someone with experience, trying to precisely grade anything according to these rubrics is no more helpful than consulting a Magic 8-Ball. Such rubrics can make grading harder, not easier. Much like *The Communist Manifesto* is a horrible set of guidelines for what to do in the real world, Bloom's Taxonomy seems to resist any useful applications.

Relating to the semantics issue is the complete unreliability of rubric construction. After I diligently Bloom's Taxonomized a course grading rubric for learners (a bunch of high-falutin' language for "told myself how to grade my own test"), if I look to see what another math professor has done for the subject, I get a somewhat different rubric. Even more hysterically, the other professor used some of the same words I used, but in different levels of the learning hierarchy. Ultimately, the rubric turns into "pass or fail" when it comes time to assess whether a student has achieved a course objective, and past that there's little overlap between rubrics. Compare this to the reliability of grading "Do 40 crunches in three minutes" in a physical training class...every instructor would grade that assignment in much the same way, viewing Bloom's Taxonomy as pointless make-work. Much like Phrenology, the study of bumps on a person's head, led to whatever interpretation the Phrenologist was looking for and varied from one "expert" to the next, any interpretation past the first level of Bloom's Taxonomy is likewise in the eye of the beholder. There is no reliability here.

Even if various professors could independently make the same rubrics for the same material with any level of reliability, there are never any given guidelines for teaching to a particular level of understanding (assuming such a level of understanding was well-defined). What type of sentence should I say to bring the student up to the next level? How can I be sure I didn't skip a level? Can you skip a level? With no scientifically recommended way to even reach the alleged levels of Bloom's Taxonomy, it seems pretty useless to apply it. This is as practical as reading extensively on how to perform surgery on unicorns.

And yet time and again this crude and arbitrary classification system is presented as critical to teaching a college course. Having it presented to faculty as established and "must follow and agree to" fact is little different than Lysenkoism, with right and wrong being purely determined by administrative force.

Let's Take A Graduate Education Course!

- *No Online courses with technology problems or cohort meeting times*

- *No reading of 300 online computer pages and then writing 50 page reports.*

- *No driving and travel time to class locations and no child care needed.*

- Great for independent learners or you can take courses with other teacher collogues (sic).

---from the instructions and promotional material for the course. Typos happen. Yikes, there are online courses where you write 50 page reports? That's scary. I bet that only happens in the most advanced graduate level online courses. We'll see later that I lose that bet.

Time and again faculty and students are subjected to the thoughts of Educationists, because administration is convinced these people really know what they are doing, and have such vastly superior capabilities they can tell everyone else how to improve learning. I had already seen at the undergraduate level, Education courses had little to offer. I resolved to take a graduate level education course and see with my own eyes what kind of skills and knowledge are necessary to master the most advanced material of Education. Since so many of Education-type degrees are offered online, I decided to take an online course for 3 graduate hours, with a public (not for profit) institution. Actually, it was more of a correspondence course, with no message boards or anything like that. At less than $400 for the course, I saw little to lose[7].

According to the course syllabus, completing the assignments should take me 45 hours, for a 3 credit hour course. This is an interesting number, as 14 weeks of meeting 3 hours a week, the typical brick-and-mortar semester, is 42 hours. It's almost as though Education doesn't really expect much effort from their specialists other than class time. What are the assignments? Read a book (amongst a wide list of choices, I picked an 8 chapter, 270 page math book with an eclectic mix of topics[8]) and write a thorough book report, three paragraphs on each chapter. Read a research paper and write a small report. Prepare a lesson plan for a single class. Write a 2 page summary of what I learned in the course.

So How Do You Feel About What You Just Read?

Educationist: "It's not about learning how to spell properly. It's about making the student feel good for what he did."

--Educationist explaining why we shouldn't really care about basic errors in student work. I give my non-native English speakers a break since I don't actually teach English, but I still write down corrections in their e-mails and notes. The concept that students will learn what they are doing is wrong even if nobody tells them is core to Education, but is completely alien to me.

The instructions for the course are a little contradictory, but doing the best I could to follow them, all four of the assignments put together consume around 25 pages of writing (and a like amount of hours of my time). I was particularly thorough in my discussions, but I could easily see someone doing it all in under 20 pages (following the rubric, a dozen pages might be passing). As per the instructions, I concatenate all my assignments into one document, and tell the instructor what grade I'm hoping for based on my following of his rubrics (!). Then I get a grade.

Student: "You gave me an F on what I wrote about Plato's thoughts."

Faculty: "Your writings clearly show you didn't understand what you read."

Student: "That doesn't matter. I wrote what I got from it."

Faculty: "What you got was wrong."

Student: "That doesn't matter."

--exchange between Philosophy professor and student, leading to an official

complaint.

The course book was an interesting read, and I certainly learned a little here, but I can't help but have reservations over this course. There's no interaction with the instructor, no feedback to know if I've done anything wrong so that I can improve my completely nonexistent Educationist skills.

My book report instructions are to primarily to write my own reflections on the material I've read; at no point am I to show that I understood the material in the book, much less take a test to demonstrate understanding. Just write my feelings down, and along with some lines about how I could use any of it in a classroom.

I chose a real research paper for my report. Again, all that was necessary was to write my feelings down; I find it unlikely the professor for the course could understand the arguments made in the paper, or even cares. With most of my teaching covering material that I learned in high school, I have to admit there's not much hope of finding much of direct use in my courses, although I do what I can to apply some of it.

In 20 years of teaching, I've never written out an Educationist-style lesson plan, but I needed to write one for this course. I just followed along the lines of a lesson plan for a different topic, I found online; I would love to know if my imitation was sufficient, or what details I missed. My first lesson plan, ever...and I have no idea if my plan, which covers some applications of ideas in the course book and research paper, is even coherent. I feel like it was, and I guess that's good enough for graduate level Education.

Finally, I wrote another two pages of my feelings about the book and course, basically summarizing the results from the previous three assignments.

Hello, Your assignments have been received and they are very good. An A Grade has been submitted to NSDU. You can order a transcript now. See attachment for directions on how to order transcripts.

--My most extensive communication with the instructor. Guess I know what I'm doing, then.

And that's the course. I actually did the work, but if I had wanted to hire someone else to do it, there's utterly no way the teacher of the course could possibly know, having never seen my face or signature. I gained some minimal skills out of it, I suppose, although I have no way of knowing for sure. Ten of these courses, twenty weeks of effort at most, and I could have a Master's Degree in Education, "specializing" in mathematics, no doubt. This education seems to be little more than a straight transfer of money from me to the school in exchange for a piece of paper asserting that I know something...an assertion based on one long e-mail that could easily not be from me.

Summary:

It would not be difficult for someone with no understanding whatsoever to get an online graduate degree in Education, and this could be why Education degrees are held in such low regard (outside of administration) that even Educationists have been known to hide what, exactly, they have an advanced degree in. Even though I did all the work in the course, I honestly don't have a clue what skills I've learned, or even know how this would help my teaching. What I've been graded on are skills I had coming into the course; this is so different from the mathematics graduate courses I've attended, filled with new information that not only was I required to learn, I was required to demonstrate what I learned in person, on tests.

A whole generation of young people infused with the utopian dream of college education is indebted via a system with few safeguards. Accreditation, which supposedly guarantees that the culture gets the education they're paying for, fails horribly. Administrators seek to present an air of legitimacy that supports also their goal of expansion at any cost, and turn to Educationists for help. The unprepared fall into a black hole of remediation often constructed by Educationists, and as insult to injury even the well prepared young people are subjected to the questionable theories and ideas of an isolated field of supposed knowledge, populated by people who quite often acquired certification of that knowledge via dubious methods of learning.

We'll see later how it happened that such a dubious field gained so much influence over higher education, but first let's look at some of the strange practices that are part of the game of getting a degree today.

Chapter 5: Online, Cheating, Technology, Fishing, and Other Games

Online Games

Administration: "We need to have more online courses, since we can offer these across the country and are more convenient to our students."

Me: "Isn't our charter as a community college to service, well, our community?"

Administration: "Expansion of our student base will allow us to provide more services here."

Me: "We're in a town with a population of 1,200. We have close to 3,000 students taking our classes. If we're not able to offer enough services to the local community now, maybe we should consider restructuring ourselves to be more efficient."

Administration: "More students is always better."

--it's so hard to argue such unassailable logic.

In 2006, nearly 20% of college students were taking at least one online course, and the growth rate of online students exceeded that of traditional brick and mortar students , a trend that has not changed[1]. The increase of students in 2011 was the largest to date. It's not a stretch to believe that online education will continue to expand despite any real consideration of sanity—are there online courses in public speaking or motorcycle repair? You bet, dozens of them, even. Apparently there is no skill that can be learned online just as well as it would be in the real world.

Online courses represent a bloated and easily squeezed cash cow for the accredited institution. Additional overhead is minimal for an already established institution, oversight is minimal, student complaints are generally easier to deal with (the student can easily be too far away to appear in person, or even in another state, which helps with legal concerns), and faculty can administer (I'm reluctant to use the word "teach") several online courses with the same effort as actually teaching a single course.

It isn't simply 2 year and 4 year degree courses that are offered online, virtually everything is available from high school to Ph. D. degrees, all accredited, most of it accredited as legitimately as can be. Before looking at how successful online education is for college, let's consider a closely regulated education system, the public high school, and compare the evidence for success there when it's tried for online students.

Colorado has invested vast sums of money into online education for their high school students, and examined the results. Dropout rates of online students were higher, by a factor of *four*. Money diverted to online courses came from closing "traditional" teacher positions, doubling up on problems when the failing online students returned to their traditional schools. Students leaving the program were further behind in their education than when they started. In short, a disaster[2].

A suggested reason for the disaster was the selection method for online students: many students chose online courses as a "last resort" for learning. These weakest students, students already with little self-drive for learning, would definitely have issues when put into an online system where the only way to learn is through self-motivation. These types of students didn't do well in online coursework, but there's more to the failure of the system than that. A look at the data showed only a few students were "at risk," with the range of ability for online students being comparable to a similar number of traditional students[3].

Perhaps Colorado was a fluke, so we look at other states. Online charter schools in Ohio, and Virginia likewise have graduation rates far below traditional schools. An online charter high school in Pennsylvania was shut down after a single year, it failed so badly, and online charter schools do worse in general than traditional schools[4]. More disaster, and there are no examples of online public schools being unarguably successful. Again, failures are attributed to marketing/recruiting at-risk students, and that these schools were targeting the vulnerable, but this argument is probably just as valid in these states as in Colorado. Even if true, some colleges likewise target the least academically inclined, and victimize students with little comprehension of what it means to take on a student loan for college, so we should nonetheless expect similar results in college as in high school.   In other words, we should expect disaster in college online courses.

"Help. I don't know how to send you an e-mail."

--e-mail from a student in my first online course.

There's a big difference that makes online high school courses not the same as online college courses, even if both provide considerable latitude for the students to work at their own pace and time. In high school, the students still, generally, have to report to some "school" with computer-filled rooms, to perform their course work. Not all schools are like this, but parents want and often require supervision of their children, and so generally that's how many online pre-college schools work. College students rarely have such supervision in an online course. While at the closely monitored primary and secondary schools, online education is far less successful than traditional education, with "disaster" as a description coming up repeatedly, online courses at the college level seem to be far more successful.

A recent comparison of 99 studies by the Department of Education showed that at the college level, online education is probably as successful as a traditional classroom setting[5], and many studies show online education to be superior. "Success," of course, is defined in the usual way—graduation rate, course grades, and other methods that are sometimes a bit suspect as far as determining if any education is going on in the course. It's positively fascinating that online education is a near total failure for 17 year olds in high school, but very effective for people in college that are 18 years of age or older.

This is quintessentially amazing, a striking demarcation in accomplishment. High school students with oversight do poorly. College students with no oversight do fine. "18" is more or less the age of adulthood in America, the age of responsibility, and it's possible that humans simply become dramatically more interested in education at this age. With "age of adulthood" varying so much around the world, however, this seems a weak argument for what is so special at this age that we see the difference in student performance rise so dramatically. What else could be the difference? Perhaps the next section can answer that.

Cheating Games

"Half a dozen students turned in the same paper, word for word, in my course. One student changed the font, but otherwise, the same paper. There's even a line in the paper where I think a cat walked across the keyboard, so the text reads 'the elDLKSNLKNLKNSGectron...", and no student chose to even edit that out."

--Physics professor explaining to me how adding writing to his course helped with learning. Any wonder at all how students got used to the idea that if they all turned in the same paper everything would be ok? This type of thing doesn't happen out of the blue.

Should the results for high school students be applicable for college? Considering how much of college work is material offered in high school, and how students are very close to the same age, the results should be similar, and yet according to many studies, they are not. The big change is now the student has money involved, his own money (or at least a portion of the loan money) to spend, and is given a much greater capacity to be responsible and trustworthy. Together, these warp the picture as the student now has the capability and opportunity to cut-and-paste or purchase his way to passing, if not necessarily learn anything.

"Mary, what did he give you on that last test? I used the answers you gave me, and he failed me."

---E-mail from a student in my online course, accidentally sent to me. More than half of the class used the answers referenced, which were correct for the test I

gave the semester before...I had changed the test, but the cheating students, all of them, had neglected to see if the questions on the current test even came close to matching the answers they gave me for the old test (it wasn't even a multiple choice test!). Admin stopped offering my course after that, though other online courses, with much higher passing rates, continued. Note carefully: catching students cheating is cause for punishment by administration, and a faculty member can never advance his career by doing so.

Cheating is rampant in online courses, overwhelming, extreme, massive even. A student with a few dollars to spare will find it's extremely easy to have a ringer to log in to his account and perform much of the work, or hire a "tutor" to sit next to him as he sits at home and takes an online test. An entire industry has arisen filled with writers that will happily write custom papers (even Ph.D. theses) on demand, with frighteningly brief turnaround time.

An exasperated—but making far more a year than I do—employee of the paper-writing industry, who claims that Education majors make up the bulk of his clients, wonders how professors can have no questions about a student that can barely speak English but write papers like his[6]. I'm also on a website of writers for hire, though not a paper-writing site, and while I agree Education majors are the majority of the higher-level assignments on offer, other fields are not without representation (I've only seen one physics thesis in ten years however, and none in mathematics). I emphasize: these are not students asking for editing help, or research assistance. They want whole papers, on demand, and are willing to pay well for them. I don't take these offers, I get enough legitimate work...but it's easy enough for anyone to do so.

Project Name: Weekely SIOP Lesson plan
Project Description:
Hello can you help with this assignment? if so what is your fee?Your final assignment for EDU...will be to develop a complete set of five lesson plans for a unit of study (approx. 1 week in length) including all elements learned in this course for effective instruction for English Language Learners. Select the

specific area and grade level for your unit of study...The completed project should be 6-8 pages in length...should incorporate at least three scholarly sources (including the textbook),...

--Another Educationist hard at work on a degree, paid for with tax dollars, and buying some coursework with tax dollars. When the Educationist graduates, he'll likely get a job paid for with tax dollars, too. At least there's balance in this.

These sites literally write an entire paper for a student willing to pay for it. A top tier term paper site gets over 8000 hits a day, over the course of a year they get nearly as many hits as there are online students[7]! That is just one site, and there are plenty of others. With these kinds of numbers, it's impossible not to consider the reality of widespread cheating in online courses. Anti-plagiarism websites are probably never going to be sophisticated enough to handle the sort of subterfuge of writing entire papers on demand—some schools encourage their students to have their papers checked first, which really is just verifying that the paper won't be detected as plagiarized (if it is, the student has opportunity to change the paper to it doesn't detect as such). High school students generally don't have the credit cards (or the money) to buy written-on-demand papers, while college students do; high school students inclined to cheat make do with purchasing pre-written papers from websites—much cheaper, and much easier to be caught. From the taxpayer's point of view, insult is added to injury as college papers are almost certainly often paid for via student loans, as is the tuition of the student, and indirectly the salary of the faculty reading the paper, and the salary of the administrator that discourages the faculty from stopping cheating. The reader is encouraged to consider which should be taken out of the relationship to improve integrity.

Those are just the papers, there are also tests to consider.

Tests administered to non-adults in public online schools are proctored and regulated, but at the college level, a student merely has to say he has integrity to be allowed to take online tests without much oversight. Most online tests are multiple choice or short answer, often with a time limit, and often the software won't allow other programs to run while the test is being taken (to prevent a student from looking up the answers on the internet, for example). For a college student at home, of course, even if no ringer can be hired, it's trivial to set up two computers if need be (a minimal laptop is easily purchased for a few hundred dollars), and simply search online for the answer to any multiple choice question...seriously, how is it that administration has never thought of this simple method to get around the *laughable* anti-cheating ideas in most online test-taking software?

Even phones can have "look it up on Google fast" functionality without much expense—teachers have a much easier time taking cell phones out of high school classrooms than faculty do in college classrooms, above and beyond the "take it in the convenience of your own home" testing of online courses. Some colleges force online students to come into campus to take critical tests and exams, and this does grant some legitimacy to online courses, but this is discouraged by administration—forcing the student to come on campus violates the entire purpose of online courses reaching a wider market, after all. "100% online" is the goal of most online developed courses for this reason. "100% online courses" maximize the increase in the potential student base, and integrity is casually sacrificed by administration for such a goal.

I can't help but suspect the widespread cheating I've observed with my own eyes is a huge factor in the greater success of college students in online courses. The primary, hysterically poor, defense colleges have against cheating is forcing students to agree to some sort of "Integrity Oath", where they promise not to cheat. Would a cheater also lie on an oath? Administration seems to think "absolutely not," and so considers such oaths to be an inviolable measure to prevent cheating. Unfortunately, the culture of the real world seems to be different than administrative culture, particularly when administrative culture seems to support cheating in action, if not in words.

"I've looked over the two papers, and the students say the similarities are because they studied together. Give both these students a passing grade."

--Administrator, overruling a faculty member who, strangely, thought it was unlikely students would type up word for word identical paragraphs in a two page paper.

Cheating in college or elsewhere isn't viewed the same as it was in times past. Although I've caught many a cheater, as have my associates, even the most egregious of violators will not be removed from college. At best, the assignment is dropped, or counted as a 0. The student rarely drops the course, forcing the faculty member to view the cheater very kindly or face a brutal evaluation—a cheating student's opinion can actually influence a faculty member's chance of keeping his job!

The penalty for getting caught cheating is, most often, nothing at all past not getting a benefit for cheating. Imagine if the penalty for getting caught robbing a bank was limited to that you had to return any money you stole; with nothing to lose, anyone would give it a try. Under these circumstances, I don't blame students for cheating, it often makes good sense to do so, and cheating can't be even be called disrespectful in a system nearly void of integrity everywhere else.

Any serious attempt to find cheating succeeds on a wide scale; even with hundreds of incidents of cheating in a University of Florida computer course, there were no expulsions[8]. The students were even warned about exactly how they would be caught cheating in that course, and it changed nothing, they went ahead and cheated anyway using a method they were informed in advance would get them caught. One student even challenged what penalties she did receive, excusing her cheating because "students cheated in years past." Hey, if one guy successfully robs a bank, that means it's ok for me to rob banks too, right?

"Grant money and special leave will be granted to faculty that translate their courses into a 100% online format."

--the notice that motivated me to create an online statistics course in the 90s.

With student integrity at this level, and administration unmotivated to remove warm bodies for any reason, it's madness to introduce a method of course delivery, *online*, that is perhaps the most conducive to cheating possible. With at least 60% of college students admitting they're cheating (some reports put it at 98% self-reporting cheating), with cheaters having higher GPAs (more than half a point higher) than non-cheaters, 85% of cheaters believing cheating is essential to college success, 95% of cheaters not getting caught, and, most damningly, with the public more concerned about cheating than college officials, it's unlikely the cheating issue will change anytime soon[9]. I have to use the word "issue" instead of "problem" when describing cheating, because my bosses don't consider it a problem, unless the student gets caught *and* complains about whatever punishment I mete out. It's been made clear that everything is best if the cheaters don't get caught in the first place.

Think about the numbers presented above. Consider the existence of paper-writing sites getting as many interested potential customers as there are online students. Realize that the majority of students admit they cheat, and consider it an essential strategy for college. With this reality, how can an administration that sets policies encouraging cheating not be responsible for it?

Even if cheating weren't a serious issue, it's fairly clear from the unprepared online students that come to my traditional courses that learning is much reduced in an online environment. Employers, the "real world" if you will, also generally hold online degrees in low regard. The exceptions are if the degree is from an accredited institution (as addressed earlier, a dubious reason for acceptance, and accreditation of online schools only helps a very little), or if the employer is likewise holding a similarly questionable degree.

Back to learning, it's completely expected that online learning is reduced; almost all students in the modern world spend a decade or more in the public school system, learning in traditional settings little different than at Plato's Academy, a few thousand years ago: a teacher stands with students gathered around, paying attention and asking questions. It would be surprising if suddenly switching to a new method of delivery were particularly useful. It's about as reasonable as a suddenly switching from holding your fork in your right hand to holding it in your left and expecting to eat a meal just as smoothly, if not better.

Is it possible to get or provide an online education? Sure, for some small percentage of the population or particularly diligent (theoretical) school. There's just no way that it could be a good option for the masses of students being suckered into it, and granted easy loans, not that it stops any institution from offering another half dozen online courses at the drop of a hat.

Educationist: "By using this software for multiple choice questions, you can give partial credit for multiple choice questions."

Faculty: "Isn't simply guessing a form of partial credit for multiple choice exams?"

Educationist: "I don't know about that, but the advantage to giving partial credit is now learners won't get frustrated if they pick an answer that's only close to correct. This will increase passing rates in your course, and retention."

(We try out the software and use the default settings for partial credit)

Faculty: "You know, the way how you've got partial credit set up here, if a student just guesses randomly on every question, he'll expect to get a 72 on any exam...that's passing, and the student doesn't have to know anything at all to pass."

Educationist: "I've heard that before."

Faculty: "..."

--With Education majors being such big customers of writing sites, perhaps it's no coincidence that Educationists are perpetually defining down achievement.

Every few years, administration gets excited about offering some new technological gimmick, always because they've been told employment of the gimmick will increase warm bodies. Despite the fact that the vast majority of studies show no significant difference between using these gimmicks or not[10], the vendors of such gimmicks always say their stuff really works, backed up with their own studies.

Often, the studies use a very biased sample (for example, preselecting only students that are interested in learning with the new technology to see if they learn using the new technology—students interested in learning generally learn better regardless of circumstance), or use a test-retest method on the same students, making it fairly easy to show improvement just by repetition. Sometimes the methods are very questionable to anyone with basic math skills, like my example above. It doesn't matter how obviously invalid the new toy is, as long as there's a promise of even a miniscule increase in retention, the new idea will be offered, and sometimes implemented regardless of what faculty have to say.

(E-mail from administrator): "I would like to see this website you're making for the online course."

(Reply from me):"Of course. Just click on this link."

(E-mail from administrator):"I don't understand. Can you come to my office and show me? I'll be here all afternoon."

(Reply from me):"Take your mouse pointer and click on the underlined words."

(E-mail from administrator):"Come to my office today and show me at your convenience."

--I had no choice but to come to the administrator's (spacious) office, and click on the link to get to my website. I note here that the administrator encouraged us, many times, to use technology. Granted, in 1998 not everyone knew all conventions of the internet. I guess.

For example, administration encourages us to use Moodle, online software, for our multiple choice exams, because it's been shown to increase retention. The default for multiple choice tests taken through Moodle is great from the student's point of view: after the student makes his guess, the software tells the student if the answer is wrong, and gives the student the chance to change his answer.

So, if the question is "DLKJFJG?", the student selects "A". If wrong, the computer warns him to select again. He then selects "B", and so on, until he is told he is right. While I grant this does represent some problem solving skill by the student, this isn't remotely learning, but that's not the point. Statistical studies doubtless show that this system will help with passing rate, but one has to wonder if students are motivated to achieve real learning in this type of test-taking environment. Such questions are irrelevant, as Moodle does help with passing, or at least retention, which is all the administration cares about.

Now, faculty giving such tests will generally notice student scores dramatically improving, and that increases passing rates. Increased passing rates result in praise from administration. Faculty could go and change the settings so that the tests are now somewhat legitimate (subject to the many possible cheating games above), but this would lead to reduced passing rates, student complaints, and pressure from administration. It…really is no wonder that student "success" improves on Moodle.

Withdrawal Games

"Ok, my course grades for assignments are F, F, F, and F. What's my average?"

--every semester, at least one student asks me this question. I find it particularly saddening when the student is in my statistics class.

If a student's GPA falls low enough, he may no longer qualify for scholarships and loans. It's crazy how little is necessary for a "scholarship"…that word means little now, though in the past it only applied to top students. Students losing scholarships and loans cuts into college revenue, and such is intolerable for the administration. While encouraging cheating and questionable course practices do much to prevent a low GPA, administration introduced a further tactic to help students get by: infinite and very late withdrawals. A student registering for a course can drop the course, with no academic penalty, past mid-terms; faculty are encouraged to make sure students have more than half their graded work done by mid-term, the better to facilitate students deciding if they're going to fail or not.

Up until now, sometimes I've referred to passing rates (the rate of students passing the course), and sometimes to retention rates (the rate of students not dropping the course). While these words should mean different things, when the withdraw deadline is deep into the semester, they really do mean the same thing, as there's no excuse for a student failing a course when he has most of his grades in front of him and has had months to figure out what kind of grader the professor is. Nevertheless, just as "remedial" turned into "developmental," so too has "passing" turned into "retention."

Keep this in mind, every time administration says to increase retention, what's really being said is to pass more students. Retention and passing are the same thing. At one university, I was called "pathetic," among other unpleasant words, for not getting 85% retention, even as the top students consistently said I was one of the few faculty that was actually teaching anything.

Fishing Games

"My father bought me this night course because I wasn't learning anything at my high school."

--explanation a 15 year old gave for being in my evening College Algebra course. She got a C on the first test, showing that indeed her background was a little weak. However, she aced everything past that point, scoring 30 points higher than the next highest score in the class on the university's departmental Final Exam. And I'm pathetic. For those reading between the lines, yes, almost all students failed the departmental final exam, although administration saw no reason that would conflict with the departmental 85% passing rate (the faculty were not obligated to make the final count for part of the course grade).

Despite all the pressure to offer ever more negligible courses, assisting the students (or should I say pseudo-learners) in their own fleecing, there are nonetheless many faculty that still try to keep some small shred of integrity, desperately clutching their legitimacy despite the endless student complaints and consequent harassment from administration.

There are also quite a few faculty more interested in pleasing administration, and students needing to pass a critical course will systematically take each faculty member in a department until they find someone compliant, one that's not interested in teaching, or even covering, material. This process is called "fishing," as in "fishing for an instructor that is easy." Adjuncts make perfect fish; they have a very tenuous, very expendable, position at the institution, and know that student complaints will be the end of even their most menial job. A student's best bet for getting an easy course is to take an adjunct, who has no security and no defense against administrative pressure for low complaints and high passing rate. This is one more reason why administrators prefer hiring adjuncts over full time faculty, especially the uppity sort that think they should challenge and educate students.

Unfortunately, fishing for an amenable instructor, withdrawing semester after semester until getting lucky, can slow down a student's progress towards graduation. Thus, the withdrawal game combines with the fishing game to create a system where most students do not get their degree (semi-bogus or not) within six years of entering college. This is something of a scandal, and administration was quick to respond with policy changes to facilitate more rapid fishing.

At one accredited institution students were allowed to register for multiple sections of the same course, dropping the redundant ones before the semester ended. How delightful! Now a student could fish out two, or even three, faculty members for a particularly problematic course (i.e., math), in a single semester, until finally landing the lunker. This was a great help for students trying to graduate quickly. For students simply looking for an easy time, this pitted members of the same department against each other to offer the simplest courses possible. As an added bonus, this made achieving a high retention rate all but impossible—20% of a class could easily be these double- or triple-registered students— leading to even more chastisement of "under-performing" faculty not making their 85% retention quota.

A slight variant of the fishing game is the ability some colleges grant for students to re-take a course they've already passed, for a better grade. So, a student who gets a B in College Algebra can go fishing with another instructor, hoping for an A on the next try. Strangely, I've had students fish me like this and improve their grade from another teacher...and had students go from me and fish a better grade from that same other teacher. Taking a course multiple times can absolutely help a student better understand the material, although for the student it's more about getting a better grade the second time around. I certainly understand the student focus on GPA, and actually respect students for doing this, but if administration wanted students to graduate more quickly, they could just stop allowing students to re-take courses for relatively frivolous reasons. This is a classic example of a stopped clock being right twice a day: administration allows this type of fishing because it obviously helps with revenue and retention...coincidentally, taking a course multiple times also helps a student get an education.

I need a paper on 15th century sewage systems in Finland by Monday. It needs to be at least 10 pages long, with citations in APA style. Can someone help me? I need someone honest."

--job posted on a site for writers-for-hire. Obviously, the professor was trying to pick a topic for which a ready-made paper would be unavailable, and was unaware that nowadays whole papers are written on demand. The request for someone honest caught my eye; in the detailed project description (which included a cut-and-pasted assignment description from the professor) the student complained the previous writer took his money and disappeared, hence the short notice. Rather makes me wonder at weaker students that ask to turn in even very brief papers a week late, and then ask for more time...they probably can't find a writer.

Summary:

So to summarize where we are in this book, vast quantities of people are suckered into taking out loans for higher education. This education is certified very questionably by accreditation, but the simple fact is a significant proportion of these victims really aren't going to benefit in any way from education, legitimate or not. Rather than being honest, and telling these people, "Look, we gave you a chance, we gave you the money, we even tried every ridiculous idea Educationists gave us, but no matter how much you cheat you're really not going to get much out of this besides a lifetime of debt, go do something productive now," numerous policies were enacted to keep these victims in the system for many years, deeply indebting them and harming their ability to earn an honest career.

Did these policies come from the President of the United States? Did they come from students? Did faculty create these policies? No, these abominable ideas came from administration, because of how administrative goals are set, and administration will, quite understandably, attempt to achieve those goals in the easiest way possible, especially if there is no oversight to assure that administration acts with integrity.

Because administration only cares about getting those checks, it becomes administration's highest goal to maximize the number of checks coming in, and this naturally translates into maximizing the number of students on campus. Up until now I've mostly pointed the finger at administration for many of the corrupted policies that define college education in America, and I admit to bias here in my estimation of ultimate responsibility. This assessment is a little unfair. If faculty, perhaps, had more of a collective spine, then maybe the corruption would not be so bad.

In the next chapter I'll discuss the kind of pressure put on faculty to submit to the unquenchable greed of administration. It takes much to become a college faculty member, and more to remain one— the latter generally requires submission to administrative desires. Many of the examples I'll give I've personally been subjected to, or witnessed, but others are those that my colleagues across the country have seen and reported.

From these examples and the information in the next chapter, I'll leave it to the reader to decide how much college faculty share the blame for the deplorable decay of college education, and then we'll examine what it takes to become a highly qualified college administrator.

"This department will now have an 85% retention rate."

--administrator explaining a new initiative to improve education. I trust the reader hasn't forgotten that retention and passing are the same thing.

Up until now, this book mostly addresses the mechanics that have led to the corruption of higher education, focusing on everything except the faculty. Outside the education industry, it's widely believed that faculty are the ultimate barrier against bogus degrees. There's certainly some truth to this, even as I've outlined many administratively created policies that have facilitated the "6 years to graduate, deep in debt, no skills or knowledge" status of so many college graduates.

"Yes, they're weaker students, so grade them more generously. This is their chance to improve themselves."

---Administrator, trying to make faculty feel good about increasing retention.

A student that knows nothing is not going to pass a course, no matter how watered down that course is, unless the faculty teaching the course passes the student. That's just one course, and there's no way to get a degree without passing thirty or more such courses. If it takes thirty or more courses to get a degree awarded, it must take a like amount of faculty failing in their duties to get a bogus degree awarded. A college that gives out bogus degrees can only do so if the vast majority of faculty members fail to act with integrity.

A case could thus be made that the massive fraud in higher education today ultimately rests at the feet of faculty. If faculty did not cave in to administrative demands en masse, perhaps the mess of higher education today would be just a little cleaner.

At the very least, it's clear there's a shortage of honest and bold faculty members in education today, too few to resist administrative demands. To see why honest faculty are such a rarity, let's take a quick look at what it takes to become, and remain, an honest faculty member at an institution.

Get the Degree

1) "A 1480 on the GRE, a national award for undergraduate research (second place went to a student at a place called "M.I.T."), and a 3.58 Honors Program GPA."

2) "Just fill in this form."

--What I needed to get acceptance into a mathematics graduate program at half of the institutions I applied to (the other half rejected me), and what I needed to get accepted into an Education graduate program, at every institution I applied to, respectively. Of course, respectively.

It takes a considerable amount of education to even become qualified to hold a faculty position. First, it takes four years to get a degree in an academic field, only achievable by a good student (typically, academics are pretty good students). It takes another two years to get a Master's degree (or an equivalent to the bare minimum to teach at an institution of higher learning), and quite possibly another four years to get a Ph.D., the terminal degree, assuming acceptance into a legitimate program, which my example above shows is not a sure thing even with solid credentials. After six to ten years of a very successful academic career, it's time to get a job.

This process alone means there will be very few potential faculty with legitimate degrees, although certainly some graduate programs are much, much, easier to get into than others.

Get and Keep the Job

"Candidates for a permanent position will have demonstrated a high retention rate."

--part of interdepartmental announcement for permanent positions opening up.

Most people outside the industry believe that college faculty have tenure, the utmost in job security. Indeed, in decades past, it was one of the biggest advantages to teaching in higher education. This presumably gave faculty the academic freedom to say unpopular things in his field, although in many fields (such as mathematics), I'm hard pressed to see what could be said that would require such job protection. Tenure is much maligned, with many semi-mythological tales of "dead wood" tenured professors that do nothing in the way of research or teaching. Certainly, there are such abuses, particularly in the primary and secondary education system, where teachers can automatically get tenure in just three years, by just barely doing their jobs[1]. In higher education, however, tenure can take seven years to even qualify for applying, and is only granted after an extensive process, assuming the often extensive qualifications are met. A professor that applies for tenure, and is rejected, can end up losing his position, making it a gamble that not everyone would be willing to take. Despite the vetting process and the risks involved, it seems every other school has a story of an unworthy professor nevertheless holding tenure. I've never met one in person, however.

"We can provide a better education if we didn't have so much dead wood," cried administration, and over the years, policies changed to the point that discussion of the value of tenure is moot in higher education: tenure is all but gone, and those that have it are an aging population. The average age of a tenured faculty member was 54 years old in 2007. While eliminating forced retirement contributes a little to the aging of tenured faculty, it's clear that most of the new faculty coming into the system in the last decade have not received tenure. Most of the over-50 crowd with tenure received it before hiring and policies were changed to make tenure no longer a realistic possibility. Today, tenure track positions where a faculty member could *theoretically* get tenure represent less than a third of full time faculty positions in higher education[2].

Tenured faculty, with no risk of losing their job by refusing to yield, could resist the corruption from the pressure to pass more students, but the administration sets policies to make such faculty an old, minority breed not long for the system. At one mature institution I taught at with over 25,000 students, the whole department had one (!) tenured faculty member, and he really did try to stop what was happening year after year, enduring open and extreme hostility by the administration until he decided to retire and be done with it. His efforts at resistance rarely accomplished anything, as he was casually outvoted by the faculty in no position to resist.

Tenure is gone. Instead of full time, tenure-track positions, many institutions hire large numbers of adjuncts[3], getting only the barest minimum number of permanent faculty. Adjuncts get perhaps $2500—that's the average, it's more like $1500 in my area--a course, with no benefits. Do the math here: an adjunct teaching 10 courses a year teaches as much or more than many full time faculty (a typical faculty course load is four or five classes a semester), for less pay than a janitor, actually much less money since benefits are out of the picture. After 8 years of schooling and advanced degrees, an adjunct position is the "best hope" for many would-be academics. An honest academic wanting to be a faculty member has to accept the possibility of spending a decade a more working for menial wages just in the hopes of landing a permanent position.

Administrator, evaluating a faculty member: "Your student evaluations for your five classes are 3.1, 2.8, 2.7, 2.4, and 2.6. That averages out to 3.6, making you the highest rated member in the department. Good job!"

Faculty member: "Thank you. Is that all?"

Administrator: "Yes. Keep up the good work!"

--A friend of mind explaining why he got kudos for high evaluations; he chose not to even try to explain to the administrator that an average can't be higher than any of the averaged numbers. I sometimes wonder if its only mathematicians that find it grating to be judged how well we do our jobs by people that clearly have no mathematical understanding of even basic concepts.

Adjuncts are trivially replaceable and in no position to resist administrative demands, making it difficult to last a long time as an honest adjunct. I've substituted for adjunct faculty when illness or other issues made it necessary, and consistently they're far behind the course material, although they have much higher retention rates than I do. Students that come to me from adjunct-taught prerequisites invariably are ill-prepared. Adjuncts are blameless; covering the material we're supposed to cover in a college level course, much less the difficult material in a course, leads to student complaints, which adjuncts can ill afford.   An adjunct who did an honest job would simply lose his position if administration found out about it.

It is quintessential *evil* for administrators to fill classrooms by telling students they'll have a better life through education...then educate them with highly educated adjuncts so poorly paid that they qualify for welfare assistance.

When permanent positions do open up, adjuncts naturally have an advantage, being already known to the institution, and are often high on the list of candidates to receive permanent positions. Having already demonstrated willingness to accede to administrative demands, and desperate to no longer live a vagabond life, these adjuncts are poor choices for standing up to the administration once they get a permanent position.

Full time faculty without tenure are in a slightly better position, but know if they lose their job, they're unlikely to get another. This is significant pressure, and it's difficult to keep much integrity in this situation. Alas, there's an additional matter that makes it difficult to expect much from faculty:

Faculty: "The committee reviewed the candidates and ranked the ones we wanted in order. Why did the candidate we rated the lowest, the one we identified as the worst possible choice, get hired?"

Admin: "Because he was the only one who accepted our offer."

Another candidate, a month after the hiring of the lowest candidate, contacted me via e-mail: "I never heard back. Did you fill the position?"

--The lowest candidate had a degree the administration wanted; he interviewed very poorly, losing his temper when he gave a sample ten minute lecture. He was let go after one year, due to repeated shouting matches with students. When we re-interviewed, we had several of the same candidates apply again, making administrative chicanery even more hysterical.

In brief, faculty don't hire faculty, administrators do. Yes, faculty can go on selection committees and go through the motions of choosing who they'll work with, but ultimately that hiring decision is made by administration. I've been on many selection committees, and the committee's selection, much like in my example above, has been overruled far more often than not. Those occasions where the person hired matches who the committee chose are few enough that it's likely the committee simply just coincidentally chose whoever administration wanted in the first place.

Institutional hiring is rather a queer process: I was hired for a temporary position without anyone with a mathematics degree of any sort looking to see if I knew what I was doing, it was an emergency situation and I was one of the few (only?) qualified candidates. When I interviewed for the permanent position, again there was nobody with an appropriate degree on the committee. Incidentally, in over ten years of job evaluations, nobody with even marginal qualifications has evaluated my teaching, or even knowledge of algebra, much less the higher level courses I teach.

If you do not have good retention, it doesn't matter how qualified you are or how well you get along with the other faculty. You will not get hired up from adjunct, it's that simple. Not all new permanent hires come from adjuncts, of course, but the point remains: administration hires the faculty and thereby chooses how much spine they want in faculty. It's only by accident that honest faculty get the job.

Since administration performs the hiring, they also get to choose what credentials are good enough for the position, leading to another problem.

Deserve the Job

"Consider the system:

2x + 3y = 7

4x + 5y = 6

The best way to solve this system is substitution, first by solving for y:

y = (-2/3)x + 7/3

y = (-4/5)x + 6/5

Now that we've solved the system, let's move on to a different type of problem common to College Algebra..."

--Discussion given as part of a sample lecture presented by a candidate for a permanent position in the math department. No math faculty were on the hiring committee, but this part was passed on to me by a committee member who knew an easier way to solve the system, and knew that the candidate had not, in fact, solved the system. Most of the committee thought the candidate unsuitable for the position, but was hired all the same. The candidate had a Master's Degree in Math Education, and was hired by an administrator also on the committee (and not capable of realizing the issues in the above discussion).

I don't know how it is in other fields, but there's considerable confusion by administration between mathematics as a field, and "math education" as a, and I hesitate to use the same word, field. As near as I can tell, administration believes the two subjects are interchangeable, and since math education degree holders promise higher retention rates, there is an additional level of competition for mathematics positions, between those that actually know the material, and those that presumably know how to teach mathematics without knowing any mathematics.

"Is f(x) = |x| differentiable at x = 1? Let me look that up."

--Holder of a Master's in Math Education trying to answer a question at a student competition. She had taught Elementary Calculus 1 many times, and this question is comparable in difficulty to identifying an adjective in a sentence.

I don't mean to cast aspersions on what might be a legitimate area of study, but having personally met so many advanced degree holders in "math education" with a stunningly limited grasp of undergraduate mathematics, I'm hard pressed to take such degrees seriously, at least when it comes to teaching college level mathematics courses.

It turns these advanced degrees are legitimate, and there's an explanation for why they don't know much math, despite the degree title being "Math Education". A quick survey of three different graduate "Math Education" degree programs reveals that 1) such programs to do not require an undergraduate mathematics degree to enter (they sometimes recommend it) and 2) the coursework for the degree does not require mathematics[5]. Math Education majors need not know math coming into the program, and will not learn math while in the program. Now, perhaps this degree is really meant for those wishing to teach high school, but these faculty apply to, and are hired for, a college position: they're teaching in a postsecondary institution, even though quite often they don't know what they're doing when it comes to what is now college level material. Since there is no process by which an administrator could tell that such people aren't qualified, people with this degree can go on for years teaching subjects they know little about...they get good retention, I'll certainly grant.

There are graduate "Subject Education" (English Education, Music Education, etc) degrees in a variety of other subjects, so it wouldn't surprise me to hear that this problem is not unique to math. An administrator sees the degree requirements as "close enough for a Subject Education degree", not realizing or caring that such a degree really isn't appropriate for teaching college courses. As long as retention rates are good, a Math Education degree holder can teach anything without interference from administration. Being barely qualified for the position, these types of degree holders are deeply unlikely to stand up to administration. I've certainly never seen one do so, or even approximate doing so.

Look Good, And That Means—You Guessed It!—High Retention

"This teacher is completely incompetent. If any of you are planning to use math for anything, you need to get out of here and take College Algebra with someone else."

--announcement a student made in a class at my institution. I gave this student a B in my College Algebra course, and he decided to take it again under another instructor, hoping to do better. He was disgusted at the lack of course content—it took a whole semester to cover in class what I covered in the first few weeks of my course. Administration doesn't like me, but LOVED the teacher of this course.

The grapevine is strong on campus: we all know what kind of instructors our colleagues are, or at the bare minimum what kind of instructors students think our colleagues are. The reader has probably picked up that I'm not a "fish" at the college, so let me go over my course structure. I cover perhaps 75% of the material that we tell SACS we cover in our courses, more than anyone else on campus. I give all my students ten points (on a 100 point scale) just for having a pulse (grading and attendance, which are given in full for every student regardless of whether they show up or do homework). My students also drop their lowest test grade or can skip a test, no questions asked. I provide the questions and answers to many of the test questions before the day of the test—very similar questions, for the most part, but word-for-word and number-for-number is common enough.

And yet, I'm the bastard, perhaps the worst teacher on campus as far as administration is concerned. My retention simply isn't high enough, because I'm just too hard.

I'm a minority among full-time faculty, as I make my students take their tests in-class under my direct supervision, no multiple choice. I don't "get" how you can give students a take-home exam in undergraduate mathematics and not simply assume cheating, and despite encouragement to use computerized multiple choice tests, I feel multiple choice in math deprives the student of a chance to demonstrate technique even if his arithmetic is poor. So I hand grade tests, cringing as the other professors generate endless staccatos off the SCANTRON machine (it's in the room I share with five other faculty), or commiserate with other faculty as they complain at grading a stack of cut-and-pasted papers, gritting their teeth at ignoring what used to be called plagiarism.

It is well known that course policies that challenge students to do the work and learn the material for themselves are also course policies that reduce retention, and are discouraged. Similarly, catching cheaters, especially with the intent of expelling them from the course, is a bad idea for faculty wishing to keep their position.

Administrator: "Do not penalize students for missing class on Saturday."

--due to administrative issues and an unfortunate hurricane, a night class didn't meet until a month into the semester. The only solution to address the class time was an extra class, given in the early morning on a Saturday. It's a miserable solution, but about the only one available (I could have provided another option, but admin didn't ask me). I'm not nasty enough to force students to come on Saturday, but it would have been nice if administration would at least support me trying to motivate students to come.

So students complain about how horrible I am, and I have low retention. On the other hand, a high retention teacher, no matter if widely regarded as incapable of doing his job (and also, actually incapable of doing his job), receives positions, promotions, and kudos from the administration.

Administrator, to groundskeeper: "Go buy as much green paint as you can, and pour it on the grass."

--Likely administrative response to an imaginary study showing campuses with greener grass have higher retention.

Retention is everything, and 100% retention all the time is the ultimate way to please administration. It should be obvious that a course everyone passes probably doesn't have content worth paying for, but administration doesn't feel that way at all. In primary school, even secondary school, perhaps it should be that most every student should pass every course. Centuries of human experience have taught us that almost all people in civilized society can learn how to read, how to write, how to perform arithmetic, all on at least a basic level. These are all things addressed before what is commonly called "higher education," or should be.

There's no mythology of "Ooh, he can read" or "Respect him, he can sign his name" or even "Only with hard work can you count to ten," or at least such myths haven't been around for centuries. Certainly, it's important when a child learns to walk, to say his first word, to tie his shoes without help...but none of these important skills are particularly prestigious past a certain age, because everyone can do these things. There is a mythology to college graduates, however, and to higher education, a mythology earned as such graduates achieve things that not everyone can do.

And yet, the path of "higher education" now is to pass everyone, give a degree to everyone, assert that everyone has every skill, no matter how difficult that skill actually is to acquire, how little effort is put into gaining that skill, or even how incapable that person is of demonstrating that skill.

"I saw one of your students today. Please give him a make-up exam."

--"Request" from administrator. I'd already offered the student a make-up at his one time of choice, which he missed. I offered him another one. He missed that. I offered him another one. He missed that, too. He asked again, and I told him I'd had enough, that he could just drop the test, no harm done. He complained to administration, who only wanted to resolve the complaint as easily as possible.

The "pass everyone" policy makes for happy customers on campus, but it also leads to a thousand people with degrees in Psychology applying for a single position that requires such a degree...and 999 eventually finding themselves trying to pay off student loans with janitor's wages. The one who manages to get the job eventually loses it because he has no skills backing up the piece of paper. A few years of such bad hiring based on degree, and a degree is no longer the sole requirement for the position; now an applicant needs a few years experience as well. The janitors with a degree won't be able to get the job this time around, either.

This scenario is playing out all across the country every day, but administrators don't mind because the customers were happy on graduation day. An honest faculty member would try to help the students gain useful skills, help his institution gain a reputation for quality graduates so they could stand out from the crowd of applicants for a job, or help his students gain real satisfaction from gaining real knowledge and abilities.

Administration doesn't want any of these things, is paid way too much to care about these things...what is desired is high retention, nothing more.

I have taught a few courses where I passed the entire class, even gave good grades to the entire class; sometimes it happens that a small collection of good students comes together. Never has administration on these occasions bothered to ask if maybe I wasn't presenting a suitably challenging course. On the other hand, there have been many occasions in other classes where I had to explain why retention was poor.

"Congratulations to [professor] for getting 100% retention in her Math for Education Majors class, and over 95% retention overall this semester."

--Special praise given to a faculty member during a departmental meeting.

Even if an honest faculty member is hired, there will be no rewards from doing an honest job, and he'll probably be discriminated against as a minority. He will face constant pressure if he dares challenge students to do more than that which anybody, even the least skilled among them, can do. As an added bonus, he'll have to sit quietly and watch copious praise heaped on associates that he knows aren't doing anything to educate students.

Avoid Student Complaints

"I think I have test anxiety but never told anyone. [The professor] doesn't seem to care..."

"I was upset because I'm failing the course. When I went to the professor the day before the final, he said that because I'd failed every assignment and missed a month of classes, there was nothing I could do."

"The tests are nothing like the material."

--Official, documented complaints against me, with implied warning from administration given about having formal complaints made. These were included with my evaluation, given as a reason for a low annual job performance evaluation. I responded with counter-arguments, including a copy of sample and actual tests, but the administrator didn't understand my assertions, and was not able to tell that the questions on both tests were very similar[5]...the low evaluation was unchanged.

Administrative oversight of what goes on day to day in the classroom is minimal. An administrator attends but a single class of a single course the whole year, and gives wide advance notice of this so that the faculty member can set up a Potemkin classroom if he so desires.

Outside of that one day, there are only two things an administrator notices about what goes on in a classroom: retention rates and student complaints. Administration knows if retention drops from 54% to 53%. Administration knows if a student is upset at failing every assignment. Administration does not know if faculty has skipped three critical chapters, does not know if faculty is just giving everyone an A, and will only know if faculty cancelled class if a student complains (a night adjunct stopped having class for a full month before a student elected to let administration know, and I've known a full-time faculty member or two to miss a like amount of time, semi-officially).

Administrators need not look over faculty shoulders at all times, but administration really should have more to the job description than "make sure retention is high." Higher education should be challenging, students should be asked and motivated to do things they wouldn't normally do…that's how people learn and grow. Some students will complain at this. Instead of coming down hard on professors who get complaints, no matter how ridiculous, administrators should be looking carefully at the faculty who *never* generate complaints. That's far more suspicious and indicative of a faculty member doing a poor job than seriously considering a student complaining about "failing every assignment and missing a month of classes, and he won't pass me."

An honest faculty member, trying to do an honest job of helping students get an education, will generate complaints as a natural consequence of doing his job. Administration will let him know of their displeasure at him doing what he knows is legitimate work. For a time, he can stand up to it, confident that the administration just made a mistake in taking frivolous complaints so seriously…but it's exhausting to work like this, knowing your bosses don't want you doing the job you agreed to do, or any other honest job.

For the Love of God, Get Good Evaluations From Students

"Half this department scored below the median on student evaluations on teaching. You need to improve."

--administrator, demonstrating a very shaky grasp of statistics. Or should I say an inadequate grasp? All the math faculty had a great laugh at this line….after the administrator left.

Every year, faculty are evaluated by their students, by definition people that have no qualifications to determine if the faculty are teaching the course properly. These evaluations cover a range of topics, such as "Instructor is prepared for class", "Instructor starts class on time", "Course materials are appropriate", "the textbook is appropriate", and others. For each question the student rates an answer from 1 to 5, with 5 being the most positive response.

Sometimes administration only cares about the response to "Instructor provided a quality education," although sometimes the average over all responses is used instead (even if, for example, the faculty member has little control over the textbook).

Usually, these evaluations are given after the drop date, so most failing students don't get the ability to evaluate the instructor (doubtless, an accidental mercy from administration). The evaluations are also given before students can know their final grade in the course, typically because they haven't taken the final exam yet. This means that the actual student grade isn't so important for student evaluations, it's the grade the student *thinks* he's going to get that influences the evaluations.

Student evaluations are anonymous hearsay; a faculty member has no defense against them beyond hoping for some decency from administration. It doesn't matter that, very consistently, studies show that student evaluations are positively correlated with the grade students think they'll receive[6], making "be an easy A" and "get good evaluations" basically synonymous. Most faculty know evaluations are only useful for identifying the worst issues an instructor might have, and that a teacher consistently getting the highest possible ratings probably isn't doing his job at all. Administration, on the other hand, believes a teacher that gets perfect student evaluations must of course be a perfect teacher creating perfectly educated students. Faculty that receive bad evaluations receive scrutiny; good evaluations, no matter how good, raise no suspicion at all.

You really do have to push a little to move people ahead, and some will push back. If an administrator sees nobody pushing back, that should raise questions, at least if administrative goals were about education, instead of retention. An educator that is loved by all his students and never challenges them is as likely to educate students as a gentle drill instructor is to take raw recruits and turn them into elite soldiers without challenging them.

Giving easy grades makes for happy students, but it's also terrible for education. This is not perversion on my part. A study of evaluations examined student performance in sequential classes, with students randomly assigned to their classes. It found very clearly that the higher a faculty member is rated by students in one course (i.e., the easier the grading of the professor), the worse those students do in future courses[7]. The more experience and rank a professor has, the lower his evaluations, and the better the students do in the next course in the sequence. While not a perfect relationship, the evidence indicates that the highest rated faculty members *literally* are the worst at providing useful education.

Administrator: "Your students are failing because you're not motivating them. Try harder."

--a rare snippet of administrative advice that isn't completely wrong.

For all intents and purposes, the absolute worst teachers are very likely to be the ones with the highest evaluations. They deceive students into thinking learning is a trivial process requiring neither work nor study, hurting those students when those students come to courses where actual learning is necessary for success.

An honest faculty member must weigh his desire to present a legitimate course with the need to be very popular with students. An honest faculty member needs to look the other way when students cheat—administration is very reluctant to remove such students, so they stay in the class, and will simply destroy the faculty member when it comes time for student evaluations. The punishment for catching cheaters just isn't worth it.

I personally manipulate the student evaluations by doing all I can to positively influence student perception of their grades around student evaluation time (for example, by covering very easy material on evaluation day and giving a few extra credit points then), and I use a few other tricks that studies show can influence evaluations. No, these tricks have nothing to do with education, but the people I, or any honest faculty member, must please don't care about education. I still don't get very high evaluations, I admit, because I feel the need to motivate my students and make them work at learning, in direct opposition to what administration wants.

Good Luck Getting Promoted

Me: "The promotion policy is explicitly clear, you can't count anything twice. Evaluations go under 'evaluations', and can't be used or represented elsewhere."

Administrator: "Just because we're using evaluations more than once, doesn't mean we're using them twice. Your complaint is rejected, and the policy gives you no further recourse for your complaint. We're done here, and you are dismissed."

Me: "…"

--It's queer how often, when an institution's written policy is detrimental to faculty, administration follows the policy to the letter. When college policy helps the faculty in any way, administration has a marked tendency to ignore the policy.

It's no surprise that administration appears to ignore the results of studies on student evaluations, and assigns much weight to them. In fact, they're not ignoring the studies at all. The studies show that good grades mean good evaluations. Good grades mean higher retention, and that's what administration wants, so naturally it believes very strongly in student evaluations as a tool to achieve its goals. That this tool is also a weapon to destroy education is not a concern.

How great is the faith administration puts in evaluations, faith that studies repeatedly show is misplaced in every way as far as contributing to education? At my institution, 22% of a faculty member's rating for purposes of promotion is dependent upon student evaluations. Developing a new course is worth 1%, at the discretion of the promotion committee. Three years of committee work on a dozen different committees is worth 10% at absolute most, at the discretion of the committee. Writing a series of books, such as the one you're holding in your hand right now? At most 5% is awarded, again at the discretion of the committee. The committee doesn't even have to award points for books, committee work, or course development, unlike for student evaluations, where the award is fixed, and out of the committee's hands. Nothing faculty can do is more important to getting a promotion than being popular with students.

Another 20% of promotion is basically a popularity contest based on how well administrators like the faculty member, little different than student evaluations, really. A faculty member would need to score above 75% to get a promotion, fundamentally impossible without being very well liked by students and nearly as well liked by administration. The remaining points come at the discretion of the promotion committee. Amazingly, my college makes much ado about how faculty "decide" who to promote from within. With 42 out of 100 points completely out of the faculty committee's hands, this is pure fiction.

An honest faculty member has no real chance of promotion, not if he tries to challenge and stimulate students, or does anything to promote education over retention. A dishonest faculty member will glide through the process.

An honest human being with a love of something in higher education will need to work for years to be qualified to teach in higher education. He will require incredible luck to get a permanent position, which he can only get if he successfully competes with a great number of less qualified applicants for the position, or somehow manages to trick administration into hiring him.

Once this honest academic somehow gets the job, he will be under constant pressure to do his job dishonestly, and will face constant penalties if he dare challenge students to learn anything new. In the face of such penalties, he will endure relentless censure. It will be miraculous if he manages to keep his job, and tenure is out of the question. Getting a promotion in the face of such penalties and censure is basically fantasy. It will be all he can do to be just barely honest enough for his own integrity, and to do what he must to satisfy the gaping maw of lack of integrity in the higher education system.

With such a series of obstacles, I think it no surprise that faculty were barely a speed bump when it came to stopping the downward spiral of higher education, although I can respect a differing opinion here.

A Look At Elsewhere

Carol J. Spencer, president of San Juan College, in New Mexico, said that regardless of how much federal money is available, the bottom line is that community colleges need to find a way to deliver more graduates.

--report from the Chronicle of Higher Education. It's not about education, and it probably never was[8]. At no point in the article does the Chronicle indicate or imply there is anything outrageous about this comment. It's about the money, after all.

Now, perhaps some will read this book and believe that this is only my interpretation, that the system is only this way in Louisiana, or strictly the institutions I've personally attended. To this assertion I answer a very simple: "No." My associates across the country, from Florida to California, from Louisiana to South Dakota, all say the same.

Consider a 2009 study, Campus Commons, which addressed the serious issues faculty believe they face on campus. They found *"Many faculty members felt that the emphasis on retention, which they believe is coming from the state and college administrations, is misdirected."* Some quotes from faculty[9]:

It bugs me that retention is the big issue. There seems to be this emphasis on retention as the indicator of success.

I disagree with that. I mean, my sense is that if a student realizes that this is not the place for me and this is where I can do better, maybe that's success.

I don't know that that's a bad thing if a student drops out...

I have students who are really doing well. They're great, and then tragedy happens in their life, they disappear. Do I get measured for that?

This is already part of our issue that they are basing funding partly on our graduation rates. It's problematic.

Definitely don't reward schools for having more students. I mean, that puts the teachers under pressure just to pass them.

So what if you graduate more people and hand more people a piece of paper? It doesn't necessarily mean that piece of paper means anything.

Yep. We'll be forced to lower standards and graduate more numbers.

Or easier classes. I could graduate a whole mess of students, I just have to, boom, lower my standards, I can get more money, easy, so no on that one.

Those quotes are from faculty at public postsecondary institutions, supposedly those for whom the student loan money is not a concern. The situation at for-profits is crass, for lack of a better word. For-profits, while not necessarily aggressive when it comes to graduating students, are relentless when it comes to having good retention, keeping students in the programs at all costs.

As one example, Kaplan has been in the news a few times, with complaints from faculty about the pressure to pass[10]. While certainly some of the activities the administration is accused of, such as changing/improving grades and manipulating attendance numbers, are more extreme than anything I've seen in public institutions, most of the accusations against Kaplan administration are basically the same as what I've witnessed any number of times by administrators at public institutions.

"Lower the bar...we were helping poor people," from the referenced article, is an example of how Kaplan influenced faculty to pass more students. This is no different from "Yes, they're weaker students, so grade them more generously. This is their chance to improve themselves." Remember that line from the top of the chapter?

Another quote from the article, that when students failed, faculty were blamed for not motivating them, also sounds familiar, as do the comments about how faculty were encouraged to ignore plagiarism. There are numerous similar complaints at other for-profits, complaints perhaps different in magnitude from public institutions but no different in kind. If mandating 85% retention at a public institution is acceptable, how is it so much worse when a for-profit institution tries to exceed 85%? The final similarity is how for-profit colleges don't have a tenure system, so faculty have no resistance to administrative shenanigans.

"Tenure? No, we won't have that here."

--Administrator explaining the plan for the tenure system at my college.

I'm not that convinced tenure is a good thing, but faculty in the for-profit system, without tenure, had no option but to cave in to administrative greed, and that collapse came quickly. The collapse of the public system has been slower, and in line with this collapse has been the steady deterioration of the tenure system. One public school merits mention in this regard: University of Maryland University College, also has no tenure system, but endured faculty protests. Faculty members complained administration "lacked interest in academic standards", and faculty "feel under pressure to pass students regardless of whether they have learned the material," complaints all but identical to those leveled at for-profit schools. As a result of such protests, over a dozen faculty were terminated for "lapses in loyalty and challenging what they perceived as the administration's attempts to water down UMUC's academic rigor."[11]

It could be a coincidence, of course, that the death of tenure and the death of standards occur at the same time, but was there ever a campus so overpopulated with tenured professors that education became meaningless? That concern seems to be a boogeyman, and it's a risk worth taking in light of the many tenure-free campuses where education is no longer on the table.

Considering that working at a for-profit institution is a "scarlet letter" that may prevent employment elsewhere, and that such institutions don't seem to have a track record for probity (despite a solid record for accreditation), an honest person probably shouldn't work for them at all.

Summary

--"pressure to raise grades, tolerate plagiarism, and dumb down courses to keep federal student aid flowing"

--Pop quiz: Do you think this is something I, a public institution faculty member would say, or a for-profit, private institution faculty member would say? Hint: trick question.

The suckers in the higher education system were failed by accreditation, failed by remediation, failed by the "masters of Education", and failed by a myriad of college policies, with administration guiding all these failures. The last chance for the suckers to be protected from receiving a bogus education was the faculty. Any con man will tell you, "never give a sucker an even chance," and administration, by completely controlling faculty, has seen to it the suckers' last chance is gone as well.

A whole culture was in awe of higher education, viewing it as an ultimate goal, a primal need to be satisfied. Vast sums of money were loaned to that culture, to pursue those needs. The accreditation process that would have kept higher education as a noble goal, that would have protected that culture from indebting itself forever just for a worthless slip of paper, failed. Accreditation could do nothing to withstand the lack of integrity by so many of those who ruled and run the system, and the rulers preyed especially on those most vulnerable, those least able to gain from higher education, indebting those most vulnerable more than any other. Those who studied Education as an end saw only the opportunity to advance themselves, and feasted no less than the rulers, assisting the rulers in creating policies to drive the system further into the abyss. Only one barrier remained: the faculty.

The fundamental corruption of the higher education system could have been stopped by a great number of honest and bold faculty, willing to face down the rulers and their often unwitting servants, the faculty could have done honest work despite the failings of accreditation, but the great hurdles placed in the system by those rulers assured that honest and bold faculty would be a tiny minority at best.

The only thing stopping administration was their own integrity, and there was none. Avarice exponentially expands into integrity's absence. It's time now to take a look at those consumed by avarice. It can be argued that administrators are no more responsible for what has happened than students, and that they have forgotten the path of enlightenment, of education. Perhaps they're not truly responsible, but they've "forgotten" nothing, college administration was never on any such path.

It's time now to examine college administrators, the better to forgive their actions and policies leading to the debasement of higher education in every possible way.

Administrator: "There's no such field as 'mathematical game theory', and frankly I'm a little bit angry that you would try to trick me."

Me: "…"

--- Key to my longevity has been keeping my mouth shut when dealing directly with administrators.

This book started with what one would suppose was the bottom of the campus hierarchy: the students. At long last, it's time to now look at the unarguable top, those with the power to hire and fire, the ultimate controllers of all things campus-related: the administration.

As a wide-eyed young student in public school, I was in awe of administrators. In public school, the dean was respected, even a little feared as a disciplinarian, and the principal was all-powerful, able to do anything he wanted, or so it seemed to a child.

In college there is still a dean, and in lieu of principal, there are people with awesome titles like vice-chancellor, or even chancellor. My respect of high school authority easily transferred to these titans of the campus.

Administrator: "We need to provide course outlines for Calculus I and Calculus II to another school. Are these ok?

Calculus I	Calculus II
The Derivative	**The Derivative**
Introduction to Limits	Introduction to Limits

Continuity	Continuity
The Derivative	The Derivative
Power Rule and Basic Differentiation Properties	Power Rule and Basic Differentiation Properties
Derivatives of Products and Quotients	Derivatives of Products and Quotients
Chain Rule	Chain Rule
Marginal Analyses in Business and Economics	Marginal Analyses in Business and Economics
Graphing and Optimization **(rest of outline removed for brevity)**	**Graphing and Optimization** **(rest of outline removed for brevity)**

--note similarities in course outlines between the two courses. Note that the administrator could not note similarities. I had to spend considerable time convincing the administrator that something was wrong here. As near as I can tell, sequential courses with identical/heavily overlapping curriculum are common in Education or Administration.

Institutions of higher learning were adapting to more of a business model early in my career, and this only increased my respect for the administrators that were becoming more and more visible on campus. Administrators were managers, after all, and the managers I knew from the real world were generally impressive. A McDonald's manager, for example, can do the job of every employee under him— operate the cash register, cook, repair the equipment, everything in the restaurant was something the manager needed to be able to do, so he could take over any employee position. It followed in my naïve mind that administrators were likewise masters of the institution, able to take over the job of any faculty member if need be. They had my respect and awe.

My first Business Calculus class at my current institution started poorly. Administration had ordered the book before I'd been hired, and had selected a graduate level mathematics textbook, suitable for an MBA program. I'd only been handed the book on my way to the classroom. I opened it, and knew there was no way freshmen community college students could handle that kind of material. The first class was brief, and I made a trip to the bookstore to correct the error as quickly as possible. In those days, the school was unaccredited, so no student loans...and yet the students had their books on the first day.

I was slow to abandon my innocence. Yes, I saw instance after instance of administrative ignorance, but I just figured they were honest mistakes, of no consequence. Besides, administrators often had Ph.D.s, they were academics, of course I could cut them some slack.

Administrator: "You need to be more clear in your writing on the board. The little numbers, the ones up top?"

Me: "The exponents?"

Administrator: "Yeah, those. You told students that there's always a one up there, but you don't always write it. You should always just put a one up there."

Me: "Thank you."

---When I do open my mouth to an administrator, it's usually to say 'thank you'.

Eventually, over the course of years, the truth finally penetrated my awe-addled skull: these guys can't do my job, mathematics was out of their ken. Still, they were administrators, with advanced degrees, they must know something.

Administrator: "I'm on this committee now."

Faculty: "You're on this committee? Considering this committee is specifically faculty-only, how are you on this committee?"

Administrator: "I put myself here ex officio."

Faculty: "Ex officio? What does that mean?"

Administrator: "I'm non-voting."

Faculty: "We'd be more comfortable if you weren't here."

Administrator: "That's not going to happen."

--The surreality of this exchange will not be reduced if the reader, unlike the administrator, knows what 'ex officio' means. I had to look it up, too. Of course, I'm not an administrator, and thus wouldn't immediately know terms about rules of order and committees and such. Administrators don't need to know, either, apparently.

After, I don't know, the thousandth time I was told to increase retention even when it was clear that doing so would not be in the best interests of an honest institution, one thing became clear: I did not understand the job of an administrator.

What Is An Administration Job?

I set out to learn what such a job is all about. The job descriptions of college administrators, for example, deans, are loaded with the corporate-speak. For example, consider this *snippet* from a position advertised on *The Chronicle of Higher Education*, for a "Campus Dean of Student Services" position[1]:

The ideal candidate must demonstrate progressively responsible higher education work experience in student services, preferably within a community college. Proven leadership in a large, complex organizational setting, preferably within a community college. Demonstrated knowledge of contemporary theories and practices affecting student services and academic programming. Demonstrated understanding of and commitment to the community college philosophy and student development. Ability to coordinate the division's service programs with other college divisions and offices so as to be responsive to the needs of a diverse student population. Proven ability to work as a team player, appropriately exhibiting a positive attitude, a sense of humor, and the ability to tolerate and flourish in an environment characterized by multiple complex factors, competing priorities, ambiguous situations, and resource challenges. Ability to supervise and evaluate assigned staff while building a highly effective working team, Excellent written and verbal communication skills. Ability to interpret and apply college policies and procedures; ability to resolve issues, resulting in mutual respect and tolerance for varying points of view. Knowledge of and ability to utilize administrative applications of information technology. Demonstrated skill in managing budgets, equipment, and other institutional resources. Master's degree in higher education, student affairs or closely related field from a regionally accredited college or university. A Doctorate is preferred.

Note how the advertisement begins: "progressively responsible...work experience." A candidate for this position will, as a matter of course, have viewed all previous positions as stepping stones for this new position. While not explicit in the advertisement, this position, too, will be considered a stepping stone. This is common to the business world—every job is another step up the corporate ladder, not that there's anything wrong with that.

This point of view, of course, is alien to an educator, who seeks to help people gain knowledge; the concept of sucking students dry and moving on just doesn't register to a person with integrity.

Sally Clausen, Louisiana's higher-education commissioner, announced on Tuesday that she was resigning, less than a month after revelations that she had quietly retired from her post and then been rehired in order to collect a lump-sum payment…

---Former president of one of my institutions. The student base vastly expanded under her watch, and all educational standards were annihilated. Her "success" at that institution was parleyed into becoming higher education commissioner, leading for more opportunity for plunder[2].

Of course, in business, one usually goes up the corporate ladder because of *successful* financial decisions. I've seen many administrators come through, establish destructive programs, sacrifice institutional prestige in the name of retention, self-declare the programs a success no matter how abominable they are, plunder the institution in any way possible...and move on and up the ladder, going to some position of even more power, influence, and especially pay. Meanwhile, those with loyalty to the institution, or standards, are left to deal with the consequences of these vagabond pirates.

Citizen: "I know your CFO. I hear she's doing very well for herself."

Me: "Yes, she sure is."

--the Chief Financial Officer was allowed to redefine her job description, greatly increasing her pay for doing the same job she had always been doing. Since her job was now so important, she moved on up the ladder to elsewhere in the system, for more, more, more. Other administrators did the same. I wish I could re-define my position for higher pay.

The rest of the advertisement is a tsunami of corporate-speak: leadership-this, organizational-that, team-player hood, positive attitude possession, and the obligatory excellent verbal and written communications skills. It's a painful read, but for such an important and extremely high paying position, all those words are necessary to describe the job, I suppose.

Then comes the education requirements: a graduate degree is required, in fields I've never heard of. A doctorate is preferred.

Wait, what?

A Doctoral Degree To Administrate?

Administrator: "A student is appealing her grade, and I need you on the appeal committee. [The professor] gave an A for final grade scores 'two standard deviations above the mean,', and an F for grades 'two standard deviations below the mean.' Can you explain what the instructor is doing?"

Me: "Uh, sure."

--an Education faculty member, for some bizarre reason, decided to give final grades based on the normal distribution. This was double-bizarre in a class with about a dozen students, since it was all but impossible for two students to get an A. The second-best student in the class complained, since her A grades weren't averaging to an A, and the better she did on tests the higher the score she needed to get an A—always out of reach. The administrator has a Ph.D., used statistics in the dissertation, but was completely clueless on basic statistics. This was my first hint that something was wonky about administrative Ph.D.s.

In the modern world, a doctorate is considered the ultimate degree for teaching or research, the terminal degree. The version of the doctorate-holding professor is a relatively recent invention in academia—in the 19th century, most academic staff or professors held no such degree (and the staff were often faculty). A Master's was sufficient for teaching, indicative of a mastery of the knowledge sufficient to help others learn. The primary difference between the two is a doctorate represents research, generally successful research that contributes to the field of knowledge. A Master's degree is obviously desirable in a teacher by a student wanting higher education. I certainly would want to be taught and trained by someone knowledgeable in the field, and I'd be willing to pay for have someone like that. A master in the field that has also extended the knowledge would be even more desirable for a student wanting to know everything. But what about for an administrator? Of what use is a research degree there?

"Your writing is just a hobby."
--Administrator, as part of an explanation of why, since my writing didn't directly relate to my job as mathematics teacher, I should expect no particular assistance or credit from my institution.

Although administrative positions command high pay for doctoral, *research*, degrees, it's a little puzzling why this would be the case. The Dean's job description, above, has nothing to do with research, or even with teaching. When I go into McDonald's, I neither want, nor am willing to pay for, a manager with a doctorate to ring up my bill on the register, just for a burger and fries no different than at any other McDonald's. If the manager pursues some arcane knowledge as a life goal, good for him. I just want my burger.

In a similar vein, I imagine if students had a choice of say, 20% lower tuition, or administrators with doctorates, they'd take the former in a heartbeat...probably why students don't ever get that option.

For all the talk about how business-style efficiency is necessary to make higher education better, it's odd that administrative positions prefer a degree that implies knowledge and skills irrelevant to the position. In fact, almost all administrative positions require, or "prefer," advanced degrees, even though advanced academic degrees are mostly desirable for teaching and research...the things most administrators don't do. A bit of hypocrisy here in light of the talk about running institutions efficiently, but administrators decide what administrators need (and their pay), the hypocrisy is merely icing on the cake.

There are a great number of institutions offering a wide variety of doctoral degrees in administrative fields. To be more clear, there are a ridiculous number of institutions, for an insane variety of degrees. Particularly disturbing is these administrative degrees are taught through education departments. It's no longer a wonder how Educationists acquired their nearly occult power over administrators. Administration and Education go hand in hand as "fields of knowledge." Hand in hand may be too tame a phrase, as it's more to the point of being incestuous: educationists hand the advanced degrees to the administrators, who use those degrees to get jobs allowing them to hand positions to Educationists.

A look at the course titles in the curriculum for these degrees only adds to the puzzlement: Progressions in Leadership Thought, Governance and Structures in Higher Education, Fiscal Management in Higher Education (sounds useful, but it's more about fundraising; you'll need actual accounting credentials to get a financial position), Strategic Planning and Change, Leading Across Cultures...again, it just goes on. There's hardly any rhyme or reason to these titles, and almost nothing relies on anything else for understanding. Much as in many bogus undergraduate degrees, each course is composed of material that requires but a few months at best to master, with no applications elsewhere. Curiously, there are no courses on "Increasing Retention." There's also no instruction on "Acting with Integrity," somewhat problematic seeing as this is key to accreditation. Nor is there anything on how to teach or how to deal with teachers, or how to deal with students—over-the-top omissions in training for an administrator at an institution where teaching happens. And yet, it's assumed these managers know these, the most important things in their job, have been trained extensively, in fact, and they're paid for it accordingly.

Not only is a graduate degree excessive for administrative positions absent of teaching or research, the specific degrees don't seem to have anything that apply to the position. Now it becomes clear why administrators seldom know anything about what goes on in my, or any other, courses, or have much respect for education in general. All those degrees, and yet completely ignorant of what their underlings do...nothing like a business model, even as they're paid as much as high level managers. My image of an administrator able to discuss Shakespearean poetry, prove a theorem in differential equations, run a biology lab, and grade a test in French collapses like any childhood fantasy: administrative training gives them nothing that relates to the primary task of many of the campuses they rule over.

Let's All Get Ph.D.s in Administration!

"Fill out this form. Next, we'll need to talk about financial aid..."

---The basic requirements for being admitted to a graduate administration program.

It's easy to sit back and laugh at administrative incompetence, and sneer at strange degrees in what seem to be silly subjects that sound like titles of self-help books in the discount rack. It's another to speak from direct observation. Having seen the curriculum, I resolved then to do what accrediting agencies should do if they were really interested in providing legitimacy: see in person that something legitimate is really going on. Curious to see what online courses are, and not wishing to travel, I elected to restrict my endeavors only to online programs; there are woefully many online accredited graduate programs in Educational Administration, probably more than there are at traditional, "brick and mortar" institutions, so this was not much of a restriction.

The mythology of graduate school might be less pervasive than for college, but it's more prestigious. It was a big deal when I applied to mathematics graduate school, decades ago. My high GRE (Graduate Record Examinations, sort of the SAT for graduate school) score, published research, high GPA, and honors program degree from my alma mater wasn't enough to guarantee admission to graduate school, and I was rejected as often as not.

I worried my admittance to an Administration program could not be a sure thing, as my degrees were issued a long time ago, and I have no training or experience in the supposedly academic field of Administration. I don't even think you could get a 4 year degree in Administration in the 80s, perhaps this is another change concurrent with the drop in academic standards.

Thus, I was pleased at being admitted in the very first accredited program to which I applied...or would have been if they'd asked for more credentials than a credit card number. Thinking it was a fluke, I decided to shop around, only to be disappointed repeatedly. Being admitted to an Administration graduate school, even a doctoral program, was a snap at the four institutions, all accredited, I applied to. I stopped at four, much like I did for my mathematics programs, years ago. Nobody asked for my GRE, or even cared about anything I did anywhere. I applied as a "freelance writer", not as faculty, as empty a qualification as could be, and it still made no difference. One, and only one, institution, needed to see a transcript from 1991...and that was it. Once it was received, I was in.

Getting in Was Easy. The Courses Must Be Tough, Right?

"Ellen Elgen Clothes Wringer"

--a lollipop was handed to me by students in some sort of social sciences course, performing some sort of assignment. Taped to the candy were those words. A year later, I found the candy shoved in a corner of my desk, and decided to find out what they meant. Probably, the student wanted me to know about Ellen Elgin, inventor of the clothes wringer. I got hungry, and I tried to get the wrapper off the lollipop, but couldn't, so I still have a lollipop with an incorrectly spelled name of an inventor on it.

With so many graduate programs, I had my pick of courses to take; almost nothing has prerequisites. As long as I was willing to blow nearly $2000 (plus a "technology fee" that could run another $400), I could take any course I wished. Ultimately, I decided on an 8000 level Educational Research Methods course[3] as the best course to illustrate for this book. This course, over all others, was determined as the best choice for several reasons.

Foremost, this is a very advanced course; doctoral candidates are intended to take this course immediately before writing a dissertation. A doctoral program is, in theory, four years. First year courses are 5000 level, second are 6000, and so on. If I chose a lower level course, I run the risk of not seeing the most challenging material in the program. I know that if I walked into a fourth year mathematics graduate course without the previous three years' preparation, I would simply be blown away (and often was outclassed even with such preparation), so I fully expected to be overmatched here.

Second, this course covers research methods. Time and again I've seen Educationists and administrators demonstrate ignorance of even the most basic concepts of statistics and experimental design. Granted, not all researchers are equal in skill, and perhaps I'd just had a 20 year run of bad luck with Educationist and administrative researchers. This course, which very clearly covers research methods, would establish if this critical topic to a social studies researcher is even addressed at the doctoral level.

Third, this particular course is from a graduate school where at least one person on my campus has received a doctorate, and promotions due to that doctorate. Thus, not only is it an accredited institution, it's an institution that is considered fully legitimate by administrators. Educationists and administrators are forever clapping each other on the back for each other's accomplishments, and one suspects they are motivated not to scrutinize each other, lest they draw scrutiny upon themselves. I always took it on faith that they knew what they were doing…it was time for me to cut the cards, so to speak.

Additionally, I took a Research Methods in Psychology course as an undergraduate, covering in detail many research methods concepts. I remember it being a difficult course that required effort on my part to narrowly get a B (as opposed to a C). Taking an 8000 level course would show clearly if graduate level courses were more difficult than undergraduate courses. I fully expected to be outclassed.

Finally, I was provided the entirety of the course within the first few days of classes, such as they are. Online courses are extremely easy to document, and I was provided with every page to be read, every assignment to be done, every grading rubric. In short, if I make a claim about what transpires in this course, I know that there is no chance of misremembering or hearsay.

Course Competencies

To successfully complete this course, you will be expected to:

1. *Evaluate the characteristics, purposes, benefits, strengths and weaknesses of research methods.*
2. *Design specific, appropriate, and feasible research questions.*

3. *Evaluate data collection strategies based on the characteristics of the research design.*

Prerequisites

There are no prerequisites for this course.

--from the course syllabus. A graduate level course in a mathematics department typically requires a year or more of advanced mathematics courses. In Administration, there are no prerequisites for even the most advanced courses. Competencies 1 and 3 are addressed to some extent in many undergraduate statistics courses, and 2 is not much of a competency (essentially, "ask good questions"). With a whole semester to cover these competencies, one might think they're covered in detail.

Despite the minimal restrictions for entry, I'm given a warning that the course requires approximately 20 hours a week to complete—this might sound excessive, but this is on a summer schedule. Presumably, it would only take 10 hours a week during the more sedate fall and spring semesters.

While the course has no prerequisites, there are some pre-requirements. A student must have fairly good computer equipment at his disposal. The course relies on special statistical software (SPSS), and it is made very, very, clear that the instructor will in no way assist the student in learning how to use this software, or deal with any technical issues. This is a bit of a pity, since gaining some technical skill would make the $2000 price tag of the course more reasonable; it's hard to justify paying this much just for a few graduate course credits. It's a straight transfer of wealth with no chance at gaining any useful skill.

There are two course textbooks that a student must acquire. One of them is a guide to the software; it's a very straightforward instruction manual, with solid examples of how to execute most statistical procedures, what buttons to press, what settings to use, and so forth. The other book lightly discusses research methods[4]. There are no explanations of the underlying ideas of statistical procedures, however, which is somewhat odd for what should be an advanced course (the manual, to its credit, states clearly it's not about underlying ideas, just about what buttons to press). While advanced degree holders in academic disciplines know what they're doing in detail, this concept is alien to an administrative degree, apparently.

To use a restaurant allegory, the guy cooking burgers might well only need to know "turn the knob to 9 to cook a burger", but the manager (or administrator) should know *why* the knob needs to go to 9---so that an improperly cooked burger doesn't kill the customer, and doesn't make the lethal mistake of "7 is close enough to 9." With so many extensively bad applications of statistics by educationists and administrators, so bad that it's causing the death of higher education, terminal degree holders probably should be required to know what they're doing. That would be the point of having terminal degree holders in such high position, after all: they know more than just barely enough to get by.

The course documentation warns me repeatedly that I'm on my own when it comes to figuring out SPSS, but the software guide looks to be very helpful. I find out in the first week of classes that we'll get an assistant, a graduate student who passed the course previously, to help with mechanical details. Before the course starts, I'm encouraged to join group study sessions with this helper and other students.

First Week

1. *Read and post a reply to the Getting Started-Experience and Goals discussion question. Posting a response will release financial aid disbursements for learners using financial aid.*

2. *Access Faculty Expectations to read and acknowledge this course's faculty expectations. (You are here.)*

3. *Click 3 Confirmation accessed through the Required–Start Here on First Day icon on your course's home page to confirm your completion of these three steps. Your confirmation will grant access to all content in this course.*
Please copy, paste, and post the following response to this Expectations Message on the discussion board below:
"I have read and understood the Faculty Expectations Message to include:
1. That the due time and day for initial posts is 4AM Eastern Time on Thursday.
(etc).

--From the first day instructions for the course. Note how step one is releasing those financial aid disbursements. Despite the fact that anyone could look in the forums and see how to respond, 3 of the first 9 respondents failed to follow the instructions of "copy, paste, and post…", simply responding with "I

agree." Reading other student (I refuse to use the word 'learner') posts, it's clear that open graduate admissions does have some issues in terms of getting students with basic writing skills. At least the general course instructions advise such students to go to the writing center for help, although one would think that help would have been taken before the 4ᵗʰ year of graduate school.

So now it is time to do some actual work. The course requires weekly reading assignments, along with posting something about those assignments in the discussion forums. The reading assignment for the first week (more like two weeks in a non-summer course) is 35 pages from the main course textbook, and the first 26 pages from the SPSS manual.

As one might expect, the manual reading is dull, and very basic. It's just the first few pages, after all, and like any good textbook it starts by defining terms and notation that will be used throughout the book. Concepts such as "right click" and "taskbar" are defined on page 10, to give an example of how thorough it is. Page 25 wraps up on how to print out and display documents. This is perhaps an hour of reading, though from experience, I know that it makes more sense to just flip through the pages initially, try to just figure things out when the software is in front of me, and come back to the book when I can't glean how to do something basic just by fiddling with the interface.

The textbook assignment is similarly light, but I'm more motivated to read every word, timing myself. Unlike using software, this is material that should be well outside my experience and knowledge, so it's best to pay attention. Fifty-seven minutes later, I'm done.

This is very light reading. For example, I'm told that according to the U.S. Department of Education, the key characteristics of reliable research are that it follows the scientific method, can be replicated and generalized, meets rigorous (but not defined) standards in design and methods, and produces findings that are consistent in various approaches. This description is hardly technical and very reasonable sounding. I'd probably study and memorize it, but there are no tests in the course. Presumably all this information is not important, and the student/administrator will just look it up when need be...why a degree for this level of "mastery," or $2000 for a course that won't legitimately certify that I have this knowledge?

"According to my dictionary, an outlier is not in the usual place of business. I asked people that were out on the street, so all my data are outliers."

--one student's response when asked to identify outliers in a data set. At least it was only one.

I emphasize again how light this material is. "A **sample** is a smaller version of the **population,**" says the book, boldfacing the new words (!) the student should learn. At least the text does later sort of touch on the idea of a simple random sample (a concept not in the book), indicating some randomness is needed in getting the sample. **Correlation Coefficient** is also boldfaced, and I'm told it ranges from -1 to 1, with no further discussion of anything about it. Granted, these are just from the first 40ish pages, so perhaps the book is just taking a very long introduction.

In addition to reading, my assignments for this week are to pay for and install the SPSS software. This takes a few minutes, but I suppose someone not particularly computer literate could take an hour on this, calling the provided number for technical support.

I also must pick a philosophical framework for how I believe knowledge is generated (as one might guess, I go with the quantitative approach), writing out a listing of pros and cons, and enter into discussion with my classmates about those pros and cons. Carefully following the information in the book, and the obligatory Taxonomized rubric, this brief essay takes about 45 minutes. Perhaps another 15 minutes could be spent exchanging posts with classmates.

That's my first week. While I'm told it should take 20 hours, I'm hard pressed to see how anyone could spend any more than 5 hours doing this "work". This supposedly represents the first two weeks of a traditional graduate course in Education Administration, and less time is spent than would normally be spent sitting in a classroom.

Granted, the first class meeting in a traditional class is usually a waste of time on bureaucratic needs like syllabus and grading discussion, so perhaps the first two weeks of an online course should go the same way.

Let's Go A Month Into The Semester

To successfully complete this learning unit, you will be expected to:

1. *Examine the factors to consider when creating a research study that affect the effectiveness of your data entry and analysis.*
2. *Examine the use of archival data and standardized instruments for measuring and understanding learning.*
3. *Analyze the advantages and disadvantages of using pre-established, standardized survey instruments in research studies.*
4. *Discuss the differences between validity and reliability in qualitative and quantitative research methodologies.*

--A month into the semester (two months for a normal semester), the course half over, and we start to see some actual skill development. The actual assignments don't quite reach toward the level of these skills.

At this stage, I've long since adapted to reading the assignments first, then reading the exactly appropriate passages from the reading assignment. There's no testing on the material, so information I've glossed over or missed completely won't be an issue—courses in this program have so few prerequisites that even if I planned to take others, information missed here will be irrelevant. There are 30 pages from the course textbook to read; I again use a stopwatch to verify it takes less than an hour to do so.

Me: "In these forms, you've confused the words "average" and "consensus." They don't mean the same thing."

Administrator: "Yes, they do."

Me: "No, they don't. It's why none of your numbers are adding up like they're supposed to. If you'd just check that dictionary on your shelf you can see it for yourself, and then we can fix this easily…"

Administrator: "I'm not going to argue with you."

Me: "…"

--conversation with an Administrative Ph.D.-holding administrator.

As usual, the reading is very light. Several dozen new terms are introduced; if I had to demonstrate actually knowing these terms, I'd have to study a little, but it's clear that I won't need that level of knowledge, *I don't need to know the meanings of the words I'm using*. The normal distribution finally gets a mention, even a picture of the bell curve, and some z-scores...no real work is done with it however, and the students, *researchers*, in the course will gain no more understanding of the normal distribution (rather a critical statistical concept) than what anyone might gain from glancing at a graph of the bell curve. The chapter exercises in the book, for example, are three questions, none of which address key concepts in statistics-based research.

While the book has some discussion of bias and other concepts, it's very clear this research methods course isn't really going to go over precise details of the statistics one might use in, well, research. All that the book wants from the student is to discuss some things, and that's all the course seems to want as well.

The SPSS book also has a 30 page reading assignment: the student is to read how to create a data file, graphs, and charts. Certainly, these are basic skills of considerable use to a researcher...the student is once again on his own for learning this, and will never be tested.

Project Name: Criminal Justice writer needed
Project Description:
Hey I have a weekly assignment in police admin and its usually in narrative format, they are usually 500 words, I also have a discussion due weekly on various of "law enforcement" topics… they are usually 150 words.. they are fairly easy but the teacher has been killing me because of grammar and spelling issues.. If your interested in this let me know.. and let me what you charge..

Here is an example of last weeks discussion..
Do you believe chain of command is important in a police agency? Would a private employer organizational structure work in law enforcement? Why or why not?

---student requesting "help" for a Criminology online course. I sometimes see requests for a writer to make weekly posts, for pay, to a message board. I didn't understand what those were about until I registered for this course.

The course assignments for the fourth week of the course (the 7th and 8th weeks of a Fall/Spring course) are slightly more involved than the first week, but only slightly. First, use a database to find examples of reliable and valid instruments created in the last five years, and, of course, discuss them. This, admittedly, takes some time, and a scholar should be able to use a database; note that the course itself doesn't really address this, merely assigns it. This is fair enough for graduate school.

Why is it important to understand the difference between [validity and reliability]?

--question from the assignment. This is an advanced graduate question, apparently. Why is it important to understand the difference in meaning between any two different words? Seriously.

The next assignment is to find the definitions of reliable and valid, and discuss why these concepts are important in both qualitative and quantitative research.

Again, I don't quite see how it takes 20 hours to do the readings and answer these questions.

Ok, So The Readings and Weekly Discussions are Easy and Require No Skills. What About the Major Assignments of the Course?

Ethics Reflection	*20%*
Qualitative Data Collection and Analysis	*20%*
Statistical Analyses	*20%*

The first assignment, Ethics Reflection, is a significant writing assignment, 8 to 10 pages, double spaced. Note that if you've read this far into this chapter, you've read about double the length of this paper. This paper is to address five issues, often, according to the rubric, asking for examples to demonstrate understanding of the issues.

hi,

I would like to rewrite my report (account management) as it was detected plagiarized. Total word count is 3548 and need to finish within 2 days…

--Administration student looking to hire help on his paper. Being caught cheating didn't deter the student or get him expelled. Obviously.

Assuming I don't want to hire someone to write the paper for me, I must first mention what general characteristics of qualitative and quantitative research methods could propose ethical issues, along with examples and ideas on how to rectify such issues. For example, a qualitative research project could easily deal with personal opinions and observations, and might cause a subject to reveal more than he initially intended. Emphasis in these types of studies should be placed on anonymity, so that a subject doesn't inadvertently incur difficulty upon himself (for example, a subject that indicates he feels attraction for 10 year old girls could easily face discrimination if identified, even if he's never engaged in any illegal or even immoral behavior), making it more difficult for the subject to exceed the informed consent agreement. The research design could also allow opportunity for the subject to amend any information he gives.

Second, the paper must describe three strengths and weaknesses of qualitative and quantitative research methods, as they relate to ethics. These are pretty much detailed in the readings for the course. Quantitative methods make provision of anonymity particularly easy, addressing many ethical issues; however, applying the results of such methods can be devastating to particular individuals. It's simple to establish from medical tests, for example, that over 99.9% of the population has no particular allergy to peanuts...putting peanut-based products into commonly eaten items can be rather devastating to those few individuals with a life-threatening allergy to peanuts, however.

Third, the paper is to address why it is important for a research methodology to support a question in terms of ethics. Probably the most important reason is if the methodology is found to be unethical, it will be impossible to replicate the results since the study cannot be repeated, making any results from the research utterly worthless.

Next, the paper must discuss why it is important that the data collection methods support the research methodology. This is fairly obvious; if the data collection doesn't support the methodology, any results that are somehow obtained would be questionable, and getting those results might be very difficult. A study examining regional tendencies towards personal color preference or racial discrimination will get no results if your data isn't collected with respect to identifying those regions, and to identifying colors, and may get skewed results regarding discrimination if there isn't some anonymity in the collection.

```
Project Name: I need help in my Phd topic
Project Description:
Hi ,

I'm Phd student in computer science and i will start my
proposal in the topic
"multimedia applications in E-Learning"

I want to help me to find problem statement in this
area and write my proposal
plane in steps to get the approval from my supervisor
in every steps

Please let me know if you can help me

I am waiting you ASAP

Thanks
```

--a student request for "help" from a professional writer. It isn't always Education and Administration majors that hire writers for these courses, although a few students in the Educational Research Methods course write about as well as this student.

Finally, the paper asks what the student can do to expedite the Institutional Review Board (IRB) process. The Institutional Review Board approves all research projects (recall, this course may be the final course before proceeding with the dissertation). Obviously, the student should follow the guidelines of the IRB to the absolute letter, and should prepare his research application with an eye towards anticipating, and answering, questions regarding all aspects of his research, especially ethical considerations.

My light outline above, addressing each topic, is nearly two pages, and took about forty minutes to write (it's basically my first draft, verifying I had all I needed to write the paper). The 8 to 10 page, double spaced paper cost me an afternoon, as these are basic questions. Granted, I'm a fast writer, but even a relatively slow Ph.D. level writer isn't going to take more than eight hours, a weekend at absolute most. So, for this one week, we're clearly at the 10 hours of effort level.

While it is nice to have institutional bosses write a paper on ethical considerations on research, it seems like something on integrity would be good. A whole course devoted to "Don't enroll every mentally disabled person you can just to maximize those sweet student loan checks" would be well recommended.

The first major assignment is little different than a high school term paper. Let's take a look at the second assignment.

Another paper. Good.

- *ix) Introduction of research.*
- *xix) Research question.*
- *1) Prepare and organize the data.*
- *2) Review and explore the data.*
- *3) Code data into categories.*
- *4) Construct thick descriptions of people, places, and activities.*
- *5) Build themes and test hypotheses.*
- *6) Report and interpret data.*

- *7) Conclusion.*

--from the instructions, addressing these concepts in the paper should take 7 to 10 pages, double spaced, not counting appendices and references, which add another few pages (much of it is transcribed material).

This paper relies on work done earlier in the course, where one creates a hypothetical research question (actual example question: "How did you discover your talent for cooking?") and conducts a mock interview with a friend (in my case, girlfriend) or family member to get qualitative information. After each section 1 through 6 (the new material for this assignment), the student is to prepare a paragraph or two of discussion on his own thoughts of the process. I honestly feel like a child imitating the adults with this assignment, as I'm simply going through the motions in a pretend assignment, spelled out completely in the course textbook.

The first three sections are fairly basic: record the data, assemble it into various displays (like a chart, or a sequential listing, or some other thing—qualitative data has fewer non-graphical ways of being shown), try to eyeball some patterns or relationships. All three steps, together, are described in perfect detail in three pages (total) in the course textbook.

Step four is the hardest part, I suppose. A 'thick' description is discussed in two paragraphs in the text: the researcher is to give detailed descriptions of all the other factors not specifically identified in the research question. Types of clothing the subject(s) wore, the weather, the background noises, and so on, helping to give a visual, auditory, even olfactory image (reasonable for cooking, as my girlfriend's pantry smells of India) of the researcher's topic. Providing such in-depth descriptions of the physical setting for the research helps to later identify possible confounding factors, I suppose, although the "why" is never really addressed. The benefit to writing thick descriptions, according to the text, is to "make readers feel like they're living the experiences described." This doesn't seem to be one of the key concepts of research mentioned earlier.

Theme-building refers to the using of key phrases or code words to help explain the underlying questions guiding the research. The researcher is to identify patterns in the raw data, to simplify it into "seven to eight" (that's directly from the book) themes.

Next comes reporting and interpreting the data, giving the researcher's interpretation of what the data mean. Such conclusions are subjective, of course, but in a qualitative study this might be unavoidable to some extent.

The course textbook highlights exactly what to do, with examples, for each of these steps; there is nothing in the book on "conclusion," although it's part of the assignment. The course instructions for the conclusion indicate the student is to address why this method of data collection (the interview) is useful for gaining the type of information in the research.

Since qualitative research is completely out of my experience, writing this all out in detail takes a full eight hours of effort (again, the book gives a walkthrough, making each step very easy once the data is collected). That might not be a fair assessment, as the data collection, done earlier, also took some time. Ten hours covers the entire assignment from scratch. While the first assignment was basically high school work, this is a fair assignment, a real college level paper, training a student in basic skills. With everything being qualitative, it's all but impossible to get this assignment "wrong," however. The textbook does a very good job here, clearly explaining and providing examples of what to do, even if it doesn't address "why" nearly enough. Overall, the assignment feels like a warm-up for a real assignment, one that never comes.

Project Name: Lesson Plans
Project Description:
Hi, I have this assignment that is 6-8 pages that is due Monday...Somebody was supposed to do it for me for $80, but…she is no longer able to do it for me. Can you please look at the details and let me know if you are able to do it and if we can stay for the long run? Please include a Reference page and use APA format for the assignment. I have attached all the pages and chapters that you might need Thanks!Final Project- Due Monday, May 9, 2011Your final assignment for EDU…

––Education student looking to hire a writer, "for the long run". Despite, possibly because of, how simple the writing assignments are in the research methods course, it would be trivial for me to hire someone else to do it if I were so inclined.

While qualitative research is interesting, even more interesting is how administrators completely disregard all qualitative issues despite this sort of training; every measure they use is quantitative, or quickly converted to quantitative. Student appreciation of teaching, for example, is converted to a 1 to 5 scale, even if a "totally awesome" teacher can't possibly be merely five times as good as a "completely terrible" teacher. Ultimately all education, as qualitative a subject as it gets, is identified by retention rate, at least for administrative eyes. In any event, I'm not sure if students really need administrators to be able to write basic qualitative research papers, even as I acknowledge it takes some effort to do so.

Regardless, while this paper took some time to prepare, anyone who can read and write at a basic level can follow along with the book's instructions and present at least a passing attempt at a paper without any particular knowledge or skills.

So We Have 2 Papers, Both Requiring No Significant Ability, For Perhaps 20 Pages Of Writing; Writers For Hire Are Standing By To Do That If Needed. What's The Third Assignment To Pass This Advanced Graduate Level Research Methods Course?

- *Descriptive Statistics, Problem #1.*
- *Crosstabulation and Chi-Square Analyses #1.*
- *T Tests #1, 2, and 3.*

--The third assignment comes from the SPSS manual, for 20% of student grade. While a tiny assignment, one might think there's some validity to it since here the answers could possibly be wrong, unlike the papers where there's very little to go wrong. A student will not get the answers wrong. The complete answers to all these problems, all five of them, are available online for free download, through the publisher's website.

The Descriptive Statistics problem is to read output from a collection of data and analyze if the data is reasonably normally distributed; this is a trivial process. Seriously, the question is to use the SPSS software to do a single problem. Or, just cut and paste the answer from the handy website. While this topic isn't in every undergraduate introductory statistics course, all that need be done is identify if some values are between -1 and +1, eliminating data that doesn't fit this description...hardly difficult, and often ignored in undergraduate courses because it's so trivial to do with software (but not so easy a task to calculate the numbers by hand).

Similarly, undergraduate statistics doesn't do chi-squared the same way as the SPSS software, but how can doing a single test, from software, answer supplied, no background information given, really teach anything about this type of analysis?

The final questions are almost aspiring to the undergraduate level. My undergraduate students in my statistics course perform dozens of t-tests; in my course, they use a pocket calculator, but similar courses at other institutions often use software that performs the tests. At the undergraduate level, students need to demonstrate they can perform a T-test in-class on a test, showing that they understand hypotheses and p-values, and that they truly understand what it means to accept or reject a hypothesis in a t-test. T-tests are a critical and very common form of statistical procedure, nearly every statistical result that makes the news uses some form of T-test. This is a concept of critical importance to a researcher, and yet no examination in this graduate course verifies that the students understand, or even have a marginal familiarity with, the underlying concepts.

The SPSS software, by the way, is very good, able to take vast amounts of data and perform a wide variety of analysis on it quickly and with little effort. It's a very useful tool, although students in this course don't actually buy it, they rent the license for six months. Considering students get no opportunity to learn the underlying ideas, and won't even exit the course owning the software that they (might) learn how to use here, it's puzzling what the benefits are to this course.

Project Name: Writer needed fo an important exam assignment
Project Description:
Hi, I have an exam that's due April 21 regard leadership management. Take a look
at it please and tell me how much would you charge me for it please. Thanks

Your exam should be indeed sent before the due day/time. Your typewritten
responses should be a maximum of one page FOR EACH QUESTION, and a minimum of 3
paragraphs long FOR EACH QUESTION (3 sentences = a paragraph). Please note this is not a group exam, this is an individual exam…

At the advanced graduate level, administration students learning how to use research methods need only answer three T-test questions...and the answers are provided. No interpretation of the results of the test occurs. Students in this course need not demonstrate in any way that they know something about the statistical tests, assuming they don't just hire someone else to do it all for them. No wonder administrators and educationists keep on using terrible statistics to advance their schemes.

To judge by the numbering, Educational Research Methods is one of the most advanced courses, if not the most advanced, in the curriculum. The primary assignments for this terminal course are simple papers demonstrating not actual research, but the ability to read and follow basic instructions from a book, and answer a handful of basic statistics questions that are undergraduate level in difficulty, or would be if the answers weren't specifically provided.

The writers for hire site I'm registered with isn't for paper-writing (more of a business writing site) but I've included a few examples above of "clients seeking writers" that are quite obviously students looking to hire writers, and in often *graduate* students hiring writers, especially in online courses. The website I'm with gets a relative few such students, as there are several sites dedicated to writing papers for students, on demand, quickly, that attract most of the students willing to pay for "help."

Even if the material and difficulty of this course were not trivial, there's no reason whatsoever not to expect a fairly significant proportion of the students are cheating by hiring someone else to write the papers, basic as they are (I'll leave it to the reader to decide if it's cheating to use the answers to the statistics problems that are provided online). In any event, this is an example of what I'm told is the most challenging course in the curriculum. Two short papers, five quick problems (answers provided).

The threat from the Education course I took earlier, about online courses requiring 50 page papers seems pretty silly now, no more a threat than the boogeyman.

How About The Dissertation?

"He didn't actually find anything in his thesis, right?"

--Administration graduate student, asking about a doctoral recipient's thesis.

I can't answer for every single thesis in these programs, but I've had the pleasure of editing a number of such theses in detail, making it very clear to the students that I only make suggestions and do no actual research work—all my edits and suggestions go in a document isolated from the thesis document, and I run no software. I simply review the text for coherency and content, check for proper applications, and check for accuracy in terms of interpreting the results.

While the theses I've edited have been well written, the research is always the same format. The candidate has some sort of theory or question about education. The candidate takes an established data set (for example, from IPEDS, the Integrated Postsecondary Education Data System), then manipulates the set in a hundred or so different ways, running a hundred or so statistical tests. Sooner or later, one of these tests gives a p-value below .01, or as low as whatever is necessary to satisfy the committee. While someone with actual statistical training would understand how dubious a p-value slightly below .01 is when running 100 different statistical tests, I'm not so convinced committees for Administration doctoral degrees seem to understand.

If through some miracle, no manipulation of the data can provide a sufficiently low p-value, an otherwise well written thesis still passes, with the conclusion that "no known relationship has been shown to exist," or something similar.

Summary:

To take this Educational Research Methods course as a guideline, the following summarizes a graduate degree in administration: pay a large sum of money ($100,000 or more) to an institution for courses (plus additional fees if you need "help"), courses where there will quite conceivably be no actual learning of anything, then write a thesis supported by questionable statistics (again, "help" is standing by), and that's it.

In terms of personal growth, I can respect that someone, especially someone with much cash to blow, might want to "learn" this stuff in detail, even if I question the possibility of doing so in online formats. But administrators are paid quite well for having these advanced degrees, which seem to serve as nothing more than indoctrination into an educationist point of view. No student coming to an institution really cares if the administrators have excellent teaching and research skills, any more than they care if their McDonald's cashier has excellent teaching and research skills.

Considering the observed high proportion of customers looking for someone to write papers in Education or Administration, it's no longer so odd that administrators don't take a dim view of cheating, or have much respect for education...only the end goal of completing the program matters, not the means to the end.

An entire culture was lured by the myths of higher education, little suspecting it was a system controlled top to bottom and beginning to end by an exclusive caste of rulers with no particular interest or respect for education, rulers that are in at least some cases holders of degrees achieved without learning anything, rulers who mutated higher education into their own image. Rulers paid very, very, well if they can but trap the culture into their own vision of education.

Institutions, run by administrators, are willing to pay quite well for administrators with such degrees, even if such degrees blatantly have nothing in them of value or use in administrating an institution. These costs are passed on to the students in the form of tuition, of course, and that merits a quick look, next.

Chapter 8: About That Tuition and Where the Money Goes

"Now I have two bongs. I've named them Pell and TOPS."

--student discussing his prized possessions (Pell and TOPS both provide money to students without much restriction)

While the previous chapters have mapped the causes of the collapse of higher education in this country, no discussion of this collapse could be complete without some mention of the most easily observed symptom: the skyrocketing costs of higher education. Foolish students, corrupt administrators, timid faculty and worthless degrees have doubtless always existed, but the cost of a college education has moved from merely expensive to a price that is utterly back-breaking for all but the wealthy.

Over the last few decades, two things have consistently increased faster than the official government rate of inflation: college tuition, and health care. The increases for medical care are usually attributed to the costs of research for new drugs and procedures, although examination of why new drugs and procedures increase so much more quickly than, say research and development of new computer gadgets is never satisfactorily addressed. In any event, no such rationalization exists for tuition, as there are no significant breakthroughs in education that could be sold to students, no expensive speculative research programs to pay for, and very seldom are even weak explanations given for the ever rising prices, prices that have risen roughly twice as fast (relative to inflation) as for medical care. While there have been some student protests, for the most part people are content to take out a larger student loan and not ask "why?" There are some answers to this question, but to address the big picture answer requires some basic economics.

Some Economics and Why Economics Doesn't Apply To Tuition.

Supply, demand, and price are three interrelated concepts for any commodity, and education is a commodity as well. If the supply is large (for example, fresh water), then the price will typically be low. If demand is high relative to supply (say, fresh water, on an island), then the price will be high. As the price increases, demand will typically drop, as people will seek ways to reduce their needs (which is why people on islands avoid having grassy yards and swimming pools). If the price drops, on the other hand, demand can increase (so one might find more swimming pools in areas where fresh water is in abundance).

Let's look at demand for higher education. The general trend for college enrollments for the last forty years has been increasing, but only recently has enrollment shot up. Enrollment in postsecondary institutions increased 9% between 1989 and 1999, little different than the general increase in population in the United States. In the decade after that, enrollment increased nearly 40%, a massive increase that cannot be so easily explained by the general increase in the population[1].

Clearly, demand has increased. Supply of education in a format people want (anyone could just go to the library and read, after all) has not been so easy to provide despite the efforts of already existing institutions. It takes time to establish and accredit a "real" educational institution able to handle the influx of new students in a given year, so from this alone one would expect the price to increase until there are enough institutions to handle the demand, and prices surely have increased. Of course, price increases clearly haven't caused the demand to drop (as enrollments are still increasing). The growth in recent years is attributed to the weak economy, but the spike in student population began well before that—and a weak economy means people shouldn't have the money for tuition. It's natural to ask what's causing such an increase in demand even in the face of rising prices.

So with the price of tuition increasing, why hasn't the demand dropped? The answer is money, particularly government loan and grant money. Vast sums of government loans are easily available to any degree-seeking student that even sort-of graduates out of high school. Student loans at the federal level headed sharply higher, starting around 1996[2]. Everyone knows what a high school graduate is, but what's a degree seeking student? Anyone who clicks off a box saying "I am a degree seeking student." That's it. There's no penalty for lying or if the student changes his mind later, as long as for that one second the box is being checked the student claims to believe it to be true, it's all good. It doesn't matter if the student is just there to take a single course in theatre or poetry, as long as that box is checked, he—or more accurately, the institution--becomes qualified to receive a huge amount of student loans and grants for his education. Federal loans, the big-big money, are only available if the college is accredited, but the difference is amazing once these loans become available: the number of students at my own college doubled and doubled again in a few short years once the free money spigot was opened.

"I'll think I'll buy another computer with it."

--student contemplating how to spend surplus loan money. In this case he is effectively going into debt to buy an unnecessary, extra, depreciating asset.

With this money gushing in, increases in tuition are not noticeable to students. In other words, the "price" isn't effectively rising, foiling the usual economic relationships. Since the loans cover the tuition and then some, the price is a non-issue for the financially unsophisticated—free money is free money, and so rising prices don't decrease demand like it would according to ordinary economic theory. All the loan receiver notices from higher tuition is that his piece of the check is smaller (as the college is taking more). It's still a check, it's still motivating the person to go to college...or at least go to college to collect the checks. Because the cost of education is "hidden" in this way from the student, the price can rise even further, motivating even larger loans. There can be complaints, but as politicians respond to the public outcry against the expense of education, still more loan money becomes available, a politically easier solution than trying to scale back institutional spending. The extra money means the demand doesn't fall, and the self-feeding cycle continues.

Keep this in mind: the sheer existence of all the student loans are, in fact, contributing to the ever rising prices of education. With no incentive to keep costs low, institutions can spend and increase overhead and pass on the costs to the student, or at least the taxpayer who ultimately pays the bill for government spending. Despite the 40% growth in the customer base over a decade and the rising revenue per customer (both of which would bode well for most any business), most all public universities are struggling to keep their budgets under control. The extra money from tuition seems to get soaked up faster than it is splashed into the budget. More accurately for public institutions, they face budget cuts even as their revenue from the student loans rises.

There is no question that there are bright, hardworking, but economically disadvantaged people that benefit from these loan programs. Because tuition is so expensive, these loan programs are the only way they can afford college now. Decades ago, before these programs and the higher tuition they caused, such people could "work their way through college," but this expression has little meaning today, where such work at best merely offsets a small part of college expenses. These people are being forced into a debt system they might never escape.

There are also very sinister elements about this process that attracts so many "students," and note how I put that word in quotes. A number of these new "students" don't come to college for the education, otherwise they would already have been in college before the free money. These "students" come to college because going to college can be as lucrative as a low wage job, with far less effort. These folk that play the system for short term game might not be true victims, but there's another cadre of students very much victimized by the loan system: the ones that truly don't understand how the system works.

"It took me six years to get this degree in psychology. I have $45,000 in student loans. I can't get a job with this degree. What am I supposed to do?"

--OWS protester sign

Recall the discussion earlier about offering remedial courses that cover material as basic as the number line. These remedial courses are paid for just like any other college course, it's all the same when it comes to the loan money. But a student who cannot perform the task of "locate 2 on a number line" without professional assistance (and I'm not exaggerating here about having such attendees at my college) likewise isn't mathematically sophisticated enough to distinguish between "student loan" and "free money." Should not college administrators show a little restraint in taking advantage of these people? If showing restraint was an administrator's job, I suppose there would be restraint. As demonstrated earlier, administrative goals, or even training, have nothing to do with restraint.

Various loan deferral programs, and the simple fact that a student can now easily take six years or more to get a four year degree, explains why the problem of student loans of the last ten years going into default hasn't materialized as yet, but it truly is just a matter of time. Student loan default rates rose sharply in 2011, so perhaps the consequences will be more apparent fairly soon[3]. The current default rate of nearly 9% is far below the high of 20% in 1990, but now there are far more students taking on loans for a greater amount (over a trillion dollars of such debt now), and the current defaults are disguised due to the many more ways repayment can be deferred, as opposed to what existed twenty years ago.

My proposed myth about "Any college will take your money, no matter what" is starting to sound more like a fundamental truth. A person merely clicks off "I am a degree seeking student," and signs up for whatever classes he wants (and, very often, these are not classes that lead to any particular degree). The college takes its cut of the loan money, and the student gets what's left over or pays the difference if he's at an expensive school, and the process is repeated semester after semester, or until the loan money runs out. It's a win-win situation for the student and the college, as long as the prospect of repaying the loan is taken out of the picture for the student, and the concept of providing an education is irrelevant for the institution.

With the endless loan money coming in, there's nothing to stop the price from rising constantly.

EDUCATION SHOULD BE FREE AND A CONSTITUTIONAL RIGHT!

AN EDUCATED SOCIETY IS A BETTER SOCIETY!

FREE EDUCATION!

--Message board post, no negative responses.

Another Point of View

While economics may be a good general explanation for excessively rising tuition costs, there's an alternative view. Health care and college do have other things in common: heavy government intervention, regulation, and, most importantly, the belief that these things are of such importance to the country that they *should be* watched over and paid for by government. Price should be immaterial in the face of how critical education supposedly is. Health care is often viewed as a fundamental right to be provided by government (regardless of whether the patients particularly want whatever government mandated health care is forcibly administered), hence the creation of various programs to provide some health care, both in the United States and in much of the world. Due to our cultural myths about college, higher education too has become more and more to be viewed as a human right, and politicians have responded with loan programs to make college more accessible on this basic idea alone. Higher education, viewed as a right, is beyond price, like any other human right. Of course, most other human rights are bestowed at birth (give or take a few months), for free, unlike education which seems to require a vast bureaucracy to grant that right. Still, health care isn't free, either, and the cost of this right is also rising faster than most everything else.

"We know that education is everything to our children's future. We know that they will no longer just compete for good jobs with children from Indiana, but children from India and China and all over the world."

--Barack Obama at a Father's Day speech June 27, 2008, presumably not implying we need to put our 10 year olds to work in the factories.

There are two important differences between health care and higher education in this regard. First, quite obviously, there will be times when a person absolutely does need health care, and in times of medical emergency, government funds allow caregivers to focus less on figuring out who's going to pay the bills and more on providing emergency care. Denying health care for a few hours to sort out who pays the bills can literally be a matter of life and death. Perhaps the rising costs of health care are forgivable in light of this clear public benefit.

On the other hand, there's no scenario where "this student must learn Gender Studies--stat!" exists. Higher education is a slow process of years, with few cases where losing a few months, much less a few hours, completely destroys a prospective student's chance for an educated future. Pursuing an education should be done with care and forethought, there's no justification for putting it all down to checking a box that essentially says "this student wants free money," particularly when that box is most often placing the student into a lifetime of inescapable debt.

"When I left college in 2000, I owed almost $4000. Now I owe almost $20,000. I still can't pay."

--recent student complaint regarding how fast the debt increases once the penalties start piling on.

The second important difference involves the payer. In government health care, the taxpayer ultimately pays the bill, and there's no deception there, at least in an electorate that understands that government can pay for nothing without first extracting the funds from a taxpayer. While it can be argued that much/some of the electorate isn't really aware of how this works, the fact still remains: a person agreeing to government health care doesn't expect to become personally liable for the results of health bills initially paid by the government, nor, generally, does he ever get such a direct liability. With student loans, on the other hand, the student does become personally responsible for the bills, eventually and with often huge interest, and this is a dramatic difference in how this "right" is paid for. If there is honest belief that higher education is a right, there should probably be less punishment for anyone exercising that right.

Education is not a right, although access to education might well be a right—it's also a right United States citizens already have through the public library system. Either way, a national guarantee of "higher education for everyone at any price" is a recipe for destruction. For an individual, price should absolutely be a factor in determining whether it is truly worth acquiring, especially if that price is to be paid via a loan (i.e, for an eventual cost that is much higher than the initial price). Even for a country, the cost of education needs to be weighed against the value of that education.

Regardless of the ultimate explanation for the rising costs, too much loan money or a belief that no price is too high, in either of the above cases there are still great sums of money flowing into institutions for education. It's natural to wonder at what is being done with all that money.

Where Goes the Money?

Answer: "Two seconds, two seconds, and depending on the last paycheck, up to two weeks."

Question: "How long can this campus function without electricity, faculty, or administrators, respectively."

--Campus joke

So where does all that extra money from student loans go? The first and natural guess would be the money goes into faculty pay. After all, it's impossible to have a class without a teacher, and the faculty must work harder to accommodate all the extra students, so it seems reasonable that the extra work would show up in the paycheck. As a faculty member, I assure you I'm paid well considering the ease of my work (this is coming from a person who has worked in sheet metal roofing in Florida for the princely sum of $5 an hour). That said, the pay isn't much. I have 20 years of experience and I'm still well below $50,000 a year. Giving my own pay is misleading, since I work in a relatively impoverished part of the county. Nationwide, it has fallen behind the rate of inflation, earning as much as any blue-collar worker with far less of my vaunted education, even if the work isn't particularly strenuous or dirty in a literal sense.

Adjunct No Longer, Jill Biden Earned $82,022 as a Community-College Professor in 2011. Chronicle of Higher Education, April 16, 2012[4].

--The wife of the vice-president has an amazing, stunningly successful career of late, skyrocketing through the ranks at a pace I just can't match, even though she teaches mostly remedial courses. In any event, it's clear faculty could be paid more, if administration felt like doing so.

The salary numbers given in reports on faculty pay are rather distorted; full professors at top tier universities do make over $100,000 quite consistently[5], but these represent a small minority of faculty (the "super earners", if you will); I don't believe I've actually spoken with a person like this, any more than most people have never spoken to a Bill Gates or Donald Trump, although I'm sure they exist.

"Celebrate! Our department of 30 is expanding. We're opening up two more permanent positions."

--pre-announcement of positions opening up in a mathematics department, in honor of doubling the number of students we were servicing in our classes.

Most institutions, rather than pay for full time faculty, simply hire a great number of adjuncts to support the additional students (who nevertheless are charged as though taught by actual faculty). Adjuncts are paid a very small fraction of faculty pay, so it's no small wonder that nearly half of college faculty are part-time adjuncts, and well over 70% of courses in this country are taught by non-tenure track/non-full-time faculty[6].

Tenure is often blamed for the ills of higher education, but nationwide, less than a third of faculty are on any sort of tenure track, and far less than that have a serious hope of ever getting tenure. Because adjuncts don't count as full time employees, they don't show up in studies of faculty pay; getting a median pay of a faculty member across the range of full professor to adjunct (much less graduate students, which often teach courses) is difficult, but would be below $40,000, less than what a plumber might hope for. If that sounds low, consider that my college could hire an adjunct to do the education part of my job (teach 10 courses) for $15,000 a year--$1,500 a course is typical adjunct pay. With the majority of courses being taught by adjuncts at about 1/10 the pay, the top salary of $130,000 by the tiny minority of full professors in top schools isn't even remotely representative of the money being spent hiring someone to educate students.

It's also worth noting that the heavy reliance on adjunct faculty does little for education, as they don't have offices or have any other reason to spend time on campus beyond teaching the course. Their interaction with students is minimal at best: show up, present the class, then go home and try to think of a way to use an advanced degree to get a living wage. These "gypsy faculty" represent the most common sort of college teacher.

The gushing money clearly isn't going to the faculty, the institutional servants that actually do the teaching work, so it must be time to look at administrative pay. Presidential salaries top out at $1.8 million a year, but the top is not a fair place to look, any more than it is for faculty. A simple look at median salaries of administrators shows that even a dean, among lowest of rungs for an administrator, commonly makes more than twice as much as permanent faculty. It's more like six times as much when you consider the more representative "faculty" pay that adjuncts receive. The median for many types of dean is over $100,000, and even *assistant* deans regularly make over $100,000[7]; virtually no administrator gets paid as minimally as a faculty member. Assistant dean…it's curious that adjuncts get so little while even assistant administrators get so much. There's no such thing as an "adjunct administrator," although there should be. As you move up the administrative ladder, pay skyrockets, with medians commonly above $200,000 for a wide range of administrative positions—these are medians, so top tier pay of above $1,000,000 a year (and that's not necessarily chief officers), while not as rare as it should be, doesn't much affect this number.

One might justify high administrative pay due to the requirements these positions have for advanced degrees. Unfortunately, this argument fails on three levels. Faculty positions also require advanced degrees, and yet don't get that kind of pay. Additionally, faculty actually need those degrees to demonstrate they know what they're doing, whereas administrative degrees have no real application to the job. Finally, those faculty degrees are desired by the students as they prefer to be trained by people that know what they're doing. On the other hand, the students, the customers of the institution, have no interest whatsoever in whatever kinds of degrees possessed by the person helping them to fill out a few forms and hand them a check.

Now, perhaps these jobs are critically important to education (education being, supposedly, what colleges are for), and if there were only a few such administrators with vast responsibilities, these extraordinary sums for low level management positions might be reasonable. Maybe. With administrators in control of salary levels, even if the student population doesn't rise, administrators still manage to funnel extra money to themselves. For example, administrative spending in Michigan went up 30% in from 2005-2010[8]. This is awesome, considering enrollments and even *budgets* were flat in Michigan for this period. This is one of the few places where enrollment has been flat for the last few years, but the state population dropped from the peak state population in 2004—a greater percentage of the population is going to school, but there's less population, evening it out. In any event, the same amount of money going into the system, but more of it goes to the managers.

Number of full time faculty: 43

Number of other employees: 44

Number of students: 4400.

--approximate numbers from a nearby institution, recently. This doesn't count administrators above the institution, who are nevertheless overseeing it. If we switched the pay between faculty and the rest, the total expenses would be the same, and the institution would be run exactly as well as before. The education would be the same, too. The only difference is the educators at the educational institution would be getting the money instead of the administrators.

Between inflation, differing tuition costs, and varying state economies, the significance and size of administrative pay can be a little deceptive, so perhaps it's better to look at ratios, which give a better understanding of how much more is proportionally going towards administrators as opposed to the educators at the institution.

Before looking at administration, we again first consider faculty. Faculty to student ratio has been roughly flat for decades, although I have to concede this ratio is suspect. Since this ratio is considered part of what makes an institution good (a better institution supposedly should have a lower ratio), it is heavily manipulated to make it look much lower than what it is as far as the students would be concerned. This manipulation is done in a variety of ways, from the simple (a librarian might count as faculty, lowering the ratio even if the librarian never steps foot in a classroom) to the not very subtle (all graduate students, whether they're teaching or not, might be forced to spend time in a "study room" where they could theoretically help undergraduates, and are thus counted as faculty for this ratio), to the blatantly crass (hiring each adjunct to teach exactly one course), with too many other tricks to list here.

That said, the official statistics say it is basically flat, even though faculty hiring hasn't jumped up that much and student population has greatly increased. Go figure. The ratio varies from school to school, of course, and nationwide it was in the area of 14 students to 1 faculty in 2007[9], essentially unchanged for decades. My direct observations from my teaching and when I was in undergraduate school would put that ratio somewhat higher, and I suspect the vast majority of students in college would also say it is higher, as well. Student to faculty ratio is *not* the same thing as average classroom size, a statistic that is similarly misleading and manipulated.

On the other hand, administrative and support staff ratios aren't manipulated, or at least not as much, because there's no real benefit to doing so—it's not considered a measure of what makes a school good, although perhaps it should be. The huge administrative pay would be far more tolerable if administrators were a rare breed. Let's take a look and see if perhaps administrators are getting such pay because there are less of them, taking on more responsibilities:

Administrator to student ratio in 1975 was 84 students to 1 administrator...you basically needed one administrator for every three classes filled with students. One might think it would be higher, considering considering how little of what the typical administrator does relates to students. The ratio in 2005 was even lower: 68 students per administrator. So now it's more like there's an administrator per every two classes. To put those in easier to visualize terms, a college with 5,000 students in 1975 had 60 administrators. In 2005, that same college, assuming it only had 5,000 students, would have 74 administrators[10]. Same students, same material, same institution....14 more administrators getting paid $100,000 or more a year, effectively tacking at least an extra $280 a year in tuition *per student* just to break even (more like $500 per student when you consider administrative benefit programs that the institution also pays for), assuming they're only getting minimal administrative pay. Note that the increase in tuition is just for the additional administrators that weren't necessary years ago; tuition can easily not even cover administrative pay at smaller public institutions. Have college students truly become that much more unruly, or is it the faculty? It appears there are more administrators, taking on fewer responsibilities...not exactly reasons for high pay, even with the useless advanced degree.

Administrators hire faculty. They do so when need be, and aren't that reluctant—having many faculty under you is a way to advance as an administrator. It's easier and cheaper to hire adjuncts, and so this option is taken far more often—why hire one faculty when you can hire six adjuncts for the same amount of money, getting more administrative clout and a lower student to faculty ratio too? Administrators also hire other administrators, a good idea when it comes time to lighten the administrative work load, although certainly expensive. Both the hiring of adjuncts and the hiring of extra administrators are represented in the above numbers, but there's one more category of institutional employee to be considered: support.

Me: "The two new trailers in the back are filthy, and haven't been cleaned even once this semester."

Administrator: "The janitor's contract doesn't cover those two rooms. Don't worry, we're hiring another janitor soon."

--the trash in that room was extreme to the point that even the students complained.

Administrators also hire support staff (janitor, secretary, and the like). Like adjuncts, these too are cheap, with no constraints against hiring them in large numbers. In 1975, the ratio was 50 students for each support staff member. By 2005, the ratio was 21 students per staffer, a huge increase[11] relative to the increase in size of the student base, comparable to some official faculty to student ratios.   While decades ago there were much more faculty than administrators and staff, now the faculty are outnumbered.

Where's the economy of scale in all this? Maybe it's wrong to think a dean can service twenty faculty nearly as easily as ten. But if one janitor can clean ten rooms, shouldn't it only take two janitors to clean twenty rooms? To put this in perspective, these numbers, or more accurately administrators, are saying "Yes, it used to take one janitor to clean everything, but now that we've doubled in size it takes *five* janitors to clean up."

Tuition rises and rises, and it takes no effort to see that the money isn't being spent on education. The incredible bloat in support staff is sometimes justified by saying how necessary an on-campus clinic, job advisors, stress counselors, and such are. This may be, but one staffer very much absent on campuses is a financial advisor. A financial advisor would doubtless tell students that taking on massive debt for degrees leading to insufficiently paying jobs (and that's most degrees, considering the debt involved) would cut into revenue. While it would be acting with integrity to hire such a critically helpful person, administrators would never do such a thing. Obviously.

"Please make allowances for students not showing up or being late on the first day. We don't have the parking to accommodate all the new students."

--administrative notice

This manner of thinking is rather disturbing, especially since administration has no difficulty inflicting the usual rules of economy of scale on faculty when it comes to dealing with a great increase in the number of students. Quite often when my institutions had an influx of students, my rooms would be filled to overflowing, sometimes with more students registered than desks in the room. Administration gives me an "attaboy" to assist with the extra load...then hires more support to handle the extra paperwork from the students, and then gets a pay raise for ruling over a larger institution.

Me, in E-mail:

To: Administrator1

Hi. I'm trying to figure out when a meeting with faculty took place last June. Was it June 4, or June 11?

Response:

From: Administrator1

CC: Administrator2

I have that information, but cannot tell you without permission from Administrator2.

Response from Administrator2, a day later:

From Administrator2

CC: Administrator1, Administrator3

Why do you want to know that information?

--It is really is amazing how many of these people are around, and how tight they can be with information. I did get the question answered, eventually.

Key to advancement as an administrator is to have and hire people under you, so it's no real surprise that the expansion in support staff growth is so large—an administrator's goal is always to advance, after all. Support staff is much easier to find and hire, for much lower pay, just as it is with adjuncts. For a teaching faculty member, when the student base doubles, the work of the faculty member doubles (but not his pay). For administrators, when the student base doubles, the work increases a little in theory, but this is offset by higher pay (larger institutions command higher pay) and the ability to hire more support staff to help with the load, to the point that such hires are out of scale with the increase in workload. The end result? As the student base increases, administrative work gets easier, with more pay. Could this be where much of the tuition money goes? Could this be why the goal of every institution seems only to grow, grow at any cost, grow?

The numbers above are over a thirty or more year period, but there's evidence that the rate of administrative bloat is increasing. Between 1993 and 2007 at the leading universities in the country, the number of administrators per 100 students grew by 39%, with inflation adjusted spending going up by 61% during the same period[12]—inflation adjusted! Higher educational institutions have more administrators, and have more money going to each administrator as well, a trend that indeed seems to be accelerating.

Certainly, some of the new money coming in can go to new computers, new buildings, new laboratory equipment, and the like, but it's clear that the bulk of the money is not being spent on education, instead it's being spent on administrative and support costs. And yet, the mission statement of no institution says anything about supporting massive administrative bloat. If faculty, instead of administrator types, were in control of accreditation, they might well have issued warnings to institutions for going so far off their mission.

My institution has lost five classrooms to administrative and support offices over the last few years, even as our student base has more than doubled. Roughly a third of floor space at my institution is devoted to administrative and support staff offices (I share my office/classroom with five other full time faculty), as opposed to classrooms and laboratories, which is what one might guess would be most everything at a teaching institution. This amount of devotion to administration and support was similar at other institutions I've worked at, and I suspect it's the same elsewhere.

Students are seldom told this when it's time for yet another tuition hike, instead being told how the money is important to provide them with a "quality education." Of course, students want a quality education, and are willing to pay for it, especially with government (or someone else's) money.

For the most part, I've been referencing public institutions, and one might think such institutions have an advantage here—public institutions aren't just trying to make a buck, so perhaps they're in it to provide an education, and it's just an illusion that administration seems to be plundering all the student loan loot. Do private institutions do any better?

America is still mostly a capitalist country, and with the huge demand by students, and the huge money offered by government sitting on the table, it's only natural that new private institutions would form, and established private institutions would grow, to soak up all that money. It's reasonable to suspect that these institutions, without burdensome government regulation, would form and grow more quickly than public institutions. Indeed, they have done so, with enrollment at for-profit institutions more than quadrupling over the last decade...that's some serious growth[13]. Much like with the public institutions the rules are the same: students take out loans, guaranteed by the government against the slight chance that the student will get an education that can be monetized well enough to pay the inflated tuition costs, and the institution gets that money regardless of student outcome.

Private institutions naturally aren't funded directly with government funds, and thus the vast bulk of their revenue, those institutions that focus on teaching, must come from tuition money (no chance of floating a public bond to construct a new campus!). In reading the literature, it's interesting how often for-profit institutions are criticized for getting the bulk of their income from student loan money...even as every public institution constantly grubs to get this same money. The only difference is private institutions have no public till to loot in addition to the student loan money; they're forced to get by just on what students are able to "pay."

Past this point, there's a sharp division between "private, non-profit" and "private, for profit" institutions. Private, non-profit institutions have significantly higher graduation rates and spending on instruction over public institutions. Surprisingly for those that believe the most in capitalism, the for-profit institutions are generally worse than non-profit, with about half the graduation rate and 2/3rds the relative spending on instruction[14].

(phone rings, I pick up)

Phone: "…"

Me: "Hello?"

(A few seconds while a computer transfers me to a salesman, after determining a human being answered the phone.)

Phone: "Hello, this is Raul. This is a recorded line. I see that you are interested in higher education. Let me recommend a college to you…"

--Upon making it known that I wished to enroll in a graduate degree program, I received one or two calls like this every day for weeks.

The for-profit institutions are criticized for low graduation rates, but this is backwards thinking. These institutions even more aggressively target anyone who can apply for a student loan, and these are often not the best students, probably not the ones most likely to graduate from a program. Around 30% of operating costs of private institutions goes towards marketing to get new students, far above other types of institutions. Instead of being praised for not giving away degrees to everyone, the low graduation rates are taken as evidence of inferiority. In light of the obvious difficulty in actually getting a degree from a for-profit institution, shouldn't such degrees be held in higher regard? One wonders if these for-profit institutions had 100% graduation, if they would be criticized for that, also, or would other institutions be pressured to increase their graduation rate to match? I suspect the latter. As a reminder, these institutions are just as legitimately accredited as public institutions.

...An investigator posing as a student in a class on learning strategies consistently submitted inadequate work, such as photos of celebrities and political figures for a written exam that required detailed answers. The student, however, received a passing grade of C- in the class...In one case an instructor appeared to show a student how to cheat on a multiple-choice quiz, noting that the same test, with the same answers, could be retaken. "It's not hard to get a 100 percent on the second try," the instructor said, "just jot down the correct answers and take the quiz again."

--some findings of a GAO secret investigation of accredited, for-profit, colleges. It's a shame the Federal government doesn't take such an interest in what's going on at public institutions[15]. How is there a class on "learning strategies", anyway? Passing grades for courses where the student does basically nothing and a multiple choice quiz that you can just keep retaking until you get it right? I'm shocked, shocked that such things happen at for-profit institutions. Such would never happen at a public institu...oh, wait, nevermind.

With much less spending on instruction, for-profits clearly don't spend their money on faculty, and are motivated to keep other expenses low as well. They've determined that the big money is simply in grabbing students in the first place, and so their tuition money goes into recruitment.

With no profit motive, the non-profits are not nearly as eager to sweep up all possible students, and often have restrictions on admission to go with their higher tuition. Overall, faculty growth has been slightly higher than administrative growth at private non-profit institutions[16].

Despite the growth in the student base, institutions of all sorts seem to constantly face budget issues, or at least to claim to have such issues. Curiously, administrators feel that the most obvious response to budget issues is to increase the teaching loads[17]—despite the relatively stable student to faculty ratios that were sufficient years ago, before the administrative bloat (caught in their own web with that!). Ideas such as not having such a heavy reliance on support staff, reducing the number of administrators, and/or bringing administrative pay in line with administrative responsibility are not on the table. Go figure, again.

"George Warshington was the furst presdent of the United States. He wun the revolutionary war against British and disgnied the flag…"

--Sample from an alleged student paper when I interviewed for a position with University of Phoenix. I and the other applicants were encouraged not to fail this level of work. Failing a student requires faculty to fill out a form justifying the failure, rather subtle pressure not to fail students.

I've never taught at a for-profit institution, so I have no direct observations of my own to add here beyond my experience above. While one can cast scorn on for-profit private institutions for their low graduation rates, it's actually illustrative of the difference between these institutions and the public institutions. In for-profit, it's all about the check. With no government bureaucracy to answer to, for-profit institutions don't need to try to inflate their graduation rates to look good…they just need to gather and keep those students, with graduation actually counter-productive to that goal. On the other hand, low graduation rates are a slur against public institutions, and thus administration is motivated to increase it.

Either way, education is not a high priority.

The worse graduation and instructional spending results at for-profit institutions might lead one to conclude that for-profit institutions should be avoided, and that might be the case, but this conclusion is tangential to education. Nevertheless, it's clear for-profit institutions are a bit of a land mine for the student when it comes to getting an education, at least if an education is all about getting a degree. Considering that degrees from many for-profit institutions are held in such low regard, it seems going there is a lose-lose proposition. These institutions are justified in spending so much money in marketing, as it must be challenging finding students foolish or desperate enough to go to such places.

Me: "Ok, suppose we know the chance of tossing a single head on one coin toss is 0.5. What would be the chance of getting a single head on 10 coin tosses?"

Student, with confidence: "The chance would be 5!"

Me: "5, you say. Are you sure the probability will be 5?

Student: "Yes, it is."

Me: "How do you get that number?"

Student: "You just multiply the chance by 10."

--exchange in my Open University statistics course at Tulane.

When I taught at Tulane (a non-profit), I presented courses both for the "usual" students (the ones with admission requirements) during the day and for "Open University" students (the ones for anyone that can get a check)—the latter are generally night classes, filled with people willing to pay to get a piece of Tulane's reputation on their transcript. According to the catalogue, I was teaching the same course to both, although my open university course had less content and far less challenging material (and more student complaints, despite that). While to Tulane's credit, I wasn't pressured to pass students, I still had little choice but to simplify the course, as the students were so inadequately prepared for the "second year statistics" course I gave during the day that had I not reduced content, I would have lost almost the entire class.

The aggressive recruiting policies at for-profit institutions lead to lower graduation rates, and those institutions have very little prestige. Public and non-profit institutions should probably be grateful to for-profit institutions for keeping their graduation rates down. It may do little for their prestige, but it does preserve the value of the degrees they, and other types of institutions, give.

But what of the degrees billowing out of other types of institutions? When a non-profit plays the "Open University" game with their prestige, they're literally cashing in the prestige for more tuition revenue, and it's hardly any better at public institutions.

"Our goal is to graduate more students than ever before!"

--Administrator at commencement address, discussing plans for improved education in future years.

The huge influx of students into colleges, paid for by government backed loans, might very well lead to more people with college degrees. It certainly leads to more people in debt and more money for administrators. Unfortunately, these degrees are cheapened and almost meaningless...even as the loans increase year after year from the rising tuition costs.

It's strange how institutions can assert the value of a degree as justification for charging so much for it, even as they expand the number of degree programs to the point that it devalues the degrees and even the institution. Should there be loans for programs offering four year degrees in Dance? Women's

Studies? Golf Management? Queer Musicology? I could list more questionable academic degrees, but it's clear these sorts of programs are more about padding the graduation numbers than advanced study. Do none of the bright and very educated people that run our institutions see a problem with this? Money poured into such "fields" is money that's being taken away from actual education and learning, the education other people are also being loaned money to receive. It's often described as some sort of national priority to have more college graduates, but it seems doubtful that America will be improved if we issue 300,000,000 degrees in Queer Musicology.

" 1/6 + 1/6 + 1/6 + 1/6 = 4/24 = 1/6"

--I gave a pop quiz in my statistics course; all students in the class had at least 6 hours of math courses coming into the class. The only question on the quiz was "What is the probability of rolling a six, four times in a row on a standard die?" The above is the answer 4 of 12 students gave; the next most common answer was sheet of paper, blank but for a student name. None were able to answer the question correctly. Yes, I covered basic probability in previous classes, and the concept of independence in the prior class. This was at an accredited public institution. Administration chastised me for "causing" so many students to drop the course, which started with over 30 students.

Summary:

   The myths of higher education created an entire population willing to go to college, and government student loans meant anyone willing to dedicate themselves to learning could have that opportunity. College administrators devised a plan to maximize their income: change the policies, removing dedication as a requirement to learning, and dilute education to the point that it was often dubious. Only legitimate accreditation could prevent this plan from working to full effect.

   Getting accredited is absolutely necessary for an institution of higher learning, as it is the source those sweet, sweet, federal student loan checks and easy growth of the student base. College administrators are the same people that work for college accreditation agencies, so it's no surprise that accreditation, if it ever was serious about education, has been diluted to the point of irrelevancy. As an added bonus, accreditation became so marginal that for-profit institutions sprang up practically overnight, easily getting accreditation even though education was blatantly never the goal of such institutions. "Diploma mills" no longer had to give themselves bogus accreditation, "real" accreditation is bogus enough.

"24%"

--the percent of students taking the ACT who meet the college-ready benchmarks in all four subjects—reading, writhing, science and math. Not all who take the ACT necessarily plan to go to college, although administrators sure wish they all would. 76% of students are not ready for college, would almost certainly be harmed by going to college, and yet still administrators push to put everyone into this system of endless debt. The percent of all students not ready for college is probably higher, as only half of high school graduates take the ACT[17].

Remediation was supposed to be an opportunity for students seeking higher education to overcome a deficiency in their early training. College administrators turned it into an opportunity, not for students wishing to learn, but for anyone wanting a little extra money to come to campus, take some pseudo-courses by semi-faculty (but paying as much as a real course with respectably paid faculty), and split the money with the institution. Years later, these victims will find themselves deep in a form of debt they can never escape, while the administrators retire to their mansions. Instead of a useful aid for students that need it, remediation has become a pit into which the most vulnerable people are thrown, with no institutional integrity to protect them.

Doug Lynch, vice dean of the graduate school of education, who claimed to have receive a master's degree and a doctorate from Columbia University in 2005 and 2007, respectively. Neither of those claims is true, according to Columbia officials.

--Despite the eensy beensy fraud, he was kept on as an administrator at accredited University of Pennsylvania, anyway. A doctorate in 2 years? One wonders how none of the administrators thought something might be wrong with that. Seeing as this wasn't a fire-able offence, he was clearly as good at his job as administrators with legitimate administrative degrees, whatever those are[18].

An entire field of Education became established at our institutions of higher learning. A legitimate field of study could, perhaps, have led to breakthroughs in ways to help people achieve higher learning. Instead, Education turned into a sub-institutional diploma mill, often turning out degree holders with no ability, skills, or knowledge. Students coming into the system gain no benefit from this field's influence on the system, except for being able to get degrees in this field (assuming this is a benefit). Even worse than simply providing no benefits, advanced Education degree holders have come to take over positions that used to be held by people that actually knew the subject being taught, making it that much harder for dedicated students to learn what they came to campus to learn.

"We had three students enrolled in courses that they didn't know they were in. Two failed, one got an A, but still complained because it was a course she didn't need..."

--Registrar explaining some glitches in the system. Think about the implications: 1/3 of the students that don't even show up for a course are still getting an A for their "effort." Administration gave no particular sanction to the "free A" granting teacher, much less investigate how common the problem really is despite the evidence slapping them in the face. It wasn't just a simple mistake: grades are calculated and reported to the institution four (yes, four) different ways. What other business doesn't care if 1/3 of its paying customers are getting no product at all? I suspect it's more than 1/3, as I conjecture many students won't complain at a free A, not that an administrator could formulate such a guess.

To deal with the massive influx of students into the system, college administrators warped the higher education system to the point of being nearly unrecognizable, just a process of payment for credit hours via loans. Online courses, degrees, and training have become commonplace and easily acquired; the incredible ease of providing such training hasn't been reflected in greatly reduced prices for the students, however—administrators see no need to reduce revenue even with overhead reduced to almost nothing. It's casually easy to cheat in such courses, but, again, expelling cheaters would cut into revenue, drastically cut into revenue, in fact, since over half of students admittedly cheat, and whole industries have sprung up to help cheaters, even as administrators do what they can to discourage faculty from catching such cheaters. Meanwhile, back on campus, administrators create a host of bizarre new policies, with the goal of keeping happy (and paying!) students on campus as long as possible, subject only to bureaucratic constraints. The fact that these policies ultimately harm the students is irrelevant.

" Of nearly 2,000 instructors, 88 percent are part time...Top administrators "can fire people at will""

--from an article indirectly discussing the status of faculty at one public institution, University of Maryland University College[19].

College faculty could have served to uphold the standards of higher education. In times past, with tenure, they even did so, but no more. They cannot. Administrators control all the hiring and employment policies, making it very difficult for honest faculty to acquire and keep a position. Any attempt to uphold standards results in sanctions, even firing, giving faculty no means of protecting education from rapacious administrators that are only interested in achieving short term goals, then moving on and up to greener pastures to plunder. Students can play no part in helping faculty, as the only input administrators accept from students is a vote on whether they are passing, student complaints of courses being "a waste of time" mean nothing…in fact, faculty that waste student's time are more likely to advance in the system.

Me: "About how much would a doctorate in administration cost?"

Salesperson: "Around $120,000."

--the cost of a doctoral degree in Administration at one accredited for-profit institution where I enrolled. The salesperson knew that answer off the top of her head, and also gave me prices for other types of degrees.

Administrators have little choice but to get their degrees from Educationists, where they learn that even the most advanced concepts in higher education are fairly trivial: follow instructions and pay no attention to underlying ideas and you can complete the course, even get advanced degrees. With "knowledge" redefined to strictly being amount of time spent taking classes, administrators have no loyalty to education, other than viewing a degree as strictly a hurdle to get a job. With neither competence nor integrity as a guide, it's no wonder "education" is reduced to "retention," or whatever the current boss says it is. Students simply become bodies, to be statistically moved through the system irrespective of any gains in skills or knowledge.

Administration: "You're a valued faculty member. We just can't afford to pay you more."

--explanation why I couldn't get a pay raise, from a boss making much, much, more than me, and receiving regular pay raises.

As a final insult to injury, the same administrators that exploit people and get them to come into the system, the same administrators that dilute the legitimacy of the system via accreditation, the same administrators that support Educationist schemes and have no respect for education or higher learning, the same administrators that have made faculty impotent to educate their students, the same administrators that developed bizarre ideas of learning while getting advanced degrees...have awarded themselves high pay and a vast legion of much lower paid underlings to assist them in doing a job that probably wouldn't merit the pay even if the administrators didn't give themselves so many support staff. Students find their tuition rising, indebting themselves for decades to support not the people that give them an education, but people that they, at best, might see for a few minutes in a graduation ceremony.

"At least 45 percent of students...did not demonstrate any statistically significant improvement...during the first two years of college."

--Academically Adrift[20]. It's not just every school I've taught at. It's not just every Education graduate school I applied to. It's nearly the entire system.

This, then, is the current status of higher education. Instead of a system of checks and balances, administrators possess broad spectrum dominance, in absolute control of all aspects of higher education. Under these circumstances, it's no surprise the system has become corrupt to the point that nearly half the customers are sold into life-crushing debt for a meaningless slip of paper while improving in no skills or knowledge.

That said, administrators are hardly to blame for exploiting and debilitating a system that, for all intents and purposes, they were invited to exploit and debilitate. Administrative positions are often filled based not on education or appreciation thereof, but instead on which candidate most credibly promises to increase retention, grow the student base, or otherwise bring in more lucre.

With each aspect of the corrupting process identified and the most debilitating symptom described, now it's time to discuss how to fix the system while there's still something left to fix.

Administrator: To address the problem of students failing College Algebra, we now have an Explorations in College Algebra course which can be substituted for the original course. It doesn't have the material the students have no use for.

Faculty: What differentiates this new course from College Algebra?

Administrator (without shame): It's algebra without the algebra.

--another year, another administrative plan to improve retention.

The first seven chapters of this book have laid out most of the primary factors that have led to the near collapse of the American higher education system, explaining how it can be that a college degree no longer is a guarantee a person can read, write, or do 'rithmetic at anything like an educated level. It is time to address each of these problems, and offer some suggestions that can allow education to return to its status of just a few decades ago. Many of these concepts are interrelated, but will be addressed as sequentially as possible.

Tell the Myths, But Tell the Truth, Too

"If I get a B, I will die."

--student complaint, in all seriousness, from early in my career. While this used to be an "every semester"-type complaint, I haven't heard the like from a college student in at least a decade, now it's more like "You need to pass me. If I fail another course, I might lose my scholarship for being a good student."

Without the myths of college and higher education, the corrupted higher education system would not have had nearly as many victims to exploit. There is nothing wrong with a mythology that inspires a people to aspire to higher things, but the myths of college, spread so liberally in primary and secondary school, need to be corrected and clarified, instead of ruthlessly exploited.

Higher education, particularly liberal arts education, needs to no longer be identified as a source of great wealth. The posters of "college graduates make a million more dollars" need to be ripped down and replaced with "people that work hard to get degrees in engineering, accounting, and some sciences make a million more dollars over a lifetime." It's the hard work and acquisition of in-demand technical skills that are responsible for the money, not the degree. Some may argue that such posters may not be much more accurate, but the current situation of students pouring into campus, indebting themselves for tens of thousands of dollars getting degrees in poetry, art, psychology, or "general studies" and then being puzzled that they are not being showered with money after graduation needs to stop.

For the sake of those that believe life choices should be about money, and there's nothing wrong with that, then high school counselors need to stop instilling awe into students about the financial glories of higher education. The high school graduate who fixes my car makes more money than I do, as does my plumber, my roofer, and many other workers. Instead of the nebulous "over a lifetime," students should be told in high school what the facts are regarding annual salaries, should be told that fixing cars, for example, is good and honorable work…and pays better than reading essays written a century or more ago. Someone who can recite a poem in 17th-century French is not, as a matter of fact, a better person than someone who can "only" repair a carburetor. Both skills have their uses, and both should be respected.

There will always be a certain minority of humanity that pursues various types of knowledge as an end, with money not a particular concern; at least, there always has been in the past. They are unlikely to be dissuaded by a high school counselor's discussion of facts, and even if they are, they can always go to college after a few years of pursuing a fortune. This is a risk this country should be willing to take, in exchange for not pulling so many people into the college system, and tricking them into wasting years of their lives trying to acquire hideously expensive degrees pursued for the wrong reasons. Without the crowds of students blinded by the dollar signs in their eyes, these few seekers of knowledge as an end will have an easier time reaching their life goals.

There are many jobs or fields of knowledge where degrees are necessary. These are the degrees where money is to be made, but this money comes from supply and demand—there are relatively few people that can master the technical skills of aeronautics or medical equipment design. Money thrown at such fields must be done carefully—a massive glut of even engineering degrees can lead to a glut of degree-holding waiters, much like today. It may be a national priority to support these people, but it should be done through targeted scholarship, not blanket provision of loans and "scholarships" for anyone that wants to poke their nose on campus to "study" any topic they wish for years on end in support of vague promises that "you'll make more money with a degree."

Outside of the sciences, it doesn't actually take degrees to achieve greatness. The great novels of the 20th century, for example, have not been written by Ph.D.s, and only a few doctorate holders have been candidates for sainthood. It's a big world, liberal arts education is not the only way to succeed in life, and students need to be told as much. Often.

In short, the myths don't really need fixing, they just need to be supplemented with a heavy dose of truth. Additionally, higher education needs to do what it takes to make the myths true again, through the fixes relating to the other issues. Doing so will reduce the number of souls willing to sacrifice everything they have for college degrees of questionable value.

Make Accreditation Meaningful

"[This college} is accredited, and I have my two year degree. Every place I want to go to has a four year degree program. They'll accept my degree, no problem. After I transfer my two year degree, it will take me at least three more years to get the four year degree. How does it all transfer, but not add up to only two more years to finish?"

--Common complaint from my students that graduate, and move on to a university. I explain that administrators don't understand why 4 - 2 should equal 2, especially since it's more profitable if 4 – 2 = 3. It's queer how it can be viewed as acting with integrity to tell students their 2-year degrees are fully transferrable when administration knows students will only get about half credit.

So much of the accreditation process has so little do with education that it's puzzling that anyone could believe being accredited legitimizes the institution. Part of this misdirection, no doubt, is that the same college administrators that have failed higher education are generally the same people who influence what comprises accreditation today. Having the watchers also be the watched is a recipe for corruption, and this alone makes it no surprise that accreditation as it stands now is meaningless.

The entire concept of accreditation began well over a century ago with educators at various institutions getting together to help each other understand how best to run an educational institution and to standardize, at least a little, what it meant to be such an institution. Accreditation was never intended to have the responsibility for the disposition of hundreds of billions of dollars of loan money; it was a huge mistake of the Federal government to indirectly assign such a massive responsibility to accrediting agencies. While administrators have their influence, many of the requirements for accrediting agencies come from the Department of Education. This is perfectly understandable, as only accredited institutions are eligible to get student loans and other money from the government: it is government money (well, after it has been "donated" by citizens), the government is entitled to set the terms under which they'll hand it away. Thus, accrediting agencies should at the minimum do what they're already doing as a matter of necessity.

This doesn't change the fact that accreditation never looks to see if there is much going on that really relates to education. Almost always, accrediting agencies allow the institution to self-report, making accreditation practically, if not completely, alone among all other forms of regulation. This made sense in the distant past when education wasn't about big money and wasn't controlled by administrators with no real interest in education, but now that accrediting is responsible for so much more than it was originally intended, it needs to be valid for the purpose of education. There are a few easy ways to make accreditation relevant to education:

The most blatantly obvious is, of course, to have evaluators, people working as faculty/teachers at accredited institutions, actually take courses at the institution wishing accreditation. I'm quite comfortable taking any undergraduate course in the math curriculum, and I would be stunned if any graduate degree holder in another field would have difficulty in courses that he is qualified to teach. The evaluators need not show up every day (students can generally miss weeks), need not submit original work (courses with writing can be time-consuming, and plagiarized papers should probably be used a few times anyway), could even try to cheat, need not even do enough work to pass the course (the better to see if grades are being given honestly), and not all courses need to be evaluated or attended for the entirety of the semester. The point is to at least have the slightest idea what goes on in actual courses at the institution.

Administration e-mail: "For night instructors, please use your class time wisely, these courses are supposed to meet for 3 contact hours a week."

--I often teach night classes, meeting once a week from 6 to 8:45. When my class takes a five minute break around 7:30, typically the parking lot has as many cars as I have students, plus my own vehicle...even when many classrooms have a class registered to it for those hours. Rumor has it, after many warnings, one adjunct did actually lose his position for ending classes so early, so often. He probably had great student evaluations.

Having faculty evaluators is important, and puts the burden on the accrediting agency to do its job, as it should be. The regulators at the accrediting agency need to *see with their own eyes what is actually going on.* There is so much bogus crap on accredited campuses, courses that absolutely are a waste of time and money for students, courses with minimal reading, minimal writing, laughable testing, and dubious lecturing, passing very happy students but accomplishing no real improvement in skills or gains in knowledge, and this is not even addressing "elective" courses that might well be of some value if minimal content. All of these shenanigans are covered up by institutions being allowed to self-report how great they are at what they do, not just in math classes or gender studies classes, but in all subjects.

Me, responding to a rumble of students outside the classroom: "Hold on while we wait for the remedial classes to finish letting out."

--It's not just night classes that let out early, I often have to pause my lecture ten to twenty minutes before my class ends and wait for "early dismissal" classes to finish up. Granted, sometimes classes end early, but any administrator that watched the parking lot could easily figure out which professors consistently shortchange their students. They'd then realize that the ones they praise and promote for having such high evaluations probably don't deserve it, however.

Administrators simply can't be trusted to do much in the way of verifying even basic educational principles. It must be faculty that do this. Yes, paying four or five experienced faculty to secretively go take a load of courses will be expensive, but the institution seeking accreditation will doubtless be willing to pay the tuition (since that's not actual money, merely replacing the money given to the institution by the evaluators when they registered for the course), and even the government might be willing to pitch in, since the savings by eliminating all the bogus courses (and hence student loan money wasted on such) could easily cover the cost of faculty salaries. It might be hard to make faculty evaluate other courses, but this needs to be part of the job description: not just teach courses, but on some occasion evaluate (and learn from) what goes on in other courses. A typical faculty member might need to do this once a decade, and taking a full load of courses of material the faculty member already knows would nearly be a sabbatical for a semester.

Once accredited, only a few courses every year would need to be surreptitiously taken, to keep the institution from simply putting up a façade of legitimacy for the accrediting process, then abandoning it once accredited. I've been behind the façade enough to know this would be necessary.

Only with approval of most of the faculty taking these courses could an institution become accredited. After accreditation, an institution could be subject to significant fines (like returning the student loan money for a year) if future course evaluations repeatedly come up as unacceptable. This touches on something markedly missing from accreditation: clear penalties for violation of accreditation principles. When accreditation was all self-regulated, penalties weren't needed because the institutions legitimately wanted to improve as an end. With "growth over all" administrators, improving education cannot be a goal. With for-profit institutions, by definition, there can be no such assumption either.

This may sound extreme, but everything else that is regulated is subject to real inspection with real penalties for violation. The current system of self-inspection is a big part of how higher education has become so corrupted, and with the prospect of returning student loan money for giving bogus courses, administrators won't be so eager to have professors offer content-free and otherwise questionable courses, or to reward professors that jeopardize accreditation by doing so.

Another part of the corruption due to the failure of accreditation is the self-feeding nature of accreditation: accrediting agencies are staffed by the same type of administrators that work at the institutions. Faculty, the ones doing the educating, need to return to having a bigger part over the agencies that certify the education is legitimate, and what the standards are for a student to come into college. Faculty don't want to do this, but faculty ceding this responsibility to administrators is what led to accreditation becoming meaningless. At the very least, the aspects of accreditation that relate to education should be controlled in a near death-grip by faculty, only being alterable by agreement from representative faculty at the institutions that are accredited by the agency. What it means for a student to be able to take college classes (i.e., not remedial classes), and what should be in a college class, should be addressed at the accreditation level. If faculty members agree to make their institutions more, or less, respectable in terms of quality of the education the member institutions provide, or to change what knowledge an educated person should have, it should be allowed. But only if the actual educators want it, as opposed to what administrators want.

Such agreement would be difficult to get, but in the past, there was some loose agreement on the body of knowledge an "educated" person had, and that can serve as a foundation for today. By ceding what constitutes an education to administrators, what constitutes a college education has been whittled down, and down, and down over the years, to what we have now, as per *Academically Adrift*, no more than a high school student of today. If it is continued to be left in the hands of administrators, education in the future will be no different than the dreaded diploma mill: any student willing to just turn over his student loan money will be handed a degree without question, without gaining any skills or knowledge.

Additionally, protections for faculty need to be hardwired into accreditation. If accredited institutions truly are supposed to be about education, they should be willing to show as much by treating educators and the educated with some sort of respect. The current situation of administrators controlling all aspects of faculty employment conditions has led to abuses without number; faculty have tried to respond by forming unions, but with administration wielding such unassailable power, these have only been minimally effective, and then only at select institutions. Accredited schools should be boasting of having the best faculty, willing to work there because of decent conditions, instead of the situation today, with institutions embarrassed at what they have done to what used to be a respectable position, even outside the top schools. If accreditation can mandate 25% of coursework for a degree being done at an institution, it can just as easily mandate 75% of the coursework be taught by full time employees instead of using mostly deplorably paid adjuncts. Accreditation always could have done such a thing, but with administrators in control of both institutions and accreditation, it's never even been on the table.

"The Dean's office and my chair 'expressed their appreciation' for me chasing such cases (in December), but six months later, when I received my annual evaluation, my yearly salary increase was the lowest ever, and significantly lower than inflation, as my 'teaching evaluations took a hit this year.'"

--NYU Professor explaining how catching cheaters lowered his evaluations, hurting himself in the process[1]. Poor guy thought that once he

acquired tenure, he'd able to catch cheaters without penalty. Over the course of the rest of his career, catching cheaters just for one semester might cost him $50,000 or more. That he waited until after tenure to try such a boneheaded move shows that he had gotten the memo from administration earlier: do not catch cheaters.

Finally, "This institution expels cheaters" needs to be fundamental to accreditation[2]. Expulsion, from a class, for a semester, or from the institution, used to be a real risk of being caught cheating, but now there are no risks. Administrative encouragement of cheating is a huge factor in the atmosphere on campus today, where the majority—the majority!—of students admit to cheating at some point in their career, and where most every attempt to catch cheaters in a course does so in abundance. Not banishing cheaters means they stay in the class, able to exert power over the faculty with the student evaluation. The cheater's "honest" evaluation of the teacher would be suspect in any thinking person's eyes, albeit not those of an administrator, who bases so much of a faculty member's career on evaluations.

Administrators don't want cheaters caught or penalized, much less expelled, because it cuts into retention rates, but this typically narrow and shortsighted view needs to be discouraged, above and beyond the stomach-churning fact that administrators penalize faculty for catching cheaters, for trying to have integrity in the institution. An institution that graduates cheaters doesn't just do the cheater a favor, it detracts from the value of the degrees granted to the honest students. Over time, the institution becomes something of a joke, although in that time the administrator has moved up and on as a result of his great success at "leadership" of an institution with many dishonest graduates.

This is what has happened to a large extent with online degrees, where any non-administrator can see the potential for cheating, a potential that has been realized to a great extent. Online degrees, even from accredited online institutions that have been around for decades, are still basically worthless pieces of paper, useful only to those that already have a position along with accommodating managers (or administrators) who know not to look too closely at the source of the degree (often because they have such degrees themselves). This near worthlessness is what all college degrees, not just online degrees, are turning into, and shutting down the cheating window would go a long way to preserving some prestigious value to a degree.

A student caught cheating is removed from the course, and probably expelled. It's that simple. There are few places in this country that are more than an hour's drive from multiple institutions of higher learning, being expelled from one institution is not a life-destroying event, the cheater can just go elsewhere. For those few students that do only have one choice and can't afford to be expelled, they still have the option of, well, not cheating in the first place.

While this might give too much power to faculty to get rid of students they just don't like, in all honesty I've never seen a professor accuse a student of cheating out of malice. This just isn't a concern, although perhaps it's possible a professor could be wrong. There are already procedures in place for students that feel they've been wrongly accused of cheating. These procedures are not much used now since faculty are penalized for finding cheaters, but this relic from a bygone era can easily return, to protect that rare possibility of harming an innocent. This is a risk higher education should be willing to take, for the sake of the millions of people that are definitely being harmed by the "open cheating" atmosphere of today, if not for the sake of the reputation of higher education, which is in real danger of being destroyed by administrative policies.

If an institution can quickly and easily lose accreditation by allowing cheaters to graduate, administrators might rethink their position on cheating. This idea might sound draconian, but higher education, in its current form, is in great danger of vanishing, and not just due to the online schools or rising tuition.

The "drastic action" of having some integrity is required because the world is changing. Free universities and the content of high quality courses are available to anyone with an internet connection. It's only a matter of time until the knowledge of most all degree programs, identical in every way to what is offered at a "traditional institution," is available online for free.

Free.

Which of the following sounds like a more likely candidate for a degree-requiring position: someone that paid $50,000 for a degree at an institution where he could easily have cheated his way through the entire program, or someone who shows up with a flash drive, containing all the work he did and skills he learned pursuing the same degree at a free university? Both candidates could be lying and know nothing, but the second at least wasn't stupid enough to waste $50,000 for a slip of paper that means nothing. Employers are already smart enough to think that through for online degrees, and students will figure it out eventually.

If "traditional" institutions don't do something, soon, to establish that they're offering something more than a piece of paper, that they're willing to honestly certify some legitimacy to what they're doing, they'll be history. It's simply a matter of time before employers realize that traditional schools no more legitimately train students than online schools, accredited or not.

It's a sign of how far institutions have fallen, how minimal the integrity is, that I feel the need to present more than a page of arguments for "get rid of cheaters." A generation or two ago, it was understood that penalties for cheating were severe and now, students literally complain when they're caught cheating, since they know administrators will rush to help them.

Remediation Should Be For The Serious, And Not A Joke

Student: "I get a gun. I get a knife. I don't know why she gotta come on up here and beef with me and my daughter. I didn't ask her husband to get me pregnant, that just happened…"

--overheard cell phone conversation. I often have parents and their adult-ish children taking my classes concurrently, or nearly so.

There was a time when entrance examinations could literally keep a student out of college, instead of merely placing them in ever lower levels of "developmental" courses. I believe in open admission, that everyone who wants to learn should be allowed the opportunity to do so.

I also believe this should be done with integrity.

Student: "Bitch, I'm up here learning."

--hastily ended phone call on campus.

Far too many people are coming to campus with no prior inclination towards learning, no current inclination towards learning, and no future inclination towards learning. They put nothing into learning. These people come to class and expect…something, and administrators lean heavily on faculty to provide it.

It's offensive to say the only reason these people are on campus is the free money, so let's charitably assume that the money isn't the reason these non-learners are swarming onto campus. Great. Get rid of the money. Stop loaning money to remedial students. Again, this sounds like a terribly mean thing to do, and so again, I present a number of arguments for what should be obvious.

Administrator: "You need better retention. These students can be anything they want to be. And you're standing in their way."

Me: "Suppose I want to be a professional race horse jockey. Are you sure that all I need is money to pay you?"

--I'm 6' 2", and 240 lbs, over twice the acceptable weight for a jockey...it doesn't matter how good the retention at Race Horse Jockey School is, the school would be acting without integrity if they accepted me as a student and talked me into taking on vast quantities of debt while telling me about the money I'd make as a professional jockey.

First, remedial students, for the most part, do ridiculously poorly in college, with over 90% of them failing to get a 2 year degree in 3 years, and a majority never getting a degree at any point. It is simply *vicious and cruel* (and not acting with integrity) to lure these people onto campus and entrap them into a lifetime of debt. If they're serious about learning, let them pay for those one or two classes with their own money before moving on to college level material. I've seen for myself that students care a whole lot more about what they buy when they pay for it with their own money. Give them the opportunity to care about what they're doing, the chance to show they care and the challenge to develop the self-reliant skills necessary to learning, rather than slap them with a ton of debt and no chance to learn life skills as well as academic skills.

Student: "I didn't do the homework because I don't have the book. The loan checks haven't come in yet."

Me: "No problem. Take out your phone, and take a picture of the relevant pages from my textbook."

--I often get students so unwilling to risk anything on their education that they won't buy the textbook[3] until they get the money for it handed to them first. It's possible they just don't have the money, but they commonly have the money for very expensive cell phones and service, not to mention cars and insurance. These complaints can go on for weeks into the semester, until the checks arrive. Then the complaints, and some of my students, disappear.

Second, remedial coursework is something that most every college-age student has already seen, and ignored, half a dozen times or more in public school. Having already demonstrated an unwillingness to learn the material, the burden should be on the student to show he's had a change of heart. This is also material that has already been paid for, at great expense, in the secondary (and often primary) school system through taxes. There's no reason the taxpayers need to pay for it twice or "half a dozen plus one" times. This material is what a child can learn, and an adult not wanting to pay for coursework can easily go to the library and read, if he was serious, or go to private tutoring services if he needs to. A serious student without a learning disability can usually pick up this material in a matter of weeks, not months, while a non-serious student will never do so, despite the passing grade administration forces faculty to give them. The learning disabled shouldn't be afflicted with a lifetime of debt in any event.

"I dropped out of college with $10,000 in loans. I haven't been able to make but a few payments in the last ten years. Now I owe almost $30,000. Even if I start making payments, which I can't, it'll take another ten years to pay it off. I have to go back to college, get a degree and get me a good job. I'll pass developmental math this time. I have to."

--A student does the math. Almost. PT Barnum was amazed at the number of people, after being tricked by The Great Egress sign, would pay admission AGAIN just to come back in and complain to him about it. Some percentage of them probably got fooled by The Great Egress sign again on their way out.

Third, this material isn't "higher" education, and so it's very questionable that a student should be charged as much for it as for any college course. Unfortunately, a loan makes the price much more than just the base cost. If the course is paid for via loan money, the student is actually paying more like three times as much over the decades it takes to pay it back, for material that should be cheaper to learn. Again, integrity is an issue here. It's simply *wrong* to do this to those least able to understand how they're being triple-charged on an already inflated price.

College administrators will screech how this would be denying those most in need of improvement, but the intellectual honesty of such complaints can be easily exposed: administrators that honestly feel this way should be welcome to donate their salaries, reducing them to say, adjunct levels, with the money going to remedial students as a grant towards their remedial education. If a significant number of administrators do this, then this point of view will be re-opened. I'll happily teach extra remedial courses for minimal pro-rated pay based on administrators sacrificing all but $15,000 a year or so of their salary and benefits. Working for people with this kind of integrity would motivate me to do the same.

Now, the natural response from administration won't be to donate their own money, of course, it will be to redefine "remedial student" until no such student exists. This might sound cynical on my part, but I speak from direct observation. Over a decade ago in Louisiana, it became apparent that the universities in Louisiana were not dealing with higher education, instead the money flowing into them was going into channeling herds of students into remedial courses, to no real benefit. Appeals to the integrity of administrators accomplished nothing, of course, so laws were written forbidding universities from teaching remedial courses, to no longer have remedial students at all, and a community college system, the one I've been a part of for over a decade, was created to give the remedial students a place to go. These laws were very clearly written, anyone reading them would think there would be no way a university could legally take in the legions of remedial students available.

I've seen the university administrators try to skirt the law in a variety of ways, with "change the definition of what a remedial student is" being the primary tactic, from "needing one remedial class" (the normal definition) to "needing two remedial classes" to "needing two remedial classes in the same subject", to simply reducing the passing scores on the placement tests to such a hysterically low value that anything with opposable thumbs would not be a remedial student. I don't blame the university administrators for doing this, they're in a fight for money after all, and dignity always loses against avarice in administrative souls.

Due to the laws, the student population of the Louisiana university system is dropping, while the community college population is exploding. Unfortunately, moving the remedial students around like this still provides no benefit to them, they're just now placed in a lifetime of debt from going to a different institution than before. The only advantage is an increase in administrative positions—each community college needs its own troop of chancellors and deans and such. Yes, I have my own job due to this, but this is immediately offset by a similar position disappearing at a university. There's no similar balance in administrative positions: add a new institution, add a chancellor and administrators and hire faculty at the new institution, fire faculty at the old institution and keep administrators at the old institution.

Remedial student, at mid-term: "Hey, how come the homework in this class don't look like nothing in my book, and how come every student in this class has a different book than me?"

--Administration accidentally scheduled a college class and a remedial class in the same room. The error was fixed on the first day, but this student had missed the first day. The faculty member, something of an old-schooler, learned the real reason why calling out attendance every day is a good idea. This student will be paying a student loan debt for this course for the rest of his life, and is it really his fault? Remedial students are often invulnerable to input, and not just with regards to academic topics.

Preventing the redefinition of a remedial student is why faculty need to control the definition of a remedial student at the accrediting level. Accreditation crosses state lines, so that the education industry can't be easily subverted by any particular state changing its laws. "Accredited institutions will not try to qualify loan money to college students that cannot perform at the high school graduate level," is integrity, nothing more. Institutions can still be open admission, any student that wants to come and take a course still can...but the "I am a degree seeking student so gimme that loan money" box needs to be just a little bit harder to check off.

Administration can still subvert this by forcing faculty to pass all remedial students, turning the above into a procedure that is only one or two semesters slower than what we have now.

As said before, the issues are interrelated, and we'll see below how we can change the way administrators think and make decisions.

Administrator 1, at a meeting: "We will be at full capacity the very first day we move into the new facility. We won't have a single office to spare."

Administrator 2, at a different meeting: "Our plan is, once we move into the new facility, to expand our student base as quickly possible, hopefully doubling it in a few years."

--Yes, these administrators talk to each other, and are both discussing the same facility. All those graduate courses in vision and leadership, but administrators still can't see when they're leading an institution to a brick wall.

Radical plans like "get rid of cheaters" and "stop taking advantage of people" might well cost me my job simply by reducing the number of souls in the system, and I can accept that. I have no faith in administrators, who can't see the big picture of what their erratic behavior and questionable schemes are doing to higher education. I'll lose my job when higher education collapses do their lack of vision anyway, and I'd rather lose it by doing the right thing.

Education Might Not Be A Joke As A Field, But It Definitely Is Not A Joker

"Once I have my Education degree, I'll be qualified to teach anything, even what you teach!"

--Student comment I've heard the like many a time, and administrators, with their own Education degrees, seem to feel the same way.

My degree is in mathematics. I can address most any undergraduate topic in mathematics and closely related concepts, like symbolic logic or arithmetic. Physics has mathematics in it, Philosophy has courses in logic, Accounting has lots of arithmetic. I don't teach these courses, although when a professor is ill, I might cover a class or two. I wouldn't dream of teaching these courses, as I don't feel I could offer the same insights as someone who truly understands the subject. This strikes me as perfectly sensible, and respectful of other people's areas of specialization.

"I will now demonstrate the FOIL technique with an example, by multiplying

(a + b) times (c + d + e)."

--Education degree holder trying to teach math. FOIL, incidentally, is a mnemonic specifically for multiplying two binomials, and makes no sense in the example given. I've given so many examples like this in this book to make it clear how ridiculous these people often are. I'm not picking on any single person here; each example comes from a different Math Education major attempting to teach mathematics on a college campus.

Time and again, I've seen mathematics positions being handed over to Math Education degree holders at the college level. I just assumed from the name of the degree that these people were well trained in how to teach mathematics, and that's what explained their higher retention. Early in my career this made sense to me, like administrators I was completely ignorant of what Math Education entails—the difference being, I'm willing make an effort to rectify my ignorance. Eager to learn their ways, I sat in courses and *saw with my own eyes* that Math Education degree holders thoroughly didn't know what they were doing, and were instead only covering the lightest material, poorly, achieving higher retention via the lowest of standards. Now that I've reviewed what a Math Education degree entails, and taken an Education course, I can say with certainty that the degrees are not interchangeable with actually knowing the subject of mathematics. It is puzzling how the holders of such degrees see nothing wrong in what they are doing when they apply for college positions.

Math Education is a splinter field, at best, addressing some minor topic which I admit I just don't understand (more accurately, I don't understand how you can study teaching of math as an end for two or more years of graduate level work that has almost no mathematics in it). A course called "Math Education" belongs on college campuses the same way courses on Gender Studies in Children belong on campus. The degree curriculum for this field has clearly been designed for people wanting to teach in public schools, and while it probably doesn't have enough mathematical training for even that, such degree holders on a college campus should only be teaching courses called Math Education, nothing else seems to apply.

Educationist: "Now let's try to do this exercise, copying the words after first turning the page upside down."

Me: "The instructions say we're to try to copy the letters as a mirror image"

Educationist: "No, it's upside down."

(I show her the handout she gave us, clearly stating to write the mirror images of the letters in our continuation of the first exercise.)

Educationist: "Well, it's all the same. Turn the page upside down."

Me: "Are we now doing the last exercise, since it's now at the top where the first exercise used to be?"

--Educationist teaching us what having a learning disability is like, probably a bit more accurately than she intended. It's nauseating how consistently Educationists don't seem to know what they are doing even when they get to pick what they're doing.

Similarly, an Education degree seems to be used as a joker, able to imitate any subject, or so Educationists claim. Much as mathematics has some application in physics or accounting, I accept the Educationist claim as some small truth, but not so much that these degree holders need to be held in such awe by administrators, and certainly not so much that everything they say should be taken as a face value undeniable truth applicable to all subjects. Educationists know about a field called Education, but past that? Not so much.

The way to stop Education from controlling everything is for faculty to reclaim a power that administrators took: the ability to hire faculty. Instead of, time and again, administrators overruling faculty and inflicting questionable "teachers" on a department, faculty should have ultimate input over who they want to work with, and why. I'm no elitist, a candidate's degree isn't nearly as important to me as ability to teach and knowledge of subject matter, but loading up departments with people whose only qualification is subservience to administration is simply not a recipe for providing a good education to students. Perhaps this, too, needs to be explicit in accreditation, although there is a distinct need for emergency appointments from time to time.

Education as a field has made inroads into math, chemistry, English, and many other subjects, watering down the curriculum in a blatant attempt to increase retention of their majors in those fields. What will happen when there are Engineering Education, Medicine Education, and, God forbid, Airline Pilot Education graduate degrees? Maybe there is a need for such specializations, but allowing such degrees to serve as wildcards for actual subject matter does a grave disservice to students that want to legitimately know these subjects.

Online Education Must End, And Other Games Cancelled As Well

"Our nearly 60 fully online doctoral programs include Marketing, Leadership, Reading and Literacy, "

--Yes, that is from an accredited school.

I've already addressed cheating above, and the technology games will disappear with faculty at other institutions directly observing courses on other campuses. But what of online degrees and coursework? This has been a huge source of money for institutions, especially private for-profit institutions that care nothing for education (or only slightly less than public institutions), caring instead only for the quick buck of student loan money.

Administrators, blinded by the dollar signs in their eyes, gave higher education cancer when they watered down accreditation, or at the very least failed to make it worthy of the immense responsibility for student loans. It's taken years to destroy the integrity of public institutions from this decision, and it's not over yet. In addition to this cancer, administrators inadvertently cut higher education's throat when they influenced accrediting agencies to allow for accredited online courses and degrees. They lacked the vision to see how quickly for-profits could spring up to take advantage of this loophole. Public institutions are bleeding students to online for-profit institutions, and have been sacrificing everything they can just to keep up. These for-profits are able to exploit the weak accreditation to casually gain legitimacy, and then slap together an online curriculum able to compete with traditional institutions everywhere, for an infinite number of students. Public institutions have been around longer, but with their integrity destroyed, their physical campuses are just not a good enough advantage over for-profits that can compete with all public institutions, everywhere, for all students.

The answer to the rise of online "competition" is easy: stop accrediting online coursework beyond some minimal amount at best (6 hours, as electives), with no such thing as accredited online degrees. It's that simple, again, and the mad scramble for every institution to offer everything online, everywhere, all the time, ends.

Why destroy online accredited "education"? The answer is obvious, and should have been understood all along.

Faculty: "They're cheating their asses off."

--a brief but accurate description of online students.

High school students that are monitored fail online courses, while unmonitored college students, just a year older, pass online courses quite easily. The capacity of the latter to casually cheat is a glaring difference.

Websites with people willing to write entire college level, even graduate level, papers are booming, with as many visitors at such sites as there are online students. Employees at such websites, paid a hundred bucks or more by the paper, make more money than online students are ever likely to make. It is obvious who their clients are.

Online courses seldom give any tests, seldom give an unethical student any reason to study. Those online courses that do give tests, are incapable of doing so in a way that a cheater cannot trivially subvert.

Online courses are nearly worthless for good reason: if you do not personally know the person with the online degree, you have no reason whatsoever to believe that the degree represents any knowledge. An online degree is just too easily acquired, by cheating or without gaining any skills or knowledge, to open doors for someone who does not have any other connections, connections that often make the degree irrelevant beyond a job requirement.

Eliminate accredited online courses because they represent nothing. It's simple.

"But there's no guarantee that traditional students aren't cheating!" is a counter-argument, but not a good one. As above, traditional schools need to start taking cheating seriously. The short-sightedness of administrators by encouraging cheating has annihilated the prestige of much of education. If all it takes to get a degree is to pay someone else to do the work, the degree simply cannot mean anything, even if merely half—and this clearly an underestimate--of degree-holders sub-contract their "education."

"But what about students that can only get a degree through online courses?" and "Why punish the minority of non-cheaters for the actions of the cheaters by denying online courses?" are other concerns, but again, only exist for the short-sighted. These online students are being robbed, paying a fortune for online degrees that are worth nothing. Accrediting online degrees *facilitates the robbery*. The students, even the honest ones, are cheated when they buy online courses only to find out much later how worthless such courses are. Only the institutions benefit from offering these courses, and only financially. Facilitating such theft is not acting with integrity.

Finally, the issue of "What about students that are learning through a life fulfillment goal?" needs to be addressed. If the goal is honestly life fulfillment, then accreditation, a certification that the education is legitimate, is unnecessary—a person knows in his heart if he's satisfied with what he's learned. If the libraries and the internet are not enough to provide training and information for a topic, then surely some entity will provide content for those that really need and want to pay for training despite the lack of accreditation/student loan loot. Accreditation was accidently turned into a source of money through student loan programs, and needs to become something of value: a seal of legitimacy.

Even a minimal guarantee of legitimacy is impossible with online courses as they are now, and no institution can have them and operate with integrity. Get rid of them.

Market realities won't let this happen, I suppose, but with administrators in control of education, corpulently obvious ideas like "online students must take tests in proctored locations" and "after papers are turned in, students will be required to write summaries of said papers in proctored locations" will never be advanced or enforced...it would cut too much into those loan checks. These testing centers already exist throughout the country and are used for a variety of tests and certifications where integrity is important, only a system with rulers that don't care about integrity would not already be using them.

Me, as a college student, whining: "How come you will only let me sign up for two electives?"

Advisor: "Because we want you to graduate in four years."

It used to be that going to college was a plan, and students were expected to choose a major within a semester or two of arriving on campus. Changing majors was allowed, but required the signing of forms and getting permission. It was not done frivolously.

This was back when institutions acted with integrity. Institutions realized that high school graduates were still quite young, and needed direction and good advice. Thus, there were policies making it very difficult for a student to spend half a dozen years wandering through dozens of introductory courses before finally settling on a "General Studies" degree. Students went to advisors, who kept them from wasting time.

Student, in tears: "But you have to pass me through College Algebra. I need this course to graduate, and I don't have any more loan money left."

Me: "This is an introductory course. You are supposed to take it your first semester. Why did you wait six years?"

--Nearly every year I have such an exchange with a student. Typically, students in this position have taken 4 or more years to get a 2 year degree, with a 2.01 GPA. A question I never ask, but should, is "Why is my introductory level, nearly remedial, course so much more difficult than the most advanced courses in your degree?"

Administrators, void of integrity and feeling no responsibility to the young in their care beyond fleecing them as thoroughly as possible, changed the policies. Now students can sign up for basically any courses they want, whenever, regardless of whether the courses lead to a degree. A student can withdraw from courses repeatedly, delaying his education and making it easy for him to blow off semester after semester, rather than develop the real skill of working hard when it's time to work hard. These changes in policies certainly went a long way to supporting bloated administrative salaries, but have obviously harmed and taken advantage of the weaknesses of a great many young students—only a concern for those acting with integrity.

With "protect the young" discarded for "grab more loot" every time, it's no wonder that typical students take 6 years or more to get a 4 year degree. Educators clearly need to have more influence in administrative policies, more influence than even that which needs to be given through accreditation.

Take the Pressure Off

Faculty: "Either I do what the dean wants, and screw over this person who deserves the position...or I get fired and lose my health benefits, which I really need right now. What do you think I'm going to do?"

--overheard faculty dilemma. The illusion that faculty have any real influence over anything on campus is casually dispelled once one realizes administrators can fire at will.

    As each fix is enabled, the problems of a corrupted higher education system get less intertwined. With faculty doing the hiring, the pressure to pass fades away. "Spineless" or incompetent faculty giving in to administrative demands will no longer be a constant issue. Ultimately, most hiring and firing would be done via a department head, with assistance of departmental committees, and this leads to a very real worry: the department head, despite being faculty, can turn into an administrator, in turn answering to the whims of those above him. There's an answer to this, an answer so seldom considered that I must build up to why it is necessary.

Student: "[That professor] is great. You won't have to learn a thing in her classes."

--student describing a professor whose courses are so popular she gets extra sections, extra money. One student saying something like this means very little, but when it's semester after semester after semester, that's a sign only an administrator could miss.

    Evaluations are key to promotion and hiring, and administrators use them to make their decisions. This is despite that it is the faculty receiving high evaluations that are not doing their job. Administration, as is often the case, has it backwards, although faculty members have always known this. I've heard it explained many times to administrators at meetings, to no effect. Evaluations need to no longer be used as the definition of good teaching, key to hiring, pay raises, and promotion.

The fix here is simple enough: instead of punishing faculty members with less than stellar evaluations, it should be understood that teaching is not a popularity contest, and student evaluations should actually count against a teacher if they're consistently too high.

This may sound wrong, but evaluations are an average of all student ratings. A great teacher should get great evaluations, but all it takes to turn a class of great evaluations into mediocre evaluations is just one angry student, just one student rating a professor negatively is sufficient.

Always, this disgruntled student is a failing student, and grades and evaluations are very closely related. The only way to get perfect evaluations is to fail nobody, and a professor that fails nobody probably isn't covering any material worth knowing (or paying for).

Changing administration's thinking on this matter, or any other matter, is unlikely to happen, not with mere words. Time and again the imperviousness of administration to common sense, even when backed by real studies, has been demonstrated to me. There is no fix that would allow administrators to become reasonable; this isn't part of their job any more than teaching or research or respect for education is part of their job. Instead of getting administrators focused on high retention, what is needed is a way to get administrators that listen to educators, and care about education. It's time to think outside the box, and change the way how institutions get administrators.

Me: "In these official documents, you assert that 1.8 + 1.4 = 3.4. It is, in fact, 3.2. Can you please at least change that much for the sake of accuracy?"

Administration: "No."

--Often I see documents that I probably should not see, but I try to help fix errors when I can. My attempts at preventing my institution from making embarrassing mistakes are hit and miss. Mostly miss.

Administrators that never serve as faculty will never understand what evaluations mean, have already ignored explanations and studies to this effect. If administrators served as faculty, they might be more willing to understand the obvious and well-documented. With administrative degrees completely unrelated to what happens on campus, administrators with such degrees will never be qualified to serve as faculty. We must go the other direction.

Administrator: "Math? That's just a bunch of formulas. A student can just look it up if he needs it."

Me: "…"

--if sometimes I seem a little disrespectful to administrators, I apologize. Respect is a two-way street, however.

Simply having a non-administrative or non-Education degree is not enough. I've seen departments where the department head is an administrative hatchetman, brought in from outside to enforce "higher retention" and destroy any academic standards that get in the way of this all-encompassing administrative goal. Despite having the appropriate degree and, presumably, respect for the subject, these well-paid assassins of legitimacy know which side of the bread their butter is on, and act accordingly. Faculty are helpless in the face of this scenario, and all they can hope to do is band together and revolt en masse against the head—a dangerous proposition as the department head, with the backing of administration, will "ease out" those faculty with the leadership ability to organize such a revolt.

I've also seen departments where the head is chosen from the faculty, and changes every year or two. This is the key to happiness, and legitimacy. Administration can no longer rig the system by bringing in an outsider to enforce their decrees. The "administrative department head" can no longer be abusive to the faculty in the department, because he'll be returning to the ranks of faculty soon enough, and will have to live with the decisions he's made and any ill treatment of his associates.

The whole reason administration managed to take over the system is because faculty, foolishly, turned it over to them, trusting to administrative integrity to keep it honorable. This happened back when administrators didn't make the extraordinary sums of today. Faculty don't want to administrate, but I suspect many would be willing to take on the bureaucratic burden, if only for a year or two, for an extra $20,000 a year (i.e., for a tiny fraction of the cost of having a professional administrator).

The same can apply to many of the lower level administrative positions. Instead of recruiting someone from outside with a Ph.D. in some strange Education field unrelated to anything that goes on in the institution, have a faculty member serve as dean, for example, for a year or two at a time, revolving through faculty at the institution, perhaps making the transition over less intense summer semesters.

"Whoa!" cries administration, claiming there are many specialized things that administrators do, things that faculty wouldn't know about. They have a point, but it's time to take a cue from the business world, since, after all, faculty have often been forced to suffer due to business concerns. Time and again faculty have been told to tighten their belts and not get a pay raise, since that's how a real business works when times are tough (although administrators clearly still get theirs). Time and again faculty have been told to always work more efficiently, because that's how a real business works (although administrators still get to hire more staff to help them). Time and again faculty have been relegated to menial, adjunct roles, and told that this is fair because that's how a business works (although administrators always work with full benefits).

Administration says these things, but they left off something else from the business world, and it's their turn to be on the business end: when an employee is about to leave, he often gets the added humiliation of training someone else to do his job, a replacement willing to do it for much lower pay. The "leaving" administrators should get the privilege of serving an extra year as an administrative assistant (or maybe in an adjunct role), teaching the faculty the critical things that are done. Think of how much more efficient this would be! In the couple of years it takes for institutions to adopt this method, administrators will have plenty of time to adjunct for various institutions, teaching the faculty what few details are needed beyond patience in meetings and willingness to fill out forms.

After he's served his time as dean or whatever, the faculty member will in turn be available to train his replacement while he returns to honest work educating or researching. Over a decade or two, campuses will be filled with faculty with the knowledge to do most basic administrative functions, functions which truly do not require Ph.D.-level understanding, since they have nothing to do with teaching or research. Faculty performing administrative work and then returning to faculty positions used to be common in the past, and it needs to be common again.

There are some limits to how far this can go, but the organizational structure of any campus should have many, if not most, administrators coming from, and returning to, faculty positions. Only administrative positions with specialized skills that absolutely cannot be filled by faculty (eg, accounting or legal) would not have this turnover. A faculty member that wants to devote his life to administration might be able to do so, but only at the tolerance of the other faculty repeatedly renewing the administrative part of the contract; the would-be administrator will be under constant pressure to do a good job to keep his position if he wants it. This pressure will also keep administrative salaries, most of them, from skyrocketing, as there will always be many candidates suitable for the position, right on campus. Since these administrative contracts are for a year or two, subject to faculty vote, "professional administrators" could still come in from time to time from outside when needed. Short contracts would help institutions avoid repeating the mistake of letting these mercenaries take over the system again. This would vastly reduce administrative abuses and bring integrity back into the system.

Certainly, there will be some faculty that will take advantage of these administrative positions, doing a terrible job in their year of servitude in exchange for extra money. Bad administrators are already a problem as it is, and can do great harm in their years of unstoppable power. In a system of rotating administrators, all that would happen is the bad administrator would be gone in a year or two, and paid much less than before. This is vastly superior to the current situation, and the eventual return to a faculty position will provide a check on power and abuse that is nonexistent now.

Make many administrative positions short-term positions filled by faculty at the institution and have them return to a faculty position afterwards. This will prevent administrative undermining of education, and allow the administration to do something they haven't done in a long while: act with integrity.

And What Of Administrators With Those Expensive Doctoral Degrees In "Administrative Leadership of Institutional Advancement Integrity Utilization"?

"Educational Leadership and Management, Curriculum and Instruction, Instructional Design for Online Learning, Leadership for Higher Education, Leadership in Educational Administration, Post Secondary and Adult Education, Professional Studies in Education, Training and Performance Improvement, General Public Administration..."

--Sampling of doctoral administrative degrees, just at one accredited institution. Wouldn't you rather someone with a doctoral degree in Physics set up the curriculum and instruction for Physics, rather than someone with a doctoral degree in Curriculum and Instruction? In what field would you NOT trust an expert in the field to do something like that? Only General Public Administration seems to make any sense as a degree field, and still is questionable for actual administration.

The chief officer of an institution is often a political position, selected as much through connections as through any demonstrated skills or knowledge, even if there is a degree requirement. With the top being a political appointee, it's only natural that the positions below it will also be similarly chosen, by the chief officer. At some point, however, that reach down will stop at the educators, who will now also hold some administrative positions. With educators in some control of administrators, education can be about education, instead of being about fattening administrators' bank accounts.

With top administrators no longer owning complete control over educators' very existence, the administrators won't be able to threaten and browbeat faculty into supporting the numbers of students needed to cover administrative pay. There will be little choice but for administrators to cut back on administrative and support positions, hopefully bringing it back to levels before the administrative takeover of higher education, back to when a college degree was distinctly worth more than a high school diploma.

There will still be a need for specialist administrators, but there also needs to be a change in the metrics for determination of what makes an institution well-run, so that administrators stop pursuing destructive goals like graduation rates and retention. Instead of focus on such things, institutions should take pride in things like "spending less on administrative and support costs" and "less floor space devoted to administration and support" relative to comparably sized *educational institutions*. Other metrics, such as "highest percentage of full time faculty," "removed more cheaters," and "lowest tuition," could also be used.

A more ambitious metric might be "Our successful graduates complete their 4 year programs in 4 years"—it's positively goofy that right now, only a small percentage of incoming students complete a 4 year program in 4 years, and it's mostly due to insane policies that string failing students along forever, and push them into questionable programs of no value after they've given up on a marketable degree. It would be a point of embarrassment, but administration today is far more focused on happy students and higher retention. Still, this metric runs the risk of focusing overmuch on forcing faculty to pass students. Perhaps a better ambitious metric would be "Our graduates have a higher average first year income after graduation than other institutions," something not so easily improved by threatening faculty.

There really are quite a few other ways to measure success than retention, and I've only just touched on some possibilities. Higher education desperately needs a measure of success better than "Our administrators are good at threatening and cajoling the educators into having the highest retention rates possible," which really shouldn't be a source of pride. How is it that all those advanced administrative degree holders lack the imagination to come up with something better, or even *different*, than higher retention?

The net result of all these fixes is clearly a greatly reduced need for so many professional administrators at our institutions, institutions that did at least as well, years ago, when they didn't even require so many administrators, much less *require* them to be highly educated and degreed in hyper-specialized fields of highly questionable applicability to the position.

I'm hard pressed to feel pity at making suggestions that would put so many administrators out of jobs, jobs that in many cases they sacrificed a fortune buying a degree for. In Imperial China, eunuchs served as the administrators to the Emperor, sacrificing their genitals for power and money. When it was found that the whole system of eunuchs was corrupt, the eunuchs were cast out, and very little pity was available for them. Simply making a sacrifice, no matter how great, is not a license to act without integrity, or grant immunity from repercussions for such behavior.

Look what we have here today in higher education. All these administrators with their administrative Ph.D.s haven't figured out that *cheating is bad,* or determined that *encouraging cheating is counter-productive to education,* or suspected that *experiments without a control are useless and the results should not be inflicted on young people*, or considered that *taking advantage of the less capable for personal profit is wrong*, or even guessed that *it is immoral to lure people into a lifetime of crushing debt for a worthless piece of paper.* I don't have a Ph.D. in Leadership or anything of the sort and gleaned what should have been obvious, and I suspect I'm not alone in having such beliefs.

Administrators, despite their research degrees, consistently ignore good research, and pursue Educationist ideas ridiculously unsupported by research. Administrators have taken control of the entire system and corrupted it as thoroughly as possible considering their brief period of ownership. Of course we need to abandon the system of administrative plunder, administrative scamming of students, and administrative abuse of faculty, and that means abandoning quite a number of administrators. That some may be in debt for purchasing advanced degrees is unfortunate, but considering the number of students indebted for worthless degrees and the food-stamp level pay administrators begrudgingly pay to doctorate-holding adjuncts, it's difficult not to see some justice in this.

Administrators, like eunuchs, still have their uses I suppose, but as the ones responsible for the corruption of the system, they seem to be a natural choice to bear some of the cost for cleaning it up.

And What Will Happen With Tuition?

"Tuition nationwide has risen 72% between 2002 and 2012, faculty pay has only risen 1%. In 2010-2011 alone, median college president salaries rose 10%."

--from an American Association of University Professors report[3]. Granted, the AAUP might have a bit of bias here, but every measure of these types of numbers shows tuition rising, with the money mostly going to administrators.

The increasingly rising tuition is a symptom of the corruption of education, and not a cause. It's only natural to ask if the fixes given here will stop the increases, or even cause a reduction in tuition. The answer, for the most part, is "no," as the increases are also due to other factors that are beyond the influence of institutions acting with integrity again. Across the country, public institutions, used to relying upon support from state governments, are finding such support draining away as state governments deal with economic shortfalls, shortfalls that are also affecting the Federal government, which likewise may be reducing student loan funding soon. Public institutions have had no choice but to respond by relying more and more upon tuition for their funding, a trend that will almost certainly continue.

So tuition will probably still continue to increase, until state budgets stop withdrawing funds from higher education. The fixes above might slow down the process, reducing institutional overhead by no longer paying for legions of overpriced administrators to perform basic tasks. This won't be much savings, however, as each administrator fired will "only" allow for four teachers to earn a living wage instead of being forced to survive on welfare as an adjunct. The fixes will help, a little, but only a little, and the money will be going to educators, instead of administrators and the staff to support administrators. This book is about identifying and stopping the fraud of education, fixing the entire country's economic system will have to wait for another time.

As education returns to legitimacy, and degrees regain their integrity, there will be many benefits. There won't be future generations of hundreds of thousands of degree-holding waiters and waitresses, deep in debt for worthless degrees that they thought would let them get a white collar job. Higher education won't be responsible for sentencing millions of people to a lifetime of debt slavery without even a worthless degree to show for it. Someone holding a degree will have something beyond a piece of paper: he'll have a trustworthy certification that he's put in the hard work necessary to be an educated person.

Higher education will become a smaller industry due to the fixes, but this is a small price to pay for the above benefits, in addition to simply being an honorable industry again. For those uninterested in legitimacy, there will always be a host of online "schools" to provide pieces of paper—and the price of such paper will drop without all the loan money.

No system is immune from corruption, but higher education is overwhelmed with it now. Many of the fixes above are trivial to implement, but the only way is if administrators allow it. Even the simplest idea of "get rid of cheaters" will not happen unless administrators acknowledge the failures of the current system, abandon hypocrisy, and decide to live an honest life where "Integrity" isn't just a doctoral degree topic.

Are there enough such administrators willing to make a difference? I don't know. But I do know that if nothing is done, very soon knowledge of how meaningless an accredited degree is will become widespread enough that the entire system of higher education will collapse: there will be no more suckers foolish enough to enslave themselves for a worthless piece of paper, and honest people seeking higher education will understand they cannot find it at our institutions, inspiring them to go elsewhere.

Footnotes:

Chapter 1:

1) United States Department of Education. "Federal Student Aid Annual Report—FY2011."
2) Bureau of Labor Statistics. "Educational attainment for workers 25 years and older by detailed occupation: 2009." The percentages there need be multiplied by the size of the workforce to get the numbers.
3) ACT. *The Condition of College & Career Readiness 2010.* As "college ready" can be redefined at the stroke of a pen, the actual proportion of incoming students ready for college varies greatly from one report to the next. "Half" is a fair estimate, however.
4) Arum, Richard, and Roksa, Josipa. *Academically Adrift*: *Limited Learning on College Campuses*. 39.
5) Ibid, Table A.3.3.
6) ASU News. "ASU Proposes Tuition Increase." November 14, 2007.
7) Clinton, Hillary. "Speech on College Affordability at Plymouth State University in Plymouth, New Hampshire," October 11, 2007.
8) Andriotis, Annamaria. "For Unpaid College Loans, Feds Dock Social Security." Smartmoney.com. August 7, 2012.

Chapter 2:

1) http://www.sacscoc.org/pdf/2012PrinciplesOfAcreditation.pdf
2) Arum, Richard, and Roksa, Josipa. *Academically Adrift*: *Limited Learning on College Campuses*. 36-37. This lack of improvement is shown through the Collegiate Learning Assessment (CLA) test. While some might criticize the validity of the test, it's difficult to imagine that courses with no reading, writing, or mathematics would do much to improve a student's skills in reading, writing, or mathematics.
3) Keathley, Michael. "Pensacola State College Fires Professor Accused of Having Bogus Degree." If you're a professor, with an unaccredited degree, you're fired.
4) The Inquisitr. *"Doug Lynch: University of Pennsylvania Dean Faked PhD ."* On the other hand, if you're an administrator and completely lie about having a degree at all...no problem. This type of double standard between administrators and faculty is quite common, though repugnant.
5) Arum, Richard, and Roksa, Josipa. *Academically Adrift*: *Limited Learning on College Campuses*. 101.

6) SACS, *Principles of Accreditation: Foundations for Quality Enhancement*. 2002-2006 Edition. http://www.sacscoc.org/principles.asp

Chapter 3:

1) Complete College America. "Remediation: Higher Education's Bridge to Nowhere." April, 2012. Since "remedial" changes definition from state to state, the numbers in this report don't necessarily match other reports, but they all say basically the same things.
2) Ibid.
3) Robe, Jonathan. "Remedial Education Is the Cause of Administrative Bloat?" The Center for College Affordability and Productivity. August, 2011.
4) Arum, Richard, and Roksa, Josipa. *Academically Adrift*: *Limited Learning on College Campuses*. 37-38.
5) www.ratemyprofessors.com is not even remotely scientific, and should mostly be used for amusement purposes, in my opinion. Thus, I won't give the name of the teacher, although a researcher could glean it from the other information provided. In fairness, I'm rather hit-and-miss on the site...at least comments on me there are not 100% negative.

Chapter 4:

1) Keller, Bess. "Education School Courses Faulted As Intellectually Thin." Education Week [American Education's Newspaper of Record], November 12, 2003, Volume. 23, Number 11, p. 8.
2) Educational Testing Service. "GRE Guide to the Use of Scores 2012-2013." 18-20.
3) Taylor, Linda Schrock, "In the Best Interests of the Children." September 4, 2006. http://www.lewrockwell.com/taylor/taylor130.html
4) Arum, Richard, and Roksa, Josipa. *Academically Adrift*: *Limited Learning on College Campuses*. 37-38.
5) Arum, Richard, and Roksa, Josipa. *Academically Adrift*: *Limited Learning on College Campuses*. 101.
6) Pierce, William. "Designing Rubrics for Assessing Higher Order Thinking." Part of a workshop delivered in Columbia, Maryland, 2006.
7) I'm not going to mention the course specifically, or the school. This is simply taken as an example course, that I took to see with my own eyes what these courses are. The reader

is strongly encouraged, if he has any doubts, to take an online Education course and see for himself.

8) Posamentier, Alfred S. *Math Wonders to Inspire Teachers and Students*. This is not even remotely a graduate level math book.

Chapter 5:

1) Allen, I. Elaine, and Seaman, Jeff. "Online Nation: Five Years of Growth in Online Learning." Sloan Consortium, October, 2007. 1

2) Hubbard, Burt, and Mitchell, Nancy. "Public Schools Also Lose When Online Students Fail." September 8, 2012. Education Week.

3) Ibid.

4) Center for Research on Education Outcomes. "Charter School Performance in Pennsylvania." April, 2011. credo.stanford.edu/reports/PA State Report_20110404_FINAL.pdf. The chart on page 8 says it all.

5) United States Department of Education. "Evaluation of Evidence-Based Practices in Online Learning A Meta-Analysis and Review of Online Learning Studies." September 2010.

6) Dante, Ed. (pseudonym) "The Shadow Scholar." *Chronicle of Higher Education*. November 12, 2010. All college faculty should read this article carefully, to get a true vision of how pervasive cheating is at the college level. http://chronicle.com/article/article-content/125329

7) Online Education Database. "8 Astonishing Stats on Academic Cheating."

8) Alcantara, Chris, "University of Florida Students Caught Cheating on Computer Science Projects." The Independent Florida Alligator. March, 13, 2012.

9) Online Education Database. "8 Astonishing Stats on Academic Cheating."

10) Russell, Thomas. *No Significant Difference Phenomenon*.

Chapter 6:

1) Sentell, Will. "Public School Tenure System Questioned." The Advocate. August, 2011.

2) Conley, Valerie Martin. "Survey of Changes in Faculty Retirement Policies 2007." *American Association of University Professors*. March 2007.

3) Hoeller, Keith. "The Future of the Contingent Faculty Movement." Insider Higher Ed. November 13, 2007.

4) Western Governor's University, Steinhardt School of Culture, Education, and Human Development, and Georgia State University all have Math Education Master's programs lacking in math. That even one such degree In Math Education can be without math means no such degree holder can be assumed to have such skills.

http://www.wgu.edu/education/teacher_certification_mathematics_master_degree,
http://steinhardt.nyu.edu/teachlearn/math/ma/program_of_study,
http://msit.gsu.edu/4833.html

5) See Appendix, Tests.
6) Millea, Meghan, and Grimes, Paul, W. "Grade Expectations and Student Evaluations of Teaching." College Student Journal. Project Innovation, Dec 2001, Volume 36 Issue 4.
7) Carrell, Scott, and West, James. "Does Professor Quality Matter? Evidence from Random Assignment of Students to Professors." March 22, 2010.
8) Gonzales, Jennifer. "At Community Colleges' Meeting, Officials Debate How to Deliver More Graduates." *Chronicle of Higher Education*. April 18, 2010.
9) Immerwahr, John, Johnson, Jean, and Paul, Gasbarra. "Campus Commons? What Faculty, Financial Officers, and Others Think About Controlling College Costs." Public Agenda. 2009.
10) Field, Kelly. "Faculty at For-Profits Allege Constant Pressure to Keep Students Enrolled." *Chronicle of Higher Education*. May 8, 2011.
11) Stratford, Michael. "U. of Maryland University College Is Said to Have Bought Silence of Former Employees." *The Chronicle of Higher Education*. March 12, 2012.

Chapter 7:

1) At no point do I quote this to report negatively on Tidewater Community College, and I hope they find a dean with integrity. http://chronicle.com/jobs/0000739837-01/
2) Kerlderman, Eric. "Louisiana's Higher-Education Commissioner Resigns Over Retirement Flap." *Chronicle of Higher Education*. June 8, 2010.
3) I'm specifically not stating which graduate school, though I repeat here that it is accredited, and promotions have been given based on a degree from this school. In reviewing other courses at other schools, the course discussed here should be taken as representative. The other courses I reviewed seemed very similar, but I did not examine them in nearly as careful detail.
4) The books for the course are Lodico, Marguerite G., Spaulding, Dean T, and Zoegtle, Katherine H. *Methods in Educational Research, 2nd Edition* and George, Darren and Mallery, Paul. *IBM SPSS Statistics 19 Step by Step A Simple Guide and Reference, 12th Edition*. I'll quote the books a few times, but the issue is what is *not* in the books, and the quotes themselves say very little.

Chapter 8:

1) National Center for Education Statistics. *Digest of Education Statistics.*

2) United States Department of Education, "Student Loan Volume Tables--FY 2009 President's Budget."

3) Lewin, Temar. "Student Loan Default Rates Rise Sharply in Past Year." New York Times. September 12, 2011.

4) June, Audrey Williams. "Adjunct No Longer, Jill Biden Earned $82,022 as a Community-College Professor in 2011." *Chronicle of Higher Education*. April 16, 2012.

5) http://www.higheredjobs.com/salary/salaryDisplay.cfm?SurveyID=3; site visited September 9, 2012.

6) McArdle, Elaine. "The Adjunct Explosion." University Business.

7) http://www.higheredjobs.com/salary/salaryDisplay.cfm?SurveyID=1; site visited September 9, 2012. This is for the same years as before, and note just how much more these people get.

8) Jesse, David. "Database: Compare salary increases for administrators at 15 state universities."

9) Mark Mongomery's posting at http://greatcollegeadvice.com/student-to-faculty-ratios-what-do-these-statistics-mean-part-i/ discusses, from an administrator's point of view, how these ratios are manipulated.

10) Ginsberg, Benjamin. "Administrators Ate My Tuition." *Washington Monthly*. September/October 2011.

11) Ibid

12) Green, Jay P. "Administrative Bloat at American Universities: The Real Reason for High Costs in Higher Education" ; site visited September 9, 2012.

13) Smith, Charles. "For-Profit Education: Milking Students and the Taxpayers for Corporate Profits." Truthout. May 2012.

14) Ibid

15) Fain, Paul. "GAO Takes Another Crack." *Inside Higher Ed.* November 23, 2011.

16) http://centerforcollegeaffordability.org/archives/6023, site visited September 9, 2012.

17) ACT. "The Condition of College & Career Readiness 2010."

18) Curry, Colleen. "University of Pennsylvania Dean Faked PhD." *ABC News*. So outrageous it bears mentioning twice: an administrator with bogus degrees will not be fired by the other administrators.

19) Stripling, Jack, and Perry, Mark. "President's Status a Mystery at Disparate Institution." *The Chronicle of Higher Education*. February 29, 2012. Read this article carefully to see just how afraid faculty are.

20) Arum, Richard, and Roksa, Josipa. *Academically Adrift*: *Limited Learning on College Campuses*. 36.

Chapter 9:

1) Parry, Mark. "NYU Prof Vows Never to Probe Cheating Again—and Faces a Backlash." *Chronicle of Higher Education*. July 21, 2011.
2) To be clear, I'm talking real cheating here, not poor attribution, bad paraphrasing, or the like, which are orders of magnitude below hiring someone else to do the class work.
3) For what it's worth, textbook pricing is another scam, but worthy of a different book.
4) American Association of University Professors. "2011-12 Report on the Economic Status of the Profession."

References:

Much of this material is available online as well as in print; I've included websites for the reader's convenience.

ACT. "The Condition of College & Career Readiness 2010." http://www.act.org/research/policymakers/cccr10/index.html

Alcantara, Chris, "University of Florida Students Caught Cheating on Computer Science Projects." The Independent Florida Alligator. March, 13, 2012. http://www.alligator.org/news/campus/article_8f6af304-6cc8-11e1-9d89-0019bb2963f4.html

Allen, I. Elaine, and Seaman, Jeff. "Online Nation: Five Years of Growth in Online Learning." Sloan Consortium, October, 2007. http://sloanconsortium.org/publications/survey/online_nation

American Association of University Professors. "2011-12 Report on the Economic Status of the Profession." AAUP. http://www.aaup.org/AAUP/comm/rep/Z/ecstatereport11-12/

Andriotis, Annamaria. "For Unpaid College Loans, Feds Dock Social Security." Smartmoney.com. August 7, 2012. http://www.smartmoney.com/borrow/student-loans/grandmas-new-financial-problem-college-debt-1344292084111/

Arum, Richard, and Roksa, Josipa. *Academically Adrift*: *Limited Learning on College Campuses*. Chicago: University of Chicago Press. 2011.

ASU News. "ASU Proposes Tuition Increase." November 14, 2007. Phoenix: Arizona State University. https://asunews.asu.edu/20071108_Tuition

Bureau of Labor Statistics, U.S. Department of Labor. "Educational attainment for workers 25 years and older by detailed occupation" Washington, D.C.: U.S. Department of Labor, 2009." http://www.bls.gov/emp/ep_table_111.htm

Carrell, Scott, and West, James. "Does Professor Quality Matter? Evidence from Random Assignment of Students to Professors." March 22, 2010. http://www.economics.harvard.edu/faculty/staiger/files/carrell%2Bwest%2Bprofessor%2Bqualty%2Bjpe.pdf

Center for Research on Education Outcomes. "Charter School Performance in Pennsylvania." April, 2011. credo.stanford.edu/reports/PA State Report_20110404_FINAL.pdf.

Clinton, Hillary. "Speech on College Affordability at Plymouth State University in Plymouth, New Hampshire," October 11, 2007. Online by Gerhard Peters and John T. Woolley, *The American Presidency Project*. http://www.presidency.ucsb.edu/ws/?pid=77063.

Complete College America. "Remediation: Higher Education's Bridge to Nowhere." April, 2012. http://www.completecollege.org/docs/CCA-Remediation-final.pdf

Conley, Valerie Martin. "Survey of Changes in Faculty Retirement Policies 2007." *American Association of University Professors*. March 2007. http://www.aaup.org/AAUP/issues/retirement/2007retsurv/

Curry, Colleen. "University of Pennsylvania Dean Faked PhD." *ABC News*. April 27, 2012. http://abcnews.go.com/US/upenn-dean-faked-phd-ivy-league/story?id=16229174#.UEv6KqNExUs

Dante, Ed. (pseudonym) "The Shadow Scholar." *Chronicle of Higher Education*. November 12, 2010. http://chronicle.com/article/article-content/125329

De Vise, Daniel. "Faculty Pay has Stalled." *The Washington Post*. April 10, 2012.

Educational Testing Service. "GRE Guide to the Use of Scores 2012-2013." http://www.ets.org/s/gre/pdf/gre_guide.pdf

Fain, Paul. "GAO Takes Another Crack." *Inside Higher Ed.* November 23, 2011. http://www.insidehighered.com/news/2011/11/23/gao-releases-new-investigation-profit-colleges

Field, Kelly. "Faculty at For-Profits Allege Constant Pressure to Keep Students Enrolled." *Chronicle of Higher Education*. May 8, 2011. http://chronicle.com/article/Pawns-in-the-For-Profit/127424/

George, Darren and Mallery, Paul. *IBM SPSS Statistics 19 Step by Step A Simple Guide and Reference, 12th Edition*, Upper Saddle River, NJ. Pearson. 2012.

Ginsberg, Benjamin. "Administrators Ate My Tuition." *Washington Monthly*. September/October 2011.

Gonzales, Jennifer. "At Community Colleges' Meeting, Officials Debate How to Deliver More Graduates." *Chronicle of Higher Education*. April 18, 2010. http://chronicle.com/article/Community-College-Officials/65161/

Green, Jay P."Administrative Bloat at American Universities: The Real Reason for High Costs in Higher Education." Goldwater Institute. August 7, 2010. http://goldwaterinstitute.org/article/administrative-bloat-american-universities-real-reason-high-costs-higher-education

HigherEdJobs. Faculty Median Salaries by Discipline and Rank, 2005-2006. http://www.higheredjobs.com/salary/salaryDisplay.cfm?SurveyID=3

Hoeller, Keith. "The Future of the Contingent Faculty Movement." Insider Higher Ed. November 13, 2007. http://www.insidehighered.com/views/2007/11/13/hoeller-

Hubbard, Burt, and Mitchell, Nancy. "Public Schools Also Lose When Online Students Fail." September 8, 2012. Education Week. http://www.edweek.org/ew/articles/2011/10/03/06enc_online.h31.html

Immerwahr, John, Johnson, Jean, and Paul, Gasbarra. "Campus Commons? What Faculty, Financial Officers, and Others Think About Controlling College Costs." Public Agenda. 2009. http://www.publicagenda.org/files/pdf/campus_commons.pdf

The Inquisitr. *"Doug Lynch: University of Pennsylvania Dean Faked PhD ."* http://www.inquisitr.com/226666/doug-lynch-university-of-pennsylvania-dean-faked-phd/#vZOj5bTwLrt4XBzF.99

Jesse, David. "Database: Compare salary increases for administrators at 15 state universities." Detroit Free Press. March 26, 2011. http://www.freep.com/article/20110327/NEWS06/110325057

June, Audrey Williams. "Adjunct No Longer, Jill Biden Earned $82,022 as a Community-College Professor in 2011." *Chronicle of Higher Education*. April 16, 2012.

Keathley, Michael. "Pensacola State College Fires Professor Accused of Having Bogus Degree." BestCollegesOnline.com. January 20, 2011. http://www.bestcollegesonline.com/blog/2011/01/20/pensacola-state-college-fires-professor-accused-of-having-bogus-degree/

Keller, Bess. "Education School Courses Faulted As Intellectually Thin." Education Week [American Education's Newspaper of Record], November 12, 2003, Volume. 23, Number 11, p. 8. http://mathforum.org/kb/servlet/JiveServlet/download/204-474848-1454755-72280/att1.html

Kerlderman, Eric. "Louisiana's Higher-Education Commissioner Resigns Over Retirement Flap." *Chronicle of Higher Education*. June 8, 2010. http://chronicle.com/article/Louisianas-Higher-Education/65811/

Lewin, Temar. "Student Loan Default Rates Rise Sharply in Past Year." New York Times. September 12, 2011. http://www.nytimes.com/2011/09/13/education/13loans.html?_r=2

Lodico, Marguerite G., Spaulding, Dean T, and Zoegtle, Katherine H. *Methods in Educational Research, 2nd Edition* San Francisco, Ca. Jossey-Bass. 2010.

Luzer, Dan.iel. "Does Tuition Rise Because of Remediation?" Washington Monthly, August 10, 2011.
http://www.washingtonmonthly.com/college_guide/does_tuition_rise_because_of_r.php

http://universitybusiness.ccsct.com/page.cfm?p=159

Millea, Meghan, and Grimes, Paul, W. "Grade Expectations and Student Evaluations of Teaching." College Student Journal. Project Innovation, Dec 2001, Volume 36 Issue 4.

National Center for Education Statistics. *Digest of Education Statistics*. Washington, D.C.: U.S. Department of Education. 2010. http://nces.ed.gov/programs/digest/d10/index.asp

Nolting, Paul. *Winning at Math, Fourth Edition.* Bradenton, Fl. Academic Success Press, Inc. 2002.

Online Education Database. "8 Astonishing Stats on Academic Cheating."
http://oedb.org/library/features/8-astonishing-stats-on-academic-cheating

Parry, Mark. "NYU Prof Vows Never to Probe Cheating Again—and Faces a Backlash." *Chronicle of Higher Education*. July 21, 2011. http://chronicle.com/blogs/wiredcampus/nyu-prof-vows-never-to-probe-cheating-again%E2%80%94and-faces-a-backlash/32351

Pierce, William. "Designing Rubrics for Assessing Higher Order Thinking." Part of a workshop delivered in Columbia, Maryland, 2006.
http://academic.pgcc.edu/~wpeirce/MCCCTR/Designingrubricsassessingthinking.html

Posamentier, Alfred S. *Math Wonders to Inspire Teachers and Students*. Alexandria, Va. Association for Supervision and Curriculum Development. 2003. (6000 Course textbook)

Robe, Jonathan. "Remedial Education Is the Cause of Administrative Bloat?" The Center for College Affordability and Productivity. August, 2011.
http://centerforcollegeaffordability.org/archives/6023

Robe, Jonathan, untitled posting. http://centerforcollegeaffordability.org/archives/5777. Visited September 10, 2012.

Russell, Thomas. *No Significant Difference Phenomenon*. Raleigh, NC. North Carolina State University 1999.

Sentell, Will. "Public School Tenure System Questioned." The Advocate. August, 2011. http://theadvocate.com/home/492228-79/story.html

Smith, Charles. "For-Profit Education: Milking Students and the Taxpayers for Corporate Profits." Truthout. May 2012. http://truth-out.org/news/item/9485-for-profit-education-milking-students-and-the-taxpayers-for-corporate-profits

Stratford, Michael. "U. of Maryland University College Is Said to Have Bought Silence of Former Employees." *The Chronicle of Higher Education*. March 12, 2012. http://chronicle.com/blogs/ticker/u-of-maryland-university-college-is-said-to-have-bought-silence-of-former-employees/41366

Southern Association of Colleges and Schools. *Principles of Accreditation: Foundations for Quality Enhancement*. http://www.sacscoc.org/pdf/2012PrinciplesOfAcreditation.pdf

Stripling, Jack, and Perry, Mark. "President's Status a Mystery at Disparate Institution." *The Chronicle of Higher Education*. February 29, 2012. http://chronicle.com/article/Presidents-Status-Remains-a/130964/

Taylor, Linda Schrock, "In the Best Interests of the Children." September 4, 2006. http://www.lewrockwell.com/taylor/taylor130.html

United States Department of Education. "Evaluation of Evidence-Based Practices in Online Learning
A Meta-Analysis and Review of Online Learning Studies." Washington, D.C.: U.S. Department of Education. September 2010. http://www2.ed.gov/rschstat/eval/tech/evidence-based-practices/finalreport.pdf

United States Department of Education. "Federal Student Aid Annual Report—FY2011." Washington, D.C.: U.S. Department of Education. 2011. http://www2.ed.gov/about/reports/annual/2011report/fsa-report.pdf

------, "Student Loan Volume Tables--FY 2009 President's Budget." Washington, D.C>: U.S. Department of Education. 2009. http://www2.ed.gov/about/overview/budget/studentloantables/index.html

Made in the USA
San Bernardino, CA
13 April 2014